RENEGADE
TEACHER

RENEGADE TEACHER

Inside School Walls with Standards and the Test

Katherine Scheidler

Renegade Teacher: Inside School Walls with Standards and the Test
Copyright © 2023 by Katherine Scheidler

All rights reserved. This book or any portion thereof may not be reproduced or used in any manner whatsoever without the express written permission of the publisher, except for the use of brief quotations in a book review.

Printed in the United States of America

Luminare Press
442 Charnelton St.
Eugene, OR 97401
www.luminarepress.com

LCCN: 2023906433
ISBN: 979-8-88679-261-4

*To Peter, and to Cath,
writing coach extraordinaire*

Contents

Author's Note x
Preface 1
Introduction 5

PART ONE
A School Called Hope

CHAPTER ONE
The "Riot" 17

CHAPTER TWO
Making a Change 26

CHAPTER THREE
A School on Shifting Sands 33

CHAPTER FOUR
Getting Noticed, Back to Old School 44

CHAPTER FIVE
Turning School Upside Down, Again 50

CHAPTER SIX
Returning to Hope 56

CHAPTER SEVEN
Small Steps to Rocky Big Change 61

CHAPTER EIGHT
Another Planet: Less is More 66

CHAPTER NINE
The Coleman Report: Demographics Matter 74

CHAPTER TEN
Dream Work and Fireworks 79

CHAPTER ELEVEN
Leadership, and Winds of Change 97

CHAPTER TWELVE
Back to School for Me 108

PART TWO
New Federal Law for Student Learning Is Unwelcome

CHAPTER THIRTEEN
Moving On: Crossing the State Line 117

CHAPTER FOURTEEN
National Mandate Isn't Welcome 130

CHAPTER FIFTEEN
Correcting Myths: It's not "Standardized" 143

CHAPTER SIXTEEN
A Wise Commissioner of Education 149

CHAPTER SEVENTEEN
Superstar Urban Teachers 160

PART THREE
Moving On, District Leadership for Change

CHAPTER EIGHTEEN
A New Position of Curriculum Director 165

CHAPTER NINETEEN
Fairfield: Involved Parents, Loving Learning 187

CHAPTER TWENTY
Sussex: More Types of Challenges 206

CHAPTER TWENTY-ONE
Paradise: Strong Teachers, Engaged Students 222

CHAPTER TWENTY-TWO
Trouble in Paradise 235

PART FOUR

Re-Envisioning School

CHAPTER TWENTY-THREE
Making A Paradigm Shift Work 249

Appendix: Ted Sizer's Coalition of Essential Schools
Ten Common Principles 262

Common Core/Massachusetts English Standards 263

Acknowledgements 267

Author's Note

The town school system names are changed (except for Hope High School, Providence, RI), because these schools and school systems simply represent common ways of working, not unique to that community. The following names, listed alphabetically, are pseudonyms: Andrea, Elizabeth, Jennifer, Richard, Steven, Suzanne.

Preface

Most everyone loves to hate what's known in conventional wisdom as school "standardized tests." These tests, coming from outside the school, are no one's preference for those within school, imposed from the state departments of education. The tests are commonly criticized as useless, and worse, called "punitive." They're also commonly called "high-stakes standardized bubble tests." These attributions are each false. State test critics also charge that the test interferes with learning, that results arrive too late, and that the test is unfair for more struggling students. Academics call it a poor test. None of this is true. I show here how testing helps enormously.

I illustrate here via story from my over twenty-five years of urban school classroom teaching and over fifteen years as school systems' leader of teaching and learning in urban districts and also in more privileged, wealthier suburban school systems how it is that this test is good, for everyone. I show how it's not simply a test hurting many, or wasting time, but instead provides useful learning goals and a gold mine of information for students, educators, and parents. It's more than just a cruel test. A student's score isn't made public or sent off to colleges; that's the SAT, a truly high-stakes test that matters for college acceptance and financial aid. The state test simply assesses for needed areas that help even higher achieving students, and helps bring basic common learning, to all, including those students formerly forgotten, marginalized. Now everyone counts. As to the test constraining teachers, educators are free to teach in whatever way they choose. Creativity in teaching and active learning are encouraged, as these heighten student engagement; the test results show if strategies work for learning.

Earlier, before this annoying accountability initiated in the mid-1990's, I saw classrooms where little to no teaching was going on. While many students in high level, engaging classes went on to fine universities, others not as well served moved into low level jobs that no longer exist. Too many fell out of the system, graduated (or didn't) and went out into the world without basic literacy and math understanding that limits advancement and continued learning. That unfair system creating "haves" and "have nots" changed under testing.

I show how the state in which I work, Massachusetts, brought the hammer down on schools and educators early, as many other states did, by initiating in 1993 the policy and practice of standards-based learning with a test written into state law. I signed up to head district work on this ambitious act for all students to learn, and saw slow and steady progress over the decades. Because Massachusetts early on began with good literacy and math standards and a fair test, though too many failed the test at first, the state continued to push hard, and Massachusetts has been and is tops nationally. Other states, as I show here, were not so fortunate with their education systems.

Then the 2020 coronavirus pandemic devastated learning, setting schools back with school and classroom doors locked, for too long. During this difficult period, when many wouldn't know if school would be open that day or not, with teachers rightfully fearful to come in to school, parents pleading for schools to open, and educators struggling to at minimum reach students remotely, many urban districts lost students, teachers quit, superintendents under duress left their jobs. National reports state that the 2020 and later school shutdown set students back by decades. Over a million students nationally left school. No one was prepared for this catastrophe for education, bringing the worst decline in student achievement in US history. I show here how the test, especially when buttressed with other aids beyond the classroom that support teachers in developing learning, helps bring learning back.

As a former classroom teacher, and now working with teachers to better develop learning, I know well the struggles, and the often surprising victories. I've seen how testing, when used as intended, to boost learning, can work well for student achievement, and I illustrate this. And I also show missteps, in "show not tell" here. I show how my urban school named "Hope" earlier went into sudden decline. I show how it was then brought back up. This improvement can happen. I show here how many educators use the test to boost learning, working alone, in pairs, in small groups, or as a school-wide or district effort. The test assesses for needed skills and understandings and provides teachers with information that can help everyone learn and grow. It's a necessary test. Does having the test mean a bit more work? Yes, one has to think about how to integrate the needed learning into one's courses. But the benefits for education equity are great. I also show how we can modify ways of working to do even better.

I show here too how it was that the standards skills and understandings tested by state tests came about. If the standards tested weren't good, I'd be among the first to complain. I report how surprising increases in learning have emerged due to the many dedicated educators. And I show how the school day use of time constrains learning.

I point out too foibles and missteps common throughout schools and districts nationally, not only at my own urban once proud school and in the school systems where I served as district administrator. My school Hope in the one state of Rhode Island, with its ups and downs, and my travels throughout neighboring Massachusetts mirror common experiences found nationally. Suburban schools fared better during the pandemic year, and in pockets even increased test scores during the pandemic, with scores tracking the decline then rise, a sign of improved learning. It's the test score decline that often motivates improvement, signaling the need to work differently.

From being inside varied schools and in district central offices, and participating in school board meetings, and in a multitude of classrooms, I show here how it's necessary to make certain fairly easy but dramatic changes to bring school back, and serve every student better. It's just not that hard, and is essential.

The large-scale data of state tests nationally and by state, district, and school is easy to find online. This data is helpful, but also hides small victories. I show here the smaller stories of successes and missed opportunities that, when taken to heart, can bring up learning, and instill confidence and pride in both students and educators, while preparing more students for their futures.

We can do better, and we must if we're to fulfill the promise of no child left behind.

Introduction

The federal policy of national standards for every student's achievement was born in large part from the 1960s civil rights movement calling for equity in education, the Sixties. During that earlier period that exposed racial injustice and where many fought for racial equity, Boston teacher Jonathan Kozol broke through to national readership on school issues by writing on the poor conditions, including overt racism, experienced by his Black students in his *Death at an Early Age: The Destruction of the Hearts and Minds of Negro Children in the Boston Public Schools*, 1967. Kozol's book swept the country, and opened eyes to disparity in public school systems. While focusing on just one urban elementary school, Kozol reported what he saw as pervasive disregard for low income African-American students, an outrageous injustice. Other teachers too at this time—James Herndon, Herbert Kohl, Nat Hentoff—wrote on similar poor conditions in which low income Black students were left behind in schools. These writers also conveyed the joy in helping all students, especially those formerly dismissed. This wave of books critical of school brought national attention to structural conditions and practices that hurt low income and racially different students. While thinking on the plight of those dismissed began to change through these stories, school structure and policies didn't. It's hard to move new thinking to long-time set practice.

Like Kozol and his fellow whistleblowers, I've had experience within the education system, in schools, with classroom teaching myself, and visiting classrooms. Since I taught before the arrival of the widely misunderstood state test, and worked in schools during the unwelcome early national testing implementation period that shook educators' world, today I see classrooms with higher expectations for all, greater success. Teachers in my online courses today strive for better work for all students, because it matters, and we now have better school support for helping each child due in large part to the fact that those test scores are linked to needed skills, and results are made public. I'm impressed with many teachers' drive for improvement. It's a delight when one sees success in good test results, validating one's classroom work, a reward I never had as a teacher. Score decline spurs better work.

A teacher posts in my online course, "We've recently looked at our test results and my teaching partner and I are talking about what we can do to do better." This isn't a statement we'd have heard twenty-five years ago. Things have improved. If success on the test doesn't translate directly to success in life, a debated topic, it's better than the past dismissal of some students. It's hard to argue that sending students off into the world with less than satisfactory literacy and math understanding, the tested areas for accountability, is acceptable.

While many if not most in schools dread and are annoyed by the test, and results may not always be what we want to see, when we look at those results as a way to help students learn and grow, we can see that it's worth the angst and hard work required to improve. But we can do even better with changes that make teaching easier, which I illustrate here. We're working with students born in this century with schools operating in a centuries-old mode. It's time for a change. The global pandemic, while causing despair and setback, motivates necessary improvement. The inventive work that every educator had to turn to during the intense Covid-19 years, with school turned upside down, shows it's possible to re-think work.

After the late 1960s and early '70s wave of teachers writing critically of schools depriving too many of a good education, another wave of books for educators and the popular audience exploded in the 1980s. University scholars, looking at research and conducting their own studies, began to produce best-selling books on school inequity, intended for and popular with both educators and the general public. These works, building on the earlier teacher stories, assessed school more broadly and forced change. Not only were urban schools in poor physical conditions, as Kozol vividly describes, recounting that as he taught in a school auditorium—a horror in itself—a piece of the ceiling fell, almost

Introduction

hitting one of his young elementary school students. But schools in the '80s still were revealed on the whole still unable to meet the needs of racially diverse students in academics—reading, writing, math. That falling ceiling was emblematic of leaving marginalized students behind. Education researchers of the '80s showed little had changed.

With the 1980s school critiques, UCLA professor Jeannie Oakes shines a light on a central and pervasive discriminatory feature of schools. From sitting in classrooms, Oakes brought to national attention the different levels of education inherent in "tracked" courses, which constituted different levels of education for different students. This strict tracking system, of what was actually termed "bottom level," "college prep," or "upper level," prevailed across the country. The course level to which a student was assigned determined teachers' view of a student's capability. I taught in that archaic structure where learning varied immensely. Reporting her studies in *Keeping Track: How Schools Structure Inequality* (1985), Oakes targets the system of creating leveled courses for students, with some (most were low-income students of color) barely taught at all, while others (white and more privileged students) soared in learning. In her classroom observations, Oakes saw some students getting college level terminology, preparing those students for that next step up, while others were sentenced to classes of little learning. Within schools, eyes were closed to this sharp disparity. It was the way school had always worked, and no one questioned leveled courses. The system both built on and fostered a belief that some students couldn't learn. Accountability, with ensuring all students are tested and results made public, aimed to turn this inequity around, and in many instances succeeded. Whatever class and whichever teacher one had, expectations are the same for each student. But I show here how we can do even better to support this ambitious goal.

A high demographic suburban district principal told me, "We don't have tracking here in Massachusetts, so we call it 'leveling.'" Words don't correct the practice. Since it's hard to eliminate leveling, with a wish to protect high levels of learning with students deemed to be able to achieve well, common national standards include all students. Common standards are color-blind and can be and are in many places taught to all students, however students are distributed in school. I love seeing in my online courses what teachers do to take steps to help more struggling students learn the higher level skills that decades ago we'd only expect for some students. We've come a long way toward equity. And we can do more.

Accountability of the mid-90s—a change hard for educators to accept, after the earlier full freedom but discriminatory practice—emerged from widespread national interest in school improvement. Some schools earlier were effective, but not all, and not necessarily for all students. My Harvard advisor Sara Lawrence-Lightfoot exposed in her study, *The Good High School* (1983), how what was considered "good schools" nationally had their weaknesses. In 1989 the national governors and—hard to believe today—both political parties in US Congress in the '90s sought school improvement, and saw the need to strive for equity in learning nationally. Federal law seemed the best way to get there, a rough but necessary path, similar to the difficulties of enforcing civil rights law.

Now many oppose this "intrusive" test. The wave of articles and books of today are anti-test polemic. And the pandemic learning setback, while revealing needs, only fosters more resentment to testing. Because I'm in schools and in touch with teachers and see both successes and needs, I show systemic roadblocks for educators to be able to boost every student's learning that remain today. I show ways where school can be designed and implemented differently to better smooth the way.

A key nationally prominent education author and critic in the 1980s explosion of books criticizing school and offering better ways was education leader Ted Sizer, who in his Nine Common Principles for his school reform effort nationally launched the "all students" goal, novel for the time:

Coalition of Essential Schools Nine Common Principles:

1. The school's goals shall be simple: that each student master a limited number of essential skills and areas of knowledge. "Less is more" should dominate.

2. The school's goals should apply to all students.

Introduction

Sizer's focus on all students initiated a turn in thinking and working.

I show here how I taught in a program which Sizer, a Brown University professor based just a few blocks away, initiated in my school. We were ready—desperate—for a change. School wasn't working well, with old-school modes not appropriate for a new student population, no longer those professors' children. Sizer effected major changes in thinking about how to help school work well for everyone. He shot a cannon ball through the tracking system that divided students into "smart" and "not smart." He also changed school day use of time to make education work better. It was Sizer's earlier US army service in training soldiers that cemented his belief that the same skills and understandings can be asked of everyone, white or black. rich or poor: All could be asked to learn the same things, with Sizer adding that learning must be "personalized," taught in different ways for different students. That old-school lecture mode of earlier years that worked for some didn't work for all.

I taught in the small program in my school named Hope that Sizer carved out, which worked dramatically well to serve all students. A major change in better use of time greatly enhanced the ability to teach and learn. Yet all was not sunshine and roses, and I show how the thorns today are dispelled. Sizer's breakthrough bestseller calling for major change, *Horace's Compromise* (1984), pointed out that it wasn't the teachers' fault that schools didn't serve all students well. It was the system of early 1900s factory model of assembly-line school—a multitude of classes and students per day, and discarding those less skilled (seen as "defective") —that was the problem. I show how change in use of time combined with new ways of teaching and new roles for teachers bring excellent new results, and in racially and socio-economically diverse settings. But for Sizer it wasn't the tinkering around the edges but a whole new mindset and mode that made school work. We need this new full framework in which to teach today. And we need other supports to buttress the long-standing need of the racial divide, a gap widened to a chasm by the pandemic.

Standards did not spring from the brain of Obama, contrary to one of the many myths that abound. These tested areas are the longtime expectations of national subject organizations of the National Council of Teachers of Mathematics and the National Council of Teachers of English. As a former English teacher, I annually read through the tests, and I see the feared test is just assessing traditional English skills of such areas as close reading, inference, and central idea with text evidence, basic reading skills, nothing new.

When I looked through the first English state test, I marveled, "Wouldn't it be wonderful for every student to learn these skills!" Today that first test would be a piece of cake for many students, as the ever-increasing test expectations raise the bar over the years. The earlier writing test question at tenth grade was a simple, "Write about a character you've read about who is a hero." This moved in 2015 to the writing expectation of reading a complex passage and writing a piece answering a specific literary analysis question, a big jump, but one needed to continue to boost learning. The math test is no longer about memorizing algorithms but tests for understanding math and writing about math, to have students explain their answers.

A dilemma though is that schools over the decades haven't provided the environment in the school day that enables all students to move up the ladder of learning. It's new wine in an old bottle. The school use of time must change to support more ambitious outcomes. The organization and focus of school have to change. This approach I present here for public education is needed not only in urban schools. Needed changes are actually in part what's done in private schools, and have long worked well in those enclaves for the rich.

Suburban districts too are plagued by unique challenges, as I show here also. The challenges here are different. I highlight dysfunctions to be corrected. I illustrate how parents in high demographic, relatively wealthier communities help schools stay on their toes, and also may need to tone down rhetoric.

I also show how what seems great teaching can miss the boat and bring low test scores if standards aren't integrated into the learning. And I show top scores result when teachers are on the money with the understandings tested, though unaware they're teaching the standards, with the standards just traditional good guides.

Introduction

Changing how our public education system works is like trying to turn an ocean liner around, land a 747. It takes time, thought, and skill. Sizer commented, "Changing school is like moving a graveyard." Among guides, he called for "conversation" among the quaint term "folks" to solve the problems. This conversation can be hard to develop but is essential. Civil discourse makes a difference. When lacking, frustration reigns, things go awry.

With a test that's moved over the years to more challenging than those relatively simpler earlier tests, on the strain and stress of testing, some urban superintendents call for a test more suitable for their students, less challenging. In 2022, a new Boston mayor calls for the state test to be in students' native language, which boggles my mind in trying to see how this would help a student in the workplace and with college acceptance, again revealing how little understood the test is. I show how it's unfair to not test all students with the same test. A student may not score at the proficient level, but may well improve in growth from year to year, which is better than no test and no growth. But more new ways to support educators in this ambitious learning are needed. Our students deserve it.

I'm a renegade for arguing for this never-loved test. I earlier saw myself a renegade because as a new teacher at my school Hope in 1969, I saw that a major school disruption—with protests common nationally in this era—carried out by disenfranchised Black students denied high quality education—was a boycott justified. My veteran colleagues remained in denial that there was a problem, and just wanted school to go back to "normal." That retreat never happened. School moved to a different and better way under Sizer's program, then, under a new superintendent with no knowledge of the program's history and aim, and without the federal push of accountability, slipped back to old school.

I show here how I left teaching during our period of low morale and a failed system, again a renegade as I leaped to a job in computer sales, which I was fully unprepared to do, dismayed by school no longer able to address needs. I returned to Hope upon learning that the faculty had voted to adopt Sizer's novel program. I was now a renegade in abandoning structures and practices that didn't work in traditional school to return to loving teaching in Sizer's program, where things worked well beyond my and others' expectations. Under better conditions, students, racially and demographically integrated, all learned well; we teachers surmounted challenges and delighted in the work. Teaching was a joy.

I then left teaching again, as a renegade, and crossed into Massachusetts at the time of the epicenter of the turn to accountability. My job was to serve as district teaching and learning head in varied districts, working to help very different communities' schools adjust to the requirement that every student is tested, head-spinning for educators.

Now, yet again as a renegade, I argue here against the tide, presenting a case for testing to show that while many consider it a waste of time—or worse, doing damage to children—that the test is actually beneficial. A friend's special education child calls the state test MCAS, the Massachusetts Comprehensive Assessment System, the "Massachusetts child abuse system." But the test simply sets out what's to be learned and assesses success. It lifts all, even if not everyone scores as high as one would like. Hurdles persist, and I show here how many leap over.

While parents earlier feared standards would "dumb down" classes, this hasn't been the case. Teachers easily see when students have the basic skills tested, and don't have to dwell on this. Higher achieving students aren't harmed by being tested, and may gain confidence seeing they do well on the test. If parents knew Advanced Placement teachers teach to the AP test, parents would lobby for more teaching to the test.

Over the years of building better learning, students improved. The 2020 pandemic crisis then changed everything. School shutdown, doors locked, hit school with a tornado. A fifth grade teacher in one of my online courses wrote poignantly, "We were told on Thursday that school would close on Friday. I didn't have the chance to tell my students take their math books home." But, as it turned out, that one year's books wouldn't have been sufficient. Learning for the most part went out the window, for longer than anyone had expected, as test scores reveal. Educators during the fraught Covid-19 era were stretched thin,

Introduction

frustrated in trying to teach students who weren't in the room. In the pandemic years' crisis, we see how important school is. Remote school worked unevenly. Too many urban students just disappeared. To more fully build back and to continue to improve, major changes are needed.

I don't supply here large scale data or charts, mainly stories that illustrate ideas. The real story is in actions and the small data points. I look at individual districts and in teachers' work and report the story behind numbers, not the large scale averages that hide smaller needs and successes. It's the behaviors that make the difference.

As I report on my work in Massachusetts and my home state of Rhode Island, and the stories behind the differences, what we see is Massachusetts tops in student learning nationally, and Rhode Island working differently, falling far behind, with lessons for states nationally. A Rhode Island reporter writes when this state finally adopts the Massachusetts standards and test in 2018, the brutal assessment is, "If Rhode Island were a school system in Massachusetts, it would be in the bottom ten percent of Massachusetts districts." Lessons are learned from both types of states and different actions, for success or its lack.

It's looking as if the test, despite critics, and due to those of good will who fight for continued equitable change, will not go away soon, despite the wishes of many. This test for every child, with its resented intrusion yet valuable reports on how well we're doing, is our best chance to continue to build good learning and skills, with the goal of no child falling through the cracks.

The May, 2020 George Floyd moment with its explosion of protests reminds us we still have a way to go in bringing greater equity. Education can be the path out of poverty and abuse. Basic other new school changes, which I illustrate more fully here, can help enormously.

The CFO of the Washington, DC-based research institute, Denise Forte, of US First, in fall, 2022 vividly details online the lasting effect of the 2020 school shutdown:

> "Earlier this week, the National Assessment Governing Board and the National Center for Education Statistics released the 2022 National Assessment of Education Progress (NAEP)

mathematics and reading results. This data includes national, state, and district-level scores for grades 4 and 8 in mathematics and reading. This year's NAEP results are sobering—showing significant declines in math and reading scores for fourth and eighth graders since 2019—but this should not be surprising.

Due to the pandemic, many students—especially Black and Latino students, English learners, and students from low-income backgrounds—disproportionately experienced significant disruptions to their learning: They experienced loss of life, food and housing insecurity, unreliable access to high-speed internet and lack of computers and other devices, reduced access to student supports and education services, limited time to build strong relationships with their teachers, as well as significant reductions to in-person classroom time.

Unless we take serious action to target resources that accelerate learning, the effects of the pandemic will be long lasting for students and will affect their ability to compete in the future economy.

As state and district leaders look to help students recover from the effects of the pandemic, continued federal and state targeted investments are crucial for students, especially students of color and students from low-income backgrounds, who are more likely to live in communities most impacted by the pandemic and who have been long underserved by our nation's schools."

Re-thinking how we do school is essential to rise above the challenges.

PART ONE

A School Called Hope

CHAPTER ONE

The "Riot"

It was a bright, sunny, blue-sky spring morning. As a new young teacher, I was conducting my first class of the day. My students were unusually quiet. I believe they knew more than I did.

Suddenly we heard the sound of an explosion. I stopped teaching. Somehow, we knew this was different.

My always closed back classroom door was suddenly wrenched open, "The library door doesn't lock," yelled a normally poised, composed, older teacher, racing in. Students poured into the back of my classroom, eyes wide. No one knew what was happening.

It was 1969, a year of school protests nationally. A small group of our African-American students had charged down the main first floor corridor with long poles, smashing high ceiling lights, to shatter our school named "Hope" forever. With this one incident, old Hope was gone.

A rumor flew around school that a teacher had been hurt. Not true, never the intent. Our Black students marginalized by the system in what was then separate courses, assigned apparently by race, just wanted to make a point. They wanted their voices to be heard. It had to be dramatic to get attention. It worked. For too long, students had been sentenced apparently by skin color to low level classes taught by teachers who didn't want to be there. We'd been told to keep learning in those classes simple. Now these students rebelled against a system that dismissed them.

Our veteran teachers were proud of their work with the more privileged middle class white students, many children of nearby Brown

University professors, easy to teach. These students went off to the Ivies.

But our students of color at this time followed a different route. Many were often suspended, kicked out for a few days. They failed, dropped out, were expelled, counselled out. Some found lucrative and more exciting activity in other quicker illegal paths, not patient for the long-term rewards school might bring that they believed they'd never have the chance for. Nothing led many of our low-income, marginalized students to believe they had the opportunity others had for a better life.

I was always sad when one of my fourteen-year-old girls—often my best, most diligent students—walked somberly into my classroom for me to sign her school withdrawal form, required to exit school when pregnant. It was always only young Black girls. One could hear a pin drop as my class strained to hear what I'd say. They all understood what this sign-out meant. I would just ask this quiet young girl to sit, and told her she could do anything she wanted, and to continue with school. I never saw these sweet, too young girls again.

My English department chair Angela had told me upon my being hired that the top track students (all white, middle class, from relatively affluent homes) should learn literary analysis and writing. This elite group read and discussed the classic novels—*The Scarlet Letter*, Dickens, and the great classic poetry that I loved. Lots of Shakespeare. They wrote essays often. The middle level group had a deadly anthology that didn't speak to them, with unconnected short readings, apparently to simply acquaint them with famous dead white males. Going through that dreary tome was a slog. Angela instructed me, as a new teacher, that for what was always called the "bottom track"—those excluded from challenging reading with lively discussion, where racially different low socio-economic students resided—these students just needed to hear me speak "proper" English. Expectations were rock-bottom. The explosion we heard was that of a system that needed to be blown up.

Angela had the prescience to retire in January, 1969.

As a new teacher, I'd been initially fearful of meeting my first "bottom track" class. It turned out this class was small; the students nice, good kids. They looked at me at first with something that seemed to be fear, expectantly, then were beautifully cooperative. There wasn't a single behavior problem. One small young Black student wore sunglasses, which slightly perplexed me. It turned out he was just shy, and simply had an eye defect he didn't want others to see. This class was fine. I loved it. I moved the small class into a circle and we talked, discussed brief, simple readings, and learned together.

This rigid tracking system dismissing some students, valuing others—primarily based on color—was old-school, a nationally traditional common system no one challenged up through the 1950s, and into the '60s. It's a system that's easy for managers to set up to control students, but totally unrelated to good schools for all. Sorting students into buckets early on limited futures. A set, longtime, traditional pattern of leveled courses where learning varied widely, expectations different, was unquestioned at this time; one simply followed the rules. But this system of who gets the better learning was deeply unfair, shutting out many capable of higher learning. It was a time bomb waiting to explode.

Keeping a lid on a system unresponsive to needs of too many is easier than trying to aim to help all students learn. But the tracking system with its simple practice of keeping some students down was a pot slowly beginning to boil. Altering that pattern that kept some students down, while lifting others, clearly racially discriminatory, would take decades to change, and not only for our school, but also with schools across the country. With the 1969 disruption, Hope High School was now set on a path to change, ideally to work better. The dramatic incident—always thereafter called by veteran teachers who'd long worked under the old system the racially tinged term "the riot"—upending an old system, had to happen to open people's eyes to all that was wrong. Moving to a way that worked would take some time.

Revolution Is In The Air

As schools across the country changed with the disruptions of 1969, some then later tightened up and moved back to the old-school pattern of better learning only for some. Others moved ahead, taking the rocky road to strong work for more students. Hope took a different route. More of a zigzag.

Renegade Teacher

We at Hope High School shouldn't have been surprised that the now old-school system, with its tracking system dismissing Black students, was disrupted, because at this time nearby Brown University, just a few blocks down the street, was taken over by students. They shut down classes, occupied the president's office, issued demands, seeking equity, such as financial support for racial minority students. It was easy in these days for students to revolt, seeking justice, with protest in the air.

I stood on the Brown main Green with my graduate student friends to listen as bold protesters with bullhorns addressed classmates with the charges. Of course, "outside" leaders up from Washington spoke boldly and eloquently, capturing attention, but blending in with students. The campus Green was filled. It was a revolution. Top university officials were as perplexed as we at Hope were on what was happening, initially oblivious to the causes of this sudden revolt. And these higher-ups too hastened to try to understand and address the concerns, out of necessity, pressured. At both Brown and Hope, school was halted, classes cancelled. This shutdown had to happen to open the door to change, to acquire concessions. Change for equity was in the air across the country. The protests couldn't be dismissed.

Early on the school day morning right before the Hope disruption, a couple of my young ninth grade students came up to me in the hallway before class to tell me, almost whispering, fearful, haltingly, "Black students came to school today with weapons." Mentored by veteran teachers on strict discipline, and in disbelief—how could this happen to our good school? —I just told these students, who were trying to alert me, to go to their classes. Even though everyone knew school riots were exploding across the country, with the hostility even just down the street at Brown, I couldn't believe this could happen at our school. We were fine. Molded by the system, and by colleagues on just how things worked, I too was blind to injustice. The set system of school was one we all just went along with. No one till now had questioned it.

Now, in the aftermath of the disruption, school was closed for two weeks, the heavy fortress-like doors locked tight, as we teachers

The "Riot"

and the building administrators all met in a school across town, presumably a safer spot. In a fog at the time, as we just did what we were told, I realized only later that this move to another site, with school cancelled, also was to allow for building repairs. To their credit, but surprising to me, the previously seemingly indifferent downtown upper-echelon administrators now paid attention, to cancel school. The disruption was hard to ignore. We met as a full school staff to be informed, as our school administrators explained what they knew to a mystified faculty.

Up to this time, I'd been bored with teaching, and often called in "sick." It was easy to leave a voicemail message that I wasn't coming in. Nothing at school engaged me. As I'd looked around the faculty lunch room, all I saw was older teachers, set in their ways, proud of their work, confident they were good at their job. With their professional attire, women in heels, stockings and businesslike suits, the men in jackets and ties, a polished look, they won their students' respect, whether they were great teachers or not. But it was because we had "good" students, with less receptive ones shunted aside, that we were considered, by ourselves and the community, to constitute a "good school." It was no wonder the "riot" shook to the core teachers who felt they were doing fine, the disruption exploding a myth. For me, while I adopted the cloak of the self-satisfied, confident faculty, for appearance, I wondered what other jobs might be more interesting. Now this more interesting job was here.

During the shutdown, I didn't miss a second of these post-disturbance meetings in which our principal, backed by other administrators, all male, in their suits and ties, attempted to explain what had happened and why. The protest leaders—teenagers speaking truth to power—weren't shy about voicing their demands. The demands were defiant, set, and clear.

Included in other information that we were told on what happened, we were informed by school leaders that three of our faculty were named racist. The student leaders called for these teachers to be removed, now. We each wondered, soul searching, who this was. In an eerie system at one of these meetings, we were all told to stand in line and each was handed a small piece of paper. Those who received a paper with an "X" on it were the ones accused of racism. This was a silent lottery-like system that we all quietly conformed to. Each of the three targeted then bravely self-identified, stood and spoke. One was the very likable and astonished longtime football coach, another an English teacher, the third a quiet teacher we barely knew. We were surprised to see this branding of our colleagues. We each wondered, "Why them?" "Why not me?"

In these weeks of meetings, with the locomotive that's school always just charging along a familiar set mode now halted, we all listened intently, more closely than ever before, to what our administrators had to say. They tried to explain what had happened. They'd met after the disruption with Black student leaders—who stormed into upper echelon offices—on the demands. In this power shift, one couldn't simply dismiss the disrupters. This inequity charge was a hard concept to comprehend, given our indoctrination into the system and our participation in established ways, like robots programmed to compliantly perform. But the reality was that our racially different students were tired of being pushed aside, not provided anything even close to the schooling of the white more privileged and relatively wealthier students who went on to fine colleges, better lives. Now it was the articulate Black student leaders, confident in their demands, who were in charge, and administrators wisely listened: They had no choice. Bringing us teachers' thinking around to see that we had to treat other students well too would be the harder task. For me, new to teaching, this was intriguing, exciting, to see a whole system blown up. The struggle to change would be very different than the boring grind. It was lots more interesting.

I can still see our handsome, muscled football and wrestling star Doug Metts, alone on the stage of our school auditorium later, alone powerfully addressing our entire faculty, with challenging charges difficult to hear. I later learned that Doug's family was prominent in the Black community. It was years of being pushed down, shoved aside, that propelled him to speak. He told us we were all racist. Not everyone heard. Denial proliferated.

The "Riot"

Also, as school re-opened, I sat alone another time in the school auditorium taking my precious class break time to observe what I could of events—in now not the entertaining spot to watch student performances but the racial divide meetings center. I watched our respected guidance department head Don, more open to new views, more cued in with the times than others on our faculty were, confer with a small group. Don was just trying to moderate, let students speak, while he listened. As talk became tense, he called on one young lady, looking quiet and meek in her long dress, As it turned out, she was Muslim, and stood and vociferously attacked white people. The meeting blew up with anger; all stormed out. Hostility to white power reigned.

Such contentious incidents became common, few able to reach the other side of the cultural gulf. It was the top level school administrators who, to my astonishment, understood that this was all a period of change, a seismic shift, not just a simple discipline problem that could be easily handled. Injustice was too deeply felt and far-reaching. With our students of color now speaking as one against racial inequity, new voices now had to be listened to. But no one really knew how to best address concerns.

Over the next couple years, consultants from our local mental health institution tried to change minds. As a full faculty, we sat through what was called at the time "sensitivity sessions," conducted by trained psychologists. These sessions were a valiant attempt to create white teacher empathy for others different from us, the students we'd paid little attention to. The mental health professionals we met with tried to break through years, even decades, of habit. The set school system instilled common thinking that lifted some, put down others. A few of us newer teachers tried hard to understand. But it seemed these meetings didn't make a dent in the mindset of older teachers long accustomed to one way of school working. When you believe some students can't learn, this belief is self-fulfilling. This discriminatory belief and the system that perpetuated it took decades to change. A whole different mode of thinking and way of working isn't easily reversed.

In these faculty meetings with psychologists over the next years, one concept we were taught was termed "overload:" A student wakes up late to the sound of parents arguing. It's often at the core a money worry. There's no time for breakfast, possibly no food. He misses the bus. It takes two cross-town busses. Coming into school late, this young man has to sign in as a late student. He walks into class only to be greeted by the now redundant, "You're late!" This is the final straw. The student explodes—he too is anxious about money, food. He feels bad he's late. He's annoyed to be yelled at by the teacher, having made the effort to get to school from across town. The teacher now retaliates at his backtalk, in a power struggle. Learning for that class is out the window. Today teachers learn to say, "Welcome!" and "Thanks for coming!" It took years to get to this empathy and support.

Our all-faculty sensitivity sessions barely scratched the surface of deeply ingrained teacher beliefs. And what we weren't getting was exactly how to behave differently. Few knew at the time a better way to work. We only knew strict discipline and following school rules to maintain a smoothly working system. But that veneer was now broken. So now, uncertain of how to approach students in new ways, school discipline deteriorated. Our low-income, racially different students became more and more empowered, with us teachers unprepared to figure out how to do better. I watched as a once well-respected teacher sharply admonished a small group of girls, charging them to move on to class. They retaliated, yelled back. She was shaken, not used to backtalk. I wasn't all that great myself with what was expected to be curtailing rapidly growing discipline problems, with students behaving increasingly unruly, countering white power. I was oblivious as to how to connect across the chasm of cultural difference as the power system of control was swept away and resistance became the norm.

I learned to surrender, not challenge when a student could out-shout me, a safe solution but also a giving-up way, avoiding modifying challenging behavior needed for a more placid school. But that earlier smooth-running system was long gone. The 1969 disruption was good, needed. But how to address concerns in a way that boosted education for those formerly dismissed was a missing link. We were clueless on how to speak to alienated students. No one said, "Do it this way." That winning strategy hadn't yet been invented.

But surprisingly to us cynics who were convinced that the remote school system central office, always called "downtown," had no idea of our challenges, top district administrators tried. To their credit, astonishing to me, they began to do the right thing. Someone was paying attention. Suddenly funds, always alleged to be tight, magically appeared for new class sets of books for us English teachers. Brightly colored, fresh new paperbacks of Richard Wright's *Native Son*, and his magnificent *Black Boy*, Ralph Ellison's *Invisible Man*, other Black writers' texts appeared, intended to replace dry barely readable texts such as the deadly *Silas Marner* (1861), which I always wondered why anyone would want scores of students to read. I learned from reading *The Autobiography of Malcolm X*, to understand lives of young people trapped in poverty and often difficult home lives. Other English teachers resented the new books. Some, with beliefs shaken, retired early. One strong, chain-smoking, outspoken large personality steeped in old school ways—earlier loved by many students, the white kids—was deeply troubled by the Black literature books. It was too hard to cross that bridge. He moved to another school in the city that was less dramatic.

As the old-school strict structure with now more empowered students declined, the old system challenged and broken, with no new model to replace it that would be a fairer way for school, faculty morale sank, many gave up. School discipline was shattered. The now empowered students were not going to accept old classrooms that didn't speak to them. It would take decades to change to school embracing a philosophy and way of working to help all students learn better. Some attempts though, were brief, bright, brilliant successes.

CHAPTER TWO

Making a Change

It was our new English department chair who helped us make a major change.

When the old-school-steeped Angela retired as department head, fortuitously in mid-year of January,1969, Paul now as chair was brought into the ways of thinking that administrators were gaining from meetings with the Black student leaders.

In addition to being an English teacher, Paul was a coach, well aware of the skills and abilities of diverse young people. Paul saw a student weak in the classroom could be a superstar on the playing field, showing brilliance and skill. He knew school had to better serve more students.

As we met as English teachers, some members of our group came kicking and screaming to Paul's attempts to enlighten us; others simply followed his wise guidance. A few, afraid to speak up, understood student concerns and knew we had to change. I looked to follow Paul. For me, complaints from colleagues who strove to defend the past grated. But I was as oblivious as everyone else as to the solution of how to bridge the gap to better engage our now changed student population.

The English department was the worst. Every student was required to take four years of English, and these yearlong courses were rigidly tracked. Once in a particular track, a student was doomed to remain there. Paul, with infinite patience and determination, led us to trash that old system that determined a student's place in the world and adopt a totally new approach.

Paul had been a professional baseball player. He had our school baseball team use "Paul Donovan" bats, his name etched in the wood, in practice, not to show off, never his style, but to encourage effort and ambition. Also, Paul had served in the army, where the same skills were expected, and demonstrated, by everyone, of any race or income level. From his own life and from what he was hearing in meetings with administrators, Paul saw what the rest of us, insulated in our own separate classroom as teachers, couldn't see: The bigger picture. The ugly truth was that the old system in which we worked had shaped our thinking so that we viewed our low-income racially different students as less capable. Paul knew better.

Paul was also a saint. Tall, gray haired, distinguished-looking, he was smarter than he tended to appear because he was always a careful listener. He mulled over what he heard, responding empathetically. His charisma was in his silence. And he connected with everyone. His ability to listen was especially therapeutic at this time of crisis, with many just venting, longing for a return to the good old days, and somehow he was able to bring out the best from all of our different personalities in the department. Paul was fighting against the tide, but he got us to give up our old ways of working to adopt something totally new: Together we leaped over a chasm, even bringing along the most defiant, locked into old-school thinking.

Much later, I learned from a former student that during the "riot," Paul's class also heard the explosion that rocked the building. Paul, as a department head, apparently had been forewarned. In response, he simply locked his classroom door and moved the class into a circle. He told students something was happening to Hope, and asked each to state whether it would be good for the school or not. Paul, it seems, had been clued in early, knew something was coming, as my own students had seen on their way to school that morning. He had both the forewarning and the presence of mind to allow his distracted class to talk about what was happening, providing a soothing influence, and possibly opening minds. This opportunity to talk happened in Paul's class as I was clueless, speechless, stymied, just down the hall in my own separate classroom. His serene presence and natural leadership, though no doubt churning inside, calmed everyone, both during the disruption and later as we struggled to understand and process what had happened to our school.

Many teachers seemed to either dismiss or fail to comprehend the significance of this national trend of schools exploding in retaliation against the old system. It was easiest to be dismissive to downplay an attack against the system one had always known. But Paul was able to bring all of us teachers—old or young, Black or white, stuck in our ways or open to new approaches—to loose consensus. Together we upset the old-school apple cart.

We had frequent English department meetings. They seemed constant. A couple teachers spoke long and vociferously, expressing their one-track mind complaint against what they saw as student rebellion that they believed should be tamped down. These insistent voices were hard to silence. But we all showed up to these painful meetings because Paul asked us to. We each attended because Paul granted each of us respect, and we in turn respected him. And Paul clearly saw there could be a better way.

One highly articulate but especially loud, continuously complaining teacher, a Cassandra, invited us to meet at her nearby house. Marge, our hostess, was a Shakespeare lover, actually living on "Montague Street," dramatic herself. But even the comfort of her lovely East Side home didn't halt the venting. We invited a local professor to meet with us, at Marge's house. He was astonished when several teachers pounced to sharply critique his writing piece he'd given us, only for only its punctuation and sentences, without paying attention to content, easier than discerning his ideas. As so often, I just sat in silence, amazed, as others tore into his writing. The professor too sat speechless, his attempt at remediating us lost.

Then, at long last, after few months, Paul presented an alternative. It was because he'd brought us all together and stayed with us that we'd formed a loose if still dysfunctional team of sorts and were able to—even if reluctantly—adopt a change in what we did. We'd had "outsiders" brought in by high-echelon supervisors from the mental health field try to tell us what we should think. But Paul was one of us. So we accepted his guidance. He was able to take us farther faster. Plus, what he suggested was what to *do* differently, not how to think. Sometimes doing the right thing trumps the thinking. It can even change thinking.

An Outlandish Curriculum Saves the Day

We moved to "mini-courses." We would each dream up a brief ten-week course. Students would select a course they wanted from our offerings, purely their choice. Each quarter of the year we'd change courses. Teachers would have a whole new group of students every ten weeks. Student choice meant racially mixed classes.

We could make up and offer any course we wanted, an opportunity for personal choice. Students would then move on to a new course, and a new teacher, for the next quarter. My creative student teacher invented a course called, "How would the world be different if there was no music?" This was popular. I taught poetry, less inventive, then dreamed up something else, such as journalism, for the next quarter. I loved this. It was fun for students to actually get to choose. This shift enlivened an old sometimes deadly curriculum and worked.

It was us formerly contentious teachers who now met together to sort students into classes based on their course selection. Generating new class lists each quarter by matching students with their course choices was done purely by hand. Remarkably, we otherwise independent thinkers simply complied with what needed to be done. We disparate teachers met together all in the same room to make piles of student names for each course, actual paper piles. This was a mindless but necessary painstaking task no guidance department, which normally scheduled students, would ever take on, but we were doing it because Paul had proposed this. As it happened, this tedious process of placing students in each next new course helped calm the waters. Once we turned to "how" to create these courses, rather than "what" was right or wrong, we moved along. Action trumped philosophy. And giving us each a choice of what to teach worked. This dramatically different approach led to basic change. The bizarre new curriculum transformed what we did. Now we teachers had to make our courses appealing to students, or we wouldn't have a class. Modes of teaching now moved more to inviting students to discuss ideas, not teacher-driven.

Students loved the mini-courses, and even we teachers adapted remarkably well to doing something different. Despite earlier devotion to year-long set courses, some simply went along with Paul's guidance, while others enjoyed solving the central problem of assigning students to different levels, constraining learning, with now creating racial diversity in our courses. Key was the fact that each of us could create our own courses, altering what's called "top down" —you must change—with "bottom up"—come up with something you want to do. Because we were all in this together, we now became something close to collegial after the divisions caused by reactions to the protest disruption. Creating piles of student choices was better than discussion, which was really just some venting.

Because we were all English teachers who, to varying degrees, were skilled in and loved reading, literary analysis, ideas, discussion, and writing, we now offered traditional English course content but with a kid-friendly surface cover. Seeing fresh new faces each quarter, for both students and teachers, was lively, even fun. Plus, someone who offered Shakespeare got those kids. But also, now teachers had to be popular with more than just some students. With each of us offering whatever we wanted, a young male teacher who spoke to young men devised a hit course on horseracing. I don't know how popular those courses on Shakespeare were.

Since classes were no longer tracked, students selected their courses based on interest, and on the teacher. Because they chose whatever they wanted, the resulting mixed-achievement-level classes were lively. Timid students began to speak up. Since students were no longer sorted into bottom- or upper-level classes, there was no way to know if teachers considered them "smart" or "not-smart." With classes racially mixed, students from different neighborhoods and home lives learned from each other. Teachers now had to engage everyone, not address only some. It worked. We didn't invent mini-courses; they were being picked up across the country at this time. But we did make these briefer courses open to all students to select from fit us. Sadly, it didn't last. After a few years a "Back to Basics" principal killed this program, puzzling to a new administrator. If we'd had a test to show students were learning well, this would have saved our program.

After this accomplishment of integrating classes, with his great success in overturning discriminatory practice, Paul was allowed to retire early. He moved across the street to an elite private school to teach in a quieter setting. The Head of School there had been an army buddy of Paul's, and had waited a long time to have Paul there. Paul had paid his dues. The deal made with the central district downtown administration was that he'd come back to Hope one day during the next year to count for the number of years for an optimal public school retirement pension. Paul's visit back across the street to Hope was in theory working in an administrative role, which he used as a time to visit us, with top administrators breaking the rules for a hero. Paul stopped me in a stairwell to talk. (We'd always joked that we both preferred to take the stairs because they were faster than the teachers' elevator.) He asked me how I was doing, and, as always, just listened. Even this brief exchange re-centered me.

When Paul left Hope, we lost a gifted leader. By changing the work of the English department, which must have created headaches for administrators, with multiple courses in place of yearlong set courses, making it hard to find a student, Paul changed a central core of the school. Other departments were then given a sign to think about how they too might work differently, especially when our principal publicly commended the English teachers—what he called "Paul Donovan's department"—on our dramatic change. A principal would never normally praise an individual or group to the full faculty, avoiding showing favoritism, risking generating resentment. But we did deserve that comment on what we'd done. We'd transformed our set curriculum, to eliminate that tracking policy and practice. It was Paul who was responsible, not us. But he didn't mind that we all were congratulated.

When the English department made a major change in response to pressing forces, and the upper administrative level approved and supported this, it reversed the common "top down" demand process of imposing ways to work that rarely works well. And excising full year traditional curriculum to set up courses in a radically different way provided a model for a process for the 1990s shift to standards learning that was to hit decades later. Paul initiated first meeting and just letting us vent, bringing very different personalities all together in the room over time, then proposing a way to solve a problem, a dramatically different way, accepted because we'd teamed up. Throwing out the old and bringing in the new disrupts and can improve. It's in winning hearts and minds that's the trick.

Paul continued to teach for years at the private Quaker school across the street. Our life at Hope never achieved the apparent serenity of that school.

CHAPTER THREE

A School on Shifting Sands

It's hard to pinpoint precisely when morale drops. A cumulation of events and people's own experiences occurs over time. Suddenly we recognize we're not doing well. A downward spiral is hard to halt. Hope sank.

When Paul left Hope, we'd had a creative period. We'd felt empowered to serve our students well. Teamwork brought collegiality. The next principal cancelled the mini-courses, and decline hit.

There was no longer a strong impetus to push us forward. Gradually, deep ties to old ways of thinking pulled us back to relying on the old past methods that didn't work. No new voices spoke up to urge us forward. After the disruption then shutting down the mini-courses, nothing inspired engagement. The lack of leadership to better work with students occurred at the same time middle-class white parents removed their children from Hope, concerned the school would not meet their expectations. And in the mid-70s, federally mandated busing intended to racially balance schools meant more poverty-level students of color were bussed from the South Side of town to the East Side, with the federal aim of integrating schools. But in a failed policy, backlash to busing only meant white flight, which occurred in urban schools nationally, creating racially segregated schools. Since we educators weren't provided with helpful information on how to meet the needs of the new population, we were stymied. White flight, along with teachers unsure about how best to serve a different demographic, left Hope with more students whom few knew how to work well with.

Standards at Hope didn't just drop, they died. Discipline issues multiplied as a result of classes that didn't work for different students. Tedious teacher talk, unengaging classes, and a punitive discipline code all met resistance. No one mentioned empathy.

It didn't take long for a new principal to cancel our mini-courses. The brief courses worked well for students and teachers, but not for the disciplinarian administrators who found it hard to locate trouble-makers when class enrollments changed frequently: It wasn't easy finding a student. Ending a lively English program that had engaged both students and teachers took the wind out of our sails. Maintaining discipline took priority under a next new principal. School reverted to old attempts at strictness and control because that was what most of us knew well. "The pendulum has swung back!" a long-time teacher cheered delightedly, as my heart sunk.

Doldrums hit. The school year pattern quickly dropped from some initial optimism at the school year start then to despair. As a too-brief summer ended at the start of a new year, we located and dusted off teaching shoes, packed away shorts and bathing suits to bring back high heels, suits, men in neckties and jackets, and organized our lives around those 6am wakeup calls. We came back to school hoping for a bright new start. The weather cooperated, suddenly turning cooler, mustering us back inside. The first day of a new school year always began with us teachers coming in out of the sunshine and sitting in the dark school auditorium, barely hearing the principal's welcome-back speech of managerial instructions, pleas for control of students. We were mainly trying to get our minds around the return to now an especially challenging job.

Always, the best part of the new year was seeing familiar faces again, greeting teacher friends with now-relaxed smiles, feeling the camaraderie we shared—younger and older, veterans and new teachers, good friends and just colleagues—now that we were back together. The harried looks of last school year's end had softened. We were even happy, somewhat, to see the principal. A common thread held us together: We were teachers. That bond bred community. On this first day back, before students arrived, we could chat in the unique collegiality of a school family.

A School on Shifting Sands

Hope High School, flowering trees planted by East Side parents

And always, the ease and camaraderie that bordered on friendship evaporated the next day with the explosion of over a thousand fresh-faced students filling the corridors and classrooms, as we each commandeered our separate posts in our own classrooms. The egg carton school design sentenced us to our own cells in which to attend to our students, demanding attention, no longer collegial dialogue.

This was a new year. We were hopeful. This year students would be cooperative. Things would go more smoothly. As we entered our own sanctuary of our classroom to host a whole new group of young people, students appeared receptive, sizing up their new teachers, attentive. This ease of connecting with students would last only a few weeks.

We always started the year with optimism. September was a time of purpose. Then the intensity—the bombardment of many students, multiple duties, fast-paced, unique challenges—would last till June, punctuated with too-brief vacations, demanding attention. While every year school was a train hurtling down the track, now, in our post-disruption phase, our lives no longer followed the earlier smoothly running pattern. School had become derailed.

Another Side of Summertime

In my earliest years of teaching at Hope, my all-white middle-class students and I would agree that summer was fun, and returning to school wasn't easy, but we'd settle in. Now, however, with our school demographic changed to the majority low-income Black students, many bussed over from crowded tenement houses, I looked at this year's group and cheerfully greeted them with the usual question: "Wasn't summer fun?"

My students' reaction shattered my own picture of summer as escape and relaxation. Their faces turned sober.

"My cousin came from New York to visit and was shot at a party," somberly volunteered a pretty sixteen-year-old, with her smartly coifed hair and carefully pressed back-to-school jeans.

Another voice quietly chimed in, "It was too hot." He didn't need to complete the thought. With no money for air conditioners, the inescapable heat added extra tension to extended-family households, crowded apartments. Other heads nodded slowly, remembering fights of all sorts, even stray bullets.

For our students, school was a safe haven. Most qualified for federally-funded free breakfast and lunch programs. They received no-cost passes for the two buses required to reach the East Side sanctuary. The structure of school, and the distance from more dangerous neighborhoods, even with the school-day fights that broke out often, provided security. We read news reports of neighborhood shootings and bystander deaths across town. At least school was safe from this kind of violence.

Conflict in the Halls and Classrooms

Since school meant safety for many students, our principal and assistant principals made it their priority to attempt to protect that atmosphere by focusing on efforts to maintain order. As we teachers were less able to work well with students of different backgrounds, we saw more open disobedience, hostility toward a system that didn't speak to them. As some teachers dropped standards and expectations, tardiness, absenteeism, and social chatting in class meant teaching was more of a struggle for everyone. Decline hit quickly, with no force to stop the fall.

When I first started teaching, under the strict behavior management system in a large mostly white school of around 1500 students, we'd had only one assistant principal in charge of discipline. The misbehavior of less than cooperative individuals of any race was halted by means of rigid rules that could mean expulsion. Anyone who seemed less than involved was in peril of dismissal. Now, even with a smaller population but larger numbers of resistant students, we had three assistant principals. The principal too spent much of his time literally chasing kids. We all-white teachers mainly knew only the administrative goal of maintaining order. That white control did not speak to students of a different income level and race never crossed our minds. It was no wonder we had problems. It seemed there was no way out of this quandary.

Hope now crackled with frayed nerves and physical fighting, often right outside my classroom door. Pent-up frustrations exploded. Corridor fights, when students left the confines of one class to move to the next, encountering others, were common. "There was a fight in the cafeteria today," a teacher would almost whisper. The few teachers monitoring the cafeteria filled with students at lunchtime were insufficient to control so many students eager to either join a fight or at minimum crowd around those engaged. A cafeteria fight wasn't just a tiff, but would explode into a sharp show of force among energetic, heated young people. At times, an ambulance was summoned. Small stresses, who-knows-what rivalries, perceived insults, and slights that struck an already on-edge raw nerve could spark a vicious brawl that instantly magnetized a crowd of onlookers. Many were excited about a distraction from class, flocking to observe, drawn to the display of angry fist fighting, hair pulling.

We adults struggled to discern who instigated a fight. Different students would volunteer different information on who did what. Administrators were too busy to spend a lot of time untangling nuance. The rule was that if two students were fighting, both were suspended. To me, this seemed unfair to the student who acted in self-defense, but the administrators were determined to discourage fights. They couldn't spend time sorting through contradictory stories, with friends on one side telling tales on the other.

So it was understandable that the principal pleaded with us, in all-faculty meetings and over the school loud speaker system, to stand in the corridor when students passed to their next classes. These school managers needed our vigilance to intervene in—or in my case, just to spot—electrifying tensions as students jammed the hallways. A coward, I would just instantly pick up the classroom phone to summon help when I saw trouble in the corridor, not leap into the fray. Always, an administrator would instantly appear.

There were too many fires to put out, and discipline problems wreaked havoc on the class learning environment. We weren't helping all kids, and we knew it. Now and then we'd hear a colleague comment that we should receive "combat pay." With the distance between teachers and students so great, a chasm seeming impossible to bridge, we became a culture of complaint.

It was almost always young men who seemed most beyond our reach, seeking action and engagement school didn't provide, with its often deadly lectures. Their disengagement from whatever we tried to teach could result in disruption that dissolved the entire class. Jack, our beloved and most effective assistant principal in charge of discipline, told us he could see our frenzied state of mind in our shaky handwriting in the reports we sent to his office citing misbehaviors. He kept us teachers sane. Tall, regal in his dark suit, not prone to small-talk, he was heaven-sent as backup. While we couldn't control the anonymous corridor fights, Jack supported us in our classrooms. He was our rock.

Students of color too respected Jack, possibly I believe due to the power he held, but also to his even-handed manner. He never showed annoyance or anger. He would simply quietly say to a student, privately in his office, "Take two days," and slip a form to the miscreant. In his shorthand method, this meant suspension from school for a couple days, and the student knew why.

No one argued with Jack. He somehow tamped down his own frayed nerves to present a calm face. His patience was infinite. Even especially troublesome students turned around one hundred percent, transformed after meeting with him. He was an urban teacher's dream. Even when Jack knew about the difficult home conditions a challenging student had, he still he insisted on good behavior. We teachers appreciated that. Jack stayed with us for many years, our hero on whose support we could always rely. We all attended his retirement party, a sad occasion, but we were happy for him. He went off to serve as disciplinarian at a small parochial boys' school. He later told us it was like being retired.

But reliance on just one person to make things work is a mistake. What's needed is a system that drives a smoothly working environment, with everyone on the same page. In fact, we'd settle for just having the same guidebook, or for half a class cooperating, for students moving from class to class without a fight.

Other heroes too came and went in those dark days, through the revolving door of urban school leadership. I gained admiration for Mary, suddenly arriving in the middle of the year as the new head of the Guidance Department, with rumored big-city political connections. Trust was hard-earned among us teachers. At first, with my skeptical eye, I felt Mary was incompetent. How could an administrator, and especially a woman, step into a troubled school in the middle of a year, without knowing the school, and not starting at the beginning of the year to see tensions slowly build up? Then I saw Mary leap over a wide desk in her skirt and high heels to race into the heart of a raging corridor fight to halt it. Another time, as I drove by the building later in the day, I saw Mary walking a female student out to her car. A brutal girl-fight had left Dakara with a bleeding face, swollen eyes. And when a university consultant—sent from out of state to straighten us out—complained that Hope had no signage for the school's name, Mary used her own money to install prominent, tasteful letters spelling out "Hope High School" above the front entrance. Mary cared.

Yet the pull of negative influences on students was overwhelming. Our school leaders futilely stressed order, and most tried to help. But the job was Sisyphean.

Small Efforts to Help

With discipline problems common, at the same time, it was a joy when I saw a fire for learning in a student, or found a voracious reader.

Letitia, a delight to have in class because of her love of learning, devoured books. We bonded. She read and re-read the thousand-page *Gone with the Wind,* and suggested we read it for class. I cringed at the racial denigration of happy servants which she chose to ignore in the book depicting racist Southern plantation homes, and I suspected few others would make it through all those pages as easily as she had. I knew she was enthralled with the love story. One day she walked into class, mildly announcing, "My father is Heathcliff," the tortured soul of *Wuthering Heights,* which she'd read over the summer.

Letitia was a fine student, and devoted to her dance class, a life-saving creative outlet essential to escape home stresses. One morning I saw an article in the statewide newspaper describing how she spent the night leaning against the family's apartment door so that her drunken alcoholic father couldn't break in to kill her mother, as he was threatening.

Another student was killed in a fatal car accident on the highway, possibly drunk or drug-fueled at the time. "Christ, What a death!" wrote one of my students in a poem. My one student who limped as a result of a gunshot wound at a young age is a sight that stays with me still. In another incident, a young woman sitting up front listed for me in class all the things a thief would take from my house, which was disconcerting since I lived so close to the school. I pretended not to hear her, a common armor we cultivated to try to keep an even keel.

When I showed my class a video of an earlier year's student presentation—made by a handsome young man with striking, easily recognized blue-green eyes—a student blurted out, "Oh! He's a big drug dealer!" and then quickly slapped a hand over her mouth. For bright, ambitious young men not captivated by school, the drug trade with its instant cash and exhilarating danger was compelling. And it was too easy for distracted and disaffected students to just not show up at school; no teacher ever complained about lax attendance of a class disrupter.

Yet while Hope was facing problems for which we did not yet have solutions, I soon then found myself at the center of a change from a school that didn't work to turn to a new system that functioned much better, even supremely well, not just for me, but for everyone.

Striving for Learning

I tried to make class work. But I began to feel more and more alone in my teaching. As the number of class disrupters grew, it became harder for me to continue to teach literary analysis and writing, a subject that had been considered "English" in my earlier years of teaching. Many of my teacher friends had given up, left, and I felt I was working against the tide. But I stayed with what I'd always known English to be: A world of ideas and a discipline that through reading opens windows on new places, people, and ideas. I was committed to helping young people see how books take us to new worlds where we learn about different people, their fine qualities and sinister ways, about values and the right thing to do, expanding perspective.

I had—and still have—faith that every child is curious. I believed—and still believe—that despite surface reactions, all young people yearn to learn more. Looking for that spark of interest and then developing it is the key, though often a challenge. And writing is self-expression that leads to self-knowledge. We learn through writing. New ideas come to us as we write. I loved having students write. Often, they did too. But at this point I and my fellow teachers just weren't capturing our students' attention. Often the gulf was just too wide. I felt terrible when I saw a determined Vietnamese student trying to decipher Hawthorne's dense prose in *The Scarlet Letter*, a language dictionary on top of the text as he strained to translate. He'd been so quiet (always a gift) that I'd neglected him. I may have helped some students; I knew I wasn't helping all.

With our school leaders pleading with us to assist in controlling the unengaged students outside our classrooms, my inclination was always love of teaching, not crowd control. I loved learning myself, and wanted my students to appreciate the beauty in words. I devoted my energy to coaxing students' insights into great literature and getting them to enjoy writing. With the school focus on management, I tried against the tide to stimulate learning.

Even with its arcane, often unfathomable language, *Romeo and Juliet* was always a hit. Mercutio trading insults with the evil Tybalt was not so foreign to my students. Teen heroes and villains, feuding families with the cause unknown, hatreds and loves, and the fatal swordfight which Romeo tragically tries to prevent—all these caught students' attention. And in discussing *The Scarlet Letter,* my students of color all condemned the centuries ago but also relevant weak men who painted Hester as the sinner, recognizing how she was shunned her in her pregnancy to conceal a man's own guilt. I loved that these young people had a deep sense of right and wrong, as they vehemently identified the woman as the victim and were outraged by the male cowards. Even with all the dense sentences, they "got it." And I was happy when a student told me he liked reading *To Kill a Mockingbird*, which I assumed was because of the Southern lawyer defending a Black man. When asked why, however, he told me he could use those big words in his rapping. But not every book caught hold in such varied ways.

Always seeking ways to get students to read, I was delighted when one happily told me that her boyfriend, now in the army, enjoyed reading a book I'd given him. I remembered handsome, polite, young Norm, but I had no idea what the book was. It turned out it was *Soul on Ice*, by Black Panther Eldridge Cleaver, a potent consciousness-raising tract on Black empowerment. It was a library copy I'd hoped to return.

Instead, it had traveled with Norm to some far-off land. Since I often tried to speak to students' interests, to help move them along when I thought there might be an inroad, I was thrilled whenever I saw I'd made a difference for one of them, as when he or she connected with a book, to hopefully launch reading. Such a small victory is a psychic reward few jobs offer.

But often in these challenging years I'd hear a quiet, non-hostile voice from the back of the room say, "This ain't English." I knew the genesis of this comment. I had students reading, discussing, writing—but it was a fragile, determined effort, and wasn't unanimous among my colleagues. With the school's focus on order, not learning, some teachers chose to take the easy route to teaching. Many hoarded stacks of the hefty beloved—but only by teachers—grammar book, the well-organized but stultifying, brain-numbing *Warriner's English Grammar and Composition*, a tome on "correct" writing. Mindless isolated word correctness, proper sentence structure, and punctuation rule exercises kept students busy, but with no transfer to their writing. All they had to do was read the book's correct apostrophe use, or see a corrected sentence fragment and then write out some hopefully correct examples, mindlessly imitating the book's usage, sometimes accurately. This activity took up time. At the end of the silent class, with the teacher treasuring the quiet, students would hand the teacher their papers, demonstrating completion of the work. I just hoped they were out the door before the teacher dumped their papers into the trash can.

That wasn't English in the sense I knew it.

A new system was direly needed at Hope. It was just around the corner. I stayed long enough to love being a part of a new way that worked.

CHAPTER FOUR

Getting Noticed, Back to Old School

Surprising to me, as I struggled to understand the 1969 disruption, and tried to help students, though school was now more challenging, my enthusiasm for attempting to work better in an otherwise confused time was noticed.

The 1969 protest impacted me and my thinking. School had been lively and engaging, even exciting, with dumping the old English department curriculum and switching to lively mini-courses. One day I walked in to the English department office to speak with the next new department chair following Paul. I don't recall what I said to Matt, but I'd been listening to bits of veterans' angst post-riot, and picking up some new thoughts. Things on how school could work better weren't crystal clear to me; I just had some sense that new and different ways of thinking and working could work better. I'd heard all the complaints with the dissolution of order. Confrontation-averse, I was reluctant to state much to colleagues or at meetings. I don't know what I said to Matt, a gentlemanly, avuncular, older teacher. He just listened.

The next thing I knew, I was meeting across town with the Superintendent of Schools, a meeting Matt had arranged and took me to. I shared with this top schools leader in his downtown quiet office alternatives to standard practice. I don't know why, but I stated such ideas as disparaging the system of teachers getting paid more just because they took more college courses. Plus, why did teaching for more years—termed "longevity"—connect with higher pay? Those earning the most were those who stuck it out longer, but not necessarily best for them or for their students. I'd seen many worn out. I wasn't myself looking for higher pay, just happy to have a paycheck, but highest paid as oldest perplexed me. These were ideas I never knew I had, really hadn't cared about, that poured out—and to the superintendent, the top ruler of the school system. I was surprised at the thoughts that came out of my mouth, all ideas contrary to long-time practice. The superintendent and Matt just listened. I wasn't used to confronting power, certainly not with those superiors in charge who wanted to hear what I had to say.

Then I kept getting phone message notices from a person I didn't know. I was busy and dismissed these. When I finally returned the call, I was offered a position to teach with the Brown University Education Department, a unique arrangement in which the superintendent would release me so that I'd still be half-time at Hope, and now also half-time at Brown. Apparently, the Education department chair had spoken with the superintendent. I was young and eager and understood nothing about what this would involve, but took the position. It amounted to two full-time jobs, and was fun.

Brown Education Department, 1970s

It took me a while to realize that I was hired at Brown because some believed I was of a generation thinking in a new way about school. People in the late Sixties and Seventies were searching for answers, for better ways for school to work. School change was in the air, even for top level school people who were those in power. I was seen as part of this movement for some change. Perhaps it had been our dynamic, more equitable mini-courses that captured some attention. Young, idealistic thinkers fueled by the civil rights movement and what's called "Sixties" energy were now entering the Brown Master of Arts in Teaching program, flocking in, hoping to be agents of change in schools. Neil Postman's 1969 bestseller *Teaching as a Subversive Activity*—an assault on old-school practices—was these students' bible. People in charge—those older—somehow thought, simply because I was younger, that I could help figure things out, to respond to calls for change in education that had become a national movement swirling around us. I wasn't sure I fully understood how schoolwork could be revolutionary, still just working in the confines of the classroom, but I found myself propelled by history, floating atop a wave.

Reverting to Old School

But then a next wave new surprise hit Hope, and not for the better.

After leaving Hope for halftime work while also teaching Methods of Teaching at Brown and supervising the new young creative student teachers, seeing them fail, and also delight, I then years later returned fulltime to a school reverting even more to the past, that dreary old mode that didn't work. This was hard. The next wave for schools was called "Back to Basics," celebrated by delighted veteran teachers. After the excitement of mini-courses and then the joy of working with new young Brown students who didn't know some strategies for teaching wouldn't work but tried these and were successful, now I was thrown back as a cog in a set system that hadn't worked well and that I wasn't cut out for. I left teaching.

I'd tremendously enjoyed working with the bright, eager Brown students, learning myself about Methods of Teaching English along the way, and then supervising these inventive young people in their transition into teaching in real schools. I loved the intensity, until after ten years of the two jobs, teaching at Hope, and teaching, then supervising, new student teachers, I hit pause. One day my car stalled in the pouring rain as I entered the highway to travel out to a suburban school. It hit me that I was tiring of these many school visits. The two jobs of Brown and Hope were draining. I had to use my weekends to prepare for my Hope classes or I'd be sunk. The Brown department on their part too decided that they wanted a doctorate-level professor in the role, so my exit was a mutually agreeable parting. But nothing prepared me for the shock of returning full-time to Hope, which not only slowly moved back to the past while I was learning lots in my Brown position, but regressed to the Dark Ages of school with a population that didn't fit old rules, a clash sure to fail.

A New Principal Moves Us Back in Time

In my half-time absence, one of our Hope science teachers, Joe, a Brown graduate, and therefore valued by superiors, had bravely stood up at our faculty meetings following the "riot," and asked hard questions. Joe challenged presenters who were trying to expand our thinking on racial issues. A cool-headed scientist just seeking answers, Joe's bold questions were nicely phrased, just a question or a comment (often a comment in the question), not seeming hostile or antagonistic, not challenging a speaker. He at times read aloud his carefully scripted questions. But he probed for explanations on problems on the minds of many: Why are we not tougher now on students of any race if that student is disruptive in class? Why aren't we grading more strictly? Why are we letting students with high absenteeism pass courses?

Joe gained a following. The veteran faculty loved him because he calmly spoke out on their concerns. But though just seeking answers, Joe was conditioned by the old way of school. Our strong science department had had superb teachers, but, again, only really successful with some students, those more privileged kids. These fine teachers, as with those in other departments, loved their discipline and were specialists in their respective areas. The longtime science department chair, tall, distinguished-looking, whom many graduates say turned them around, was a model of professionalism and dedication. But these greats taught well students who showed up prepared to comprehend their expertise. Others found it hard to grasp concepts. More struggling low income students of color didn't always fit their classes.

With a revolving door of school principals attempting to make Hope work, one only lasting six weeks, and with a groundswell of support from a frayed faculty, perplexed with the challenges of a different school population, under the mysterious ways of the district central office, Joe, only licensed as a teacher, was anointed our new principal. The deal with the central office administration, bending the rules, was that while in the job, he'd have to take the college courses that would qualify him for this position.

Joe moved simmering concerns off the back burner. In the years after the revolt, as behavior standards had slipped, we were stymied for a new and better way to help struggling and recalcitrant students work well. Since we were told we were doing things wrong, but not helped with what would work well, the result was that upon my return full-time to Hope, I now saw more fully that order had deteriorated. We missed the influence of more engaged students who could pull up others in a class. Those students had pulled out. Administrators couldn't keep up with the dissolution of discipline. Veterans who hadn't retired or transferred to other schools turned angry and cynical, longing for the mythic Golden Years when Hope was a "good school."

As teachers bemoaned our challenging students, and no one had solutions, Joe cracked down. Exasperated with the lack of discipline we'd had in earlier days, Joe decided it was Back to Basics. Suburban teachers too struggled with the '70s counter-culture movement. It was those more outspoken veterans of earlier years, whom other teachers call "loud and proud," "Napoleonic" who argued for stricter discipline, not in the "Let's figure out another way" mode, who now dominated.

The first thing to go with Joe was eliminating a nice "rotating schedule" that we'd adopted in a more creative era. This schedule mystified anyone who didn't work in schools because it seemed odd that the time of a class moved each day. We teachers loved it. Students figured it out. Everyone benefited. With this schedule, a class that met at the end of the school day on Friday, when everyone's brain was fried and students were restless at best, or brain-dead, just ready to explode from boredom, would then rotate to meet first on Monday, when the teacher was fresh and students more receptive. Students easily adjusted to this complex rotating schedule. Joe eliminated this class period rotation. Each day's class schedule would be the same. Friday's deadly last-period class would remain a challenge for the entire year. It was easier now for those seeking disciplinary culprits to locate a student with a set schedule, but for teachers interested in moving learning along, we could write those last period of the day students off. Always, management for order trumped what was best for learning.

There were now no more department meetings where we gathered on issues, if not always well-behaved ourselves. No leader moved us forward, with good new ideas to accommodate our current students. Stuck in the plight of school not speaking to our students, with no one having answers, Joe just pressed for order. He launched a crackdown period in an attempt to bring back old Hope, ignoring the fact that our student population had changed. Those attempting to help had pulled out. I lost interest in my work.

No one had a plan anymore. Since all we knew well was the old-school rigid system, then demands and reaction to demands, then failure in our response to a type of student whom we teachers didn't understand well, it was only inertia that kept me at Hope. I was just sad. Teaching lacked appeal. Then, finally, once again, things changed, for me.

CHAPTER FIVE

Turning School Upside Down, Again

During our back-to-basics period, all that was expected now was that we were in the spot assigned and that we kept the lid on a class. No one cared about the quality of learning. Engaging all students in learning wasn't yet a concept even imagined. I wasn't fit for this mode of just maintaining order.

In this back-to-the-past period welcomed by others, school for me was not just boring but also I felt stymied by lack of any success that I was making with students. We weren't going anywhere. In these less than dynamic, stagnant years, one day I sat at my desk in my empty classroom in late spring and pondered my work. What was I accomplishing?

We teachers now operated in isolation in our separate classrooms, with no lively meetings to stir discussion. Even contention would have been welcome. And there were no expectations for how and what to teach. There was no conversation. Teaching was independent and random. Who doesn't love independence? The problem with no outside stimulus, annoying as it might be, was that I for one knew I was making little progress. As the end of the year loomed, I saw that a student who was a "C" student at the start of the school year still had a "C" at the end of the year. He or she was just a "C" student and would remain so. Also, if in some way I was helping a student, there was no recognition; it didn't count. I felt no one cared, a constant drumbeat in my head. Frustration grew; younger teachers who had other options came, tried their best, and left. For veteran teachers, stuck paying their mortgages and kids' college tuitions, with little alternative options, their frustration with an increasingly more challenging population turned to a wave of cynicism. Rejected applicants for the rarely available small steps up become disaffected. When a colleague who also coached applied for the step up to school Athletic Director, and also for English department chair, and was rejected for both, he turned sour, always complaining. When colleagues help foster an atmosphere of despair, all-school morale plummets. School is a burden. It becomes hard to drag oneself into work each day. The system held little reward now for me. The freshness of early years of teaching, and then awakened to a new way of thinking about school, then shutting down those changes, shifted to burnout. So when a friend asked me to help out at her husband's new store, I had no second thoughts.

I took off a year from teaching to move into the computer area. Computer sales were hot. This great new job would give me a better life. I imagined that now I could have leisurely, civilized lunches with a friend, not locked into the tight schedule of twelve minutes for the one break of the teachers' lunch squeezed in between classes. At the end of the day I'd feel like a truck had run over me. In sales, I could think for myself, as an independent entrepreneur. There'd be no bosses such as the principal ordering me to do what didn't fit my own thinking, such as the mindless job of standing in the corridor while students changed classes, rather than remaining in my now quiet empty classroom in the brief break to think about the next class coming in, with the non-stop barrage of classes, an overload of students. I found that order and status quo mode deadly.

In my new job, I'd get rich, with better than a teacher's salary. Computers were selling at lightning speed, and I'd be great at it because I love the excitement of a challenge. I'm Type A. I'd have independent work, and a free, open schedule to do as *I* wanted, not the rigid schedule with bells ruling my work, marking the change in classes. I'd have time to think, escaping from a system that didn't match my spirit.

I signed out of school and walked right into the new job.

Well, that joy didn't last long. There was no training for this new work. I was astonished when I hit the correct switch and the computer turned on. People walked into the shop wanting to buy a computer. But I was on "outside sales." I was somehow magically supposed to drum up my own business. Where were those outside people who were eager to buy computers?

Lunch? While we didn't get just our quick run four floors down to the basement cafeteria to stand in line for a cafeteria tray lunch—it was amazing that we teachers didn't all have ulcers, though at least we saw our adult colleagues, if only momentarily—I could never really plan on having lunch, not knowing what would be going on in the store. A downtown law office might call looking for new computers and I wouldn't be there. Then next I was put only on commission, with no regular paycheck. I think an "Aha!" epiphany moment was when I was at a large sales conference presentation and I looked around the room. These others attending weren't teachers. I just felt out of place.

A School Surprise

Finding computer sales not all I'd hoped for, in a pivotal moment, I attended Hope's graduation in June. I never did this while teaching, few did. We were too tired after the demanding school day. I now had a vague sense of wanting to re-connect. It was fortuitous that I'd only taken a year's leave from school.

At the graduation ceremony, with few seats available in the crowded auditorium filled with delighted families, I happened to sit by accident—at first I felt by mistake —next to the veteran, bright, but relentlessly dramatic, venting teacher Marjorie, with whom I normally felt I had little in common. Marge and I had together survived the riot, the switch to mini-courses, and now the deadly "back to basics." Though she had graciously invited our department to her house during our seemingly endless meetings to react to the change thrust upon us, and seeking what to do next, Marge was always the complainer.

Turning School Upside Down, Again

    To my astonishment, Marjorie now was excited about school. In my year's absence from Hope, an event comparable to an earthquake—a next tectonic shift—had occurred. Our latest principal—there were many, in a revolving door of challenged school leaders—had met with the new Chair of the Brown Education Department, a giant of education, Ted Sizer. While I was away, full Hope faculty meetings had taken place with this professor that resulted in a faculty approval to create a new program. Marge loved this. I was stunned.

    Remarkably—Hope teachers at this time were not an optimistic, let's-all-make-a-change group—the required eighty-five percent had voted for a different way of working within the school. Discussions on this venture over the year in my absence were open to all teachers. Marge was excited, thrilled. I was riveted by her enthusiasm. She was clearly enthralled by Sizer, a tall, handsome, boyish-looking, astonishingly well educated professor, whom we later learned was a national education reform guru now right in our neighborhood. The silver-tongued Sizer had spoken in his relaxed, confident, charming and respectful, plain-speaking yet brilliant manner to our entire faculty, to win over a formidable group. We didn't often see such intelligence and eloquence at school. At a time when the only thing that teachers could agree on was payday was good, now teachers voted for major change.

    During our post-riot all-faculty meetings period, Marge had stood and told us she'd been dubbed "racist." Coming from a more privileged background, her father a prominent doctor, she'd attended a small parochial girls' school and Pembroke, the women's college that later merged with Brown. Nothing in Marge's background had prepared her for the disruption by our students of color that turned Hope upside down. She found our current students exasperating, flaunting rules. The punctual Marge locked her classroom door when the bell rang to start class, to student dismay, insisting on promptness to class. The students complained to the principal, to his alarm. Now, to her credit, Sizer's innovative concepts excited her. Marge, along with most of us, longed for change.

    It turned out that Sizer was well experienced at speaking even to tough crowds like our demoralized faculty. Many, though discouraged, were moved by the knowledge, personable manner, and charisma of this man from another world, a scholar, but one who was informed on education and who'd spent quite a bit of time in public schools, and saw something different about school. Sizer jump-started a spark. He spoke broadly about what school should be, presenting a new vision. We all deep down needed some hope. Many could go with his inspiring words on doing things differently.

School reform giant, Ted Sizer

Ted Sizer was a Yale graduate, with a Harvard Ph.D. in Education and American History, former boy dean of the Harvard Graduate School of Education at age 31. A product of boarding schools, and former headmaster of Phillips Andover Academy, Massachusetts, boarding school, he'd completed a national study of school, and called for change.

Why would Sizer come to our urban high school which seemed hopeless to speak to teachers? Who could be that brave? As an example of Sizer's big idea, refined thinking, and always civil manner, he used the quaint terms "folks," and "conversation." In discussing hard issues, folks would have conversation, serving up open exchange of ideas. For people with lots of opinions, this was a new way to operate. He believed in people.

Wisely, in Sizer's approach to sway the needed percentage of teachers to vote in favor, his proposed program wouldn't necessarily affect a teacher. Teachers would choose to apply. The plan was that this would just be a program within the school. In theory, the rest of the school wouldn't be affected. Little did anyone know how that selection process would work out. And more, what wasn't stated, but later became increasingly clear to me, was that his proposal was all experimental, based on a vision. For me, and others at this time, anything different was good.

Teachers joining this new program would be guinea pigs for what no one was certain would work out. Other schools hadn't made this same shift. We'd be among the first to put Sizer's concept into practice. No research found that our particular model would succeed. While 1980s era studies were critical of school, no one had a model of how school *should* work. That would in theory be us. It was backwards: We'd have the program, and researchers would use us to study success. I naively signed up.

But since Sizer had studied schools nationally, in personal visits, sitting in numerous classrooms, combined with his research knowledge, he knew things had to change. He bravely stepped in to help. He put his theories into practice. Even we teachers—with not all caught on to his specific ideas, and not fully understanding this next step—had to say he was on the money about that need for a change.

CHAPTER SIX

Returning to Hope

Now with this highly informed and visionary professor's entrance on the scene, I was torn on whether to go back to Hope or not. Listening to Marge's enthusiasm, I had a dilemma. Should I quit teaching? Since I'd taken only a year's leave, I had to consider whether or not to return to my position. School system rules, written into the teachers contract, were strict. More than one year off wasn't allowed.

I talked with my brother, who visited that summer. Frank was an accomplished civil rights attorney, winning Supreme Court decisions. He was heading north for a brief vacation from his work as a civil rights lawyer and dedicated head of the JFK-initiated Lawyers Committee for Civil Rights Under Law office in Jackson, Mississippi. He stopped at our house en route to an island in Maine for an August week's rest.

Frank took on civil rights cases such as when a Mississippi Black man is tried by an all-white jury, not a jury of peers. He won every case. Honed by the Oberlin College debate team, Frank was Harvard Law School-educated, intense and committed. His book *Black Votes Count* cites his extensive legal work on voting rights. He'd been recruited at Oberlin to register Black voters in the South during the summer at the time that Black activist Medgar Evers was shot in his home driveway. Evers had been named as Frank's contact by the Freedom Summer organizing group that recruited college students for Black voter registration in the South, dangerous at the time. Frank was devastated as we watched the report of Evers' murder on TV. He was committed to social justice.

I told Frank of my difficult choice of whether to stay in computer sales—where my husband Peter claimed I'd initiated the downturn in computers due to the drop in sales nationally when I entered the field—or return to Hope. Choosing his words carefully, as always, Frank said, "Kay, try it (the new program at Hope). At least it will be interesting." Frank had the big picture perspective on racial equity that I lacked from just the confines of my classroom.

It was hard to argue with his point. Little did I know how "interesting," and in what ways. No one at the time fully realized how revolutionary school would be under Sizer's plan. Peter's contribution was his smiling, "Teaching is the next best thing to stealing," voicing the common view that since teachers have school vacation weeks and summers off, unlike those in the business world, teaching is easy. Facing such a weighty decision, I didn't bother countering that view.

I stayed in our back yard hammock that warm August night until three in the morning, contemplating returning to Hope. I had to get my head around what it would mean. The constraints of the tight work schedule, the constant demands, the lack of thinking time, the bombardment of a hundred students a day, the isolation from other adults, and school management, not learning, as the main focus weren't my cup of tea. I'd return to a system that didn't care, with few rewards. But the enticement of Sizer's involvement was compelling.

Luckily, I'd taken a leave of absence from Hope, not resigned. The remote downtown district central office official who answered when I called to say I was returning from my leave told me I'd called just in time to go back to my position. Surprised, I hadn't known there was a deadline; not surprisingly no one in the large bureaucracy had informed me. Perhaps this stipulation was buried in the small print of the massive eminently unreadable teachers union contract, the bible of work rules. Plus, the impersonality of a large school system that relies on people to do the hard work of educating students was no stranger to me. I was just relieved I'd called in time.

The other surprise was that it wasn't automatic that I'd be able to go back to the same nearby school I'd left. Schools didn't necessarily keep positions open for a returning teacher. But, mysteriously, when the Hope administrators checked with their central office superiors, they were told to hand me a teaching schedule. I later learned it was the former principal Joe—awarded a quiet central office job after his work for us—who sent me back to Hope. I didn't know Joe had even known who I was.

First Year Back

Now in the back-to-school mode as August moved into September, I enjoyed the start of a new year, the return to the familiar building, with the initial collegiality, rested co-workers, receptive students. The easy month of September assured me I'd made the right decision to return to teaching.

But the freshness of the new school year as usual lasted just a few weeks. By early October, again I felt trapped. The window of fresh air closed. We were no longer in old-school Hope, with college-bound students ready and eager to learn. With the population now tipped to largely more challenging students, school remained difficult. Sizer's entrance on the scene was timely.

Attempts to Spark Students' Attention

With school in its all about being "on time," and "where you're supposed to be" mode, I was a renegade with my attempts to engage students. At times I purchased my own set of books for a class that needed a different text. I searched for reading more relevant to students' own lives, to stimulate engaged reading, dynamic discussion, good writing. I'd buy copies of paperbacks on sports, to entice a class athlete to read, or on the hot topic of the day, anything to spark reading, not uncommon for teachers. I felt it futile to deal with the cumbersome process of school bureaucracy to go through the process to order certain books, with rejection quite possible, not to mention taking a year to actually receive the books. This tactic of using different readings to light a spark for better learning wasn't the school agenda. But no administrator ever seemed to notice. They were only looking for things that weren't working, which at times was fortunate for me, as I found my own ways to connect.

James, a heavy-set ninth grader, who always sat up front, always with something to say, mostly off-topic, became riveted as the issues raised in a particular book sparked his thinking. While he was a valued member of the football team, he seemingly had no use for school otherwise. But James quickly became the class leader, outspoken, stimulating ideas in others. Together James and I stirred all-class debate that led to good writing. So often the student who could be the trial of a lifetime when turned around to be engaged was the brilliant class leader in a good way. I relied on this. Others relied on lecture to hold a class together, whether they listened, or not.

In another challenging situation, I finally learned, through a book selection, that almost all the students in one class were from the Dominican Republic. I dropped the unsuccessful text we were using—*The Autobiography of Malcolm X*—which intrigued Black students, but was a bust in this class—and distributed a new book that had somehow appeared in our English book room. It was Julia Alvarez's *How the Garcia Girls Lost their Accents*. One troublesome, annoying young man, José, quietly for a change, scrutinized the fine print on the back of the book—I hadn't known if he could read, since he was always jabbering—and called out, pounding the book, "She's from the Dominican!"

Though the author was a middle-class female, and the book was not about boys or sports, which would normally capture more interest, the entire class enthusiastically embraced the work. It was their homeland. As we read and talked, they explained to me the evils of the Trujillo regime, and in the dead of a cold, dark New England winter, they brought in pictures to show me sunshiny, warm island beaches. We fantasized planning a field trip. The students read intently, and we had lively discussions of each chapter. Students wrote expressively on the issues Alvarez raised. We had a food day, in which students brought in their island's foods, such as plantains. They loved explaining things to me. Administrators—who might normally forbid food in class—were apparently just happy kids were in the classroom, not escaping to roam the hallways.

But these moments of success were serendipitous. In general, malaise ruled.

However, slowly, at a glacial pace, the ground was moving in response to Sizer's initiative. Under his leadership, changes were happening in connection with a major national shift. These were, of course, initially management kinds of changes, setting the stage for the new approach. I had no idea at the time how shattering the move would be. What was coming would break the longtime traditional system that held back so many.

CHAPTER SEVEN

Small Steps to Rocky Big Change

Upon returning to Hope, even while immersed in the same old challenges, I could see some small steps moving toward bigger change, bright spots in the fog. In my absence, one teacher, Steven, had been anointed head of Sizer's new program. Several had applied for this position—it was a coveted new job away from classroom struggles, with an office, a computer, a phone. Others who'd applied were hit with the sting of rejection.

Right at the beginning, an incident occurred that was to be the start of many clashes to prevent the new program from sailing along smoothly. It wasn't a positive incident, and could have been avoided. Steven wanted to take over a large double-classroom space, a dumping ground devoted to piles of old English department books no one ever used. Steven wanted the books out.

Since nothing was moving along toward cleaning out the space, Steven took it upon himself to trash the books. Jennifer, the English department chair, was a rejected contender for this new program position that Steven now held. She was not only livid about not being selected as program head, but she now felt that dumping these old long-unused English books in a power play was a final straw. Jennifer went ballistic, complaining to whoever would listen.

This incident was only the beginning of not-so-collaborative relations between the regular school and the new, more elite, program.

Jennifer could complain, but no one was going to salvage those books. And no one missed them. I admired Steven's take-charge move, but he could have gone to talk with Jennifer first.

A bit later, Steven located me sitting alone reading my students' work in a remote empty computer lab. I'd been invited to join the new program for the coming year. No one else had applied in this teacher rejection system with my position now as the second English teacher in the program. Steven asked me if I'd like to be in the now cleaned-out double classroom. This was new. We'd never been asked before which room we'd like to teach in; it was just assigned. I'd taught in every space in the building, including as a new teacher in a basement woodworking classroom, with students sitting on high stools, not at desks. Now, I was surprised that Steven sought me out. He said, "This is just if you and John (a new teacher I'd gotten along with) want to teach together." Always isolated, I'd never taught with another teacher before. Astonished to be asked, I think I might have said something like, "Okay" to these two new offers, Do you want this classroom, and do you want to team-teach?

Steven assured me there would be a movable partition between the two classrooms. I worried about sound from the class on the other side of the partition disturbing my work. Steven said, "This wouldn't be a flimsy partition. It'll be soundproof." Of course it wasn't soundproof, but it turned out that John and I worked in sync beautifully. I smiled when our students complained about how loud the class behind the partition was, because that same class when it was the class over there was them talking loudly when they were in John's class. John didn't mind noisy. I did, but got used to it. From John I also learned to just laugh at what to us seemed bungling administrators' missteps, different from our view from the classroom.

John and I often moved the not so soundproof partition to allow our classes to meet together. Creating the full double classroom area opened up a large space that invited others in, a sign of a new era. Opening the partition was like unveiling a portrait for a new day. Bringing classes together and working with another teacher were real change, a dramatic shift in work that was like taking on a new job, but right there in the same old building. Teaming up brought huge support.

But joining the new Sizer program wasn't automatic. One didn't just sign up, step into it. Sadly, old-school union-determined ways of getting a new position ruled. For any new position, the process is set: Applicants apply, a team interviews, one is selected. Losers get no feedback, not even a "Thank you for applying," or a "Good morning" smile the next day. The rejected teacher was just dismissed. Bad feelings linger.

This unsupportive set process for joining the program was just another twist that didn't win a lot of friends for the new venture. In my seeking to join this new program, I shouldn't have been surprised when I saw Suzanne, a fairly new teacher, walking out of the building on the day of the first interviews with a fellow teacher on the selection committee whom she'd never talked with before. In my year of absence, Suzanne had befriended both school and university initiators of the program. Joining it was a step up. I had some credentials. But I didn't know how to single out deciders and sidle up to them. This seemed to me unprofessional. The broaching of boundaries never occurred to me. How could one suddenly be friendly with a more powerful colleague in order to petition for a new and better position? Naïve, I applied, had an interview, and was rejected for the position of teacher in the first year of the program.

The next year I was *asked* to join. Others who may once have been interested no longer applied. Setting up a system that's perceived as elite, with teachers who rise into positions that seem above colleagues doesn't work well in a school, especially when conversation to restore confidence for the losers is lacking. The sniping and parking lot complaints that result from dismissal in applying for a coveted position undermine the good that might happen with a quick supportive comment to the one rejected.

When I went to the chair of the social studies department, a group against changes, holding fast to old-school ways, to explain to the longtime veteran teacher Jim about why—after long reflection—I was looking to join the experimental program, he looked at me kindly and shook his head. "You don't have to explain to me," he said quietly. I sensed he understood why I chose to make this move, while it wasn't his own preference. His response helped smooth my feelings of rejecting an old way of working with longtime colleagues. Jim had the sensitivity others lacked.

But that brief talk with Jim was just one small connection with others in the building, a place soon called, "A house divided against itself." If we'd all been better at communicating with the rest of our colleagues, in thoughtful and open discussion, there might have been a chance for full school change, for the better. That brief window of opportunity was quickly lost, as our new program grew and attained national attention, which didn't make us popular with our fellow teachers. Ignoring the other half of the school proved a mistake, as some rose to a new position, while others were left behind, even though it may have been their choice.

Jim's department became known as open protesters, even though they were happy to not be a part of the change. It just wasn't for them. The new program head had used the term "Naysayers" in a written document on the program in relation to critics. Believing themselves criticized, this department posted a sign on the social studies department door: "Naysayers only. All others keep out." They were poking fun at being derided.

To be fair, although this division in the school at large was pervasive, there was also some intense internal conflict that distracted us from reaching out to others. Nothing in our earlier experience of separate classrooms, just obeying administrators, had prepared us to work well together in a new way in the new program. Putting teachers together doesn't automatically create a smooth-running cohesive team. When I briefly visited the Harvard Graduate School of Education, where I'd earlier gotten a degree, I saw a research study posted that likened teachers fighting with each other during school change to the chaos of small Balkan countries newly released from the Soviet regime. I smiled to see that teacher collaboration during change was a national problem.

When I visited Boston University, looking at graduate school programs, I saw they advertised a course on "Group Problem-Solving." "That's an oxymoron," I told the professor. He calmly said, "There are ways a group can work together well." I signed up.

CHAPTER EIGHT

Another Planet: Less is More

Teaching in the new Sizer program was like moving to another planet. School was turned upside down. It was like real school, a world I'd never dreamed of.

One major shift was a dramatic new use of time. I'd come from teaching several different courses a day and more than one hundred students a day, large numbers moving in and out of the classroom. Especially in an urban school, there was no way teachers could do their best work with so many students, many of them needy, tired, itchy, some outright recalcitrant when school didn't speak to them.

And it was no wonder students couldn't keep up well with switching from art class to math, then English, then Spanish, then science class, with just snippets of fifty-minute class time, with very different teachers, different expectations. Plus, sitting and being quiet six hours a day isn't adolescent-friendly.

A radically different use of time was the foundation that allowed those of us in this new program to teach well. Instead of a chopped-up school day, divided into brief classes, with no time to breathe in between, we now had lengthier one-hundred-minute double-period class time. And we had only two of these longer classes a day, instead of five. The next day, alternating, we taught our other two. With multiple classes a day that accomplished little now out the window, we could teach well in the longer time period, and students had a better shot at learning.

Also as part of Sizer's "Less is More" approach, instead of teaching several different courses and different tracks of students, I now taught just one course, a huge benefit for class planning. All students were integrated into classes, rather than being separated by perceived level of ability. In one course of mixed students replacing multiple classes, more academically inclined students—once pulled out for advanced classes—learned from demographically mixed classes. And more struggling students learned from higher-achieving classmates. Ideas discussed in this more elevated work for everyone caught each student's attention. No one was deemed less smart.

In addition to this powerful change of teaching just one course and only two classes a day, to have a chance to do better, time was set during the day for us to meet with other teachers *who shared the same students.* Each team at each grade level was made up of a math, science, English and social studies teacher. We could confer on issues, help one another out. A student who plagued one class could be discussed for ways to better engage that student. Conferring with other adults during the school day helped tremendously as a break from the relentless stream of students. Now we could think, confer, plan, share thoughts.

This different use of time, seeming simple, worked miracles. The old-school rigid, brain-stifling schedule of many classes a day was an industrial-period factory model that dished out knowledge to whoever showed up, an outdated assembly-line job that never changed students' learning. In that system, students who had trouble learning stayed that way. Now that we spent more time in each class to attend to each student, and also with time to confer with our team, I was no longer a wiped-out bundle of nerves with a brain of mush at the end of the day. I was a teacher. Instead of beating kids out the door after school, escaping to breathe. many of us lingered after dismissal, met with students, who also voluntarily stayed, or we conferred with colleagues. We were a team of adults centered on doing our best with our students, which provided great personal and professional satisfaction. It took the respected outsider—and one who knew well private school ways of working—to see that a simple schedule change could make so much difference, change one's life as a teacher. Sizer, not caught up in this is how we always do it, knew of another way, and it made all the difference.

Other supports helped, too. Our program came with a "teacher as advisor" role, a longstanding private school expectation new to public schools at the time. Traditionally, teachers' first daily meeting with students was attendance-taking and listening to mostly irrelevant all-school announcements blasting from the public address system into everyone's classroom. Now we were to use this otherwise just sitting empty period as advisory time to confer on non-class issues, see how students were doing, talk about concerns. In the role of advisor, I learned to see students from a different perspective. And they learned to see us as caring adults, not just their teacher. This advisory role helped transform our ways of working with students. In a new light, students saw me as a person; I saw them as kids to help. This lessening of the "I'm in charge" attitude, instead of opening things up to too much freedom to rebel, brought greater cooperation, when students saw that their teacher cared. Dropping the strict boundary line between teacher and a caring person helped with students connecting more easily with the teacher, breaking down that barrier.

Another Sizer Principle was "Parents as partners." I kept my advisees' parents' phone numbers in my sacred gradebook, the detailed record of a student's work. One day I called Tracy's mother because her daughter was habitually late to school. I suspected she got off the bus, then walked down the street to the shops. "If I have to drive her up to the third floor to get her into your class, I will," her mother immediately responded in this brief phone call. I was bowled over by her cooperation. Tracy was never late again. "It's best when it's two against one," joshed Raju's father when we met later, only half kidding.

A team of teachers sharing the same students with common planning time to confer worked nicely. Collaboration with us teachers connecting our courses all with the same grade level, the same students, emerged because we had time to meet and talk in person, with my having the math teacher for our team located across the hall, social studies next door. Formerly teachers were separated out by departments located in various parts of the building. Now those sharing the same students in a student-centered way helped forge connection and work across boundaries. The focus was on students, not the adult subject departments. This interconnectedness made a difference.

Kay and John teach together

One day during the common meeting time for all four members of our team, John, the social studies teacher, and I were talking about our joint unit. I was teaching John Hersey's *Hiroshima*, and John was covering the Cold War period. Merriam, the science teacher on the team, listened and said, "If you're doing that, I can teach nuclear energy." I was delighted when my class was writing their papers on this topic in the computer room, and some had their social studies books out, while others consulted their science books. When a Harvard researcher came to interview our students on their writing, one talked about this paper, saying, "I never knew totally different subjects could connect." Too much under the earlier system was disconnected.

Now things were coming together, a huge help for learning. John and I meshed our yearlong history and English courses with history chronology, and I matched literature to the time period, providing reading to deepen the history taught, and history providing context for the literature. This collaboration was successful in part because we were in adjacent classrooms in our large double room where we could easily meet to confer, even in spur of the moment thinking. Joining both our courses, we'd planned our yearlong course before the start of the year, but new ideas always popped up to make things work better. We'd have just a brief check-in to confer, with next-door proximity. Always, we reached mutual agreement, not one subject area dominating over the other, to preserve the integrity of the discipline. By having classes relate to each other, going into greater depth by matching literature with history, students learned and retained more than when courses were disjointed. Students themselves would bring up connections. When we read Melville's "Bartleby the Scrivener," they associated the protagonist's statement, "I prefer not to," with the industrial period in history. And they provided historical context I hadn't known about for *Huck Finn*.

John and I were a real team. We conferred on students. He supported some who were challenging for me, so they behaved better. John had attended boarding school, and only knew how to treat young people with respect. No longer left on my own, I could now appreciate his view of a student, how he connected with those not so easy for me to warm up to. I can still see small Evans Duré from Haiti, sitting next to John at the teacher's desk, pouring over his history text as his idol John did. Students didn't mind this special seat. They saw their teacher treating a student well, as he treated them all. This respect helped us other team members, as one teacher's good ways of working carried over to others, and students reciprocated.

We were also helped by our colleague Nancy, a science teacher who was committed to using small group learning to encourage students to confer and figure out issues together, as an alternative to teacher talk. Nancy understood that student discussion allows them to process information and helps internalize learning. A student can clarify what another was confused on, often working better than a teacher explanation. Nancy trained all the students in our team in this way of conferring. Knowing a colleague was successful with small group work made it easier to latch onto than hearing an outside presenter make the same point as a theory. I feared students would just socialize if I asked them to sit together to talk in a small group. To my amazement, when I asked them to confer, they did, all on task. I was astonished. Now with us sharing the same students, a teacher's work in one area helped others, multiplying positive effects.

In another helpful incident that lifted students, I heard that our guidance department head Shirley's son Ron was at historically Black Howard University. I asked her if he could come to speak with our students. Shirley graciously said, "Sure." We opened the partition for the full group. It turned out Ron was eloquent, charismatic. Our students were mesmerized, clinging to his words. After the talk, an ongoing debate about whether to attend an historically Black college or not would pop up in a class discussion. There was now no question that our students were going to go on to college; it was just which type.

The combination of having my teaching partner John as a colleague to plan and confer with and being a member of a team of four teachers committed to making things work felt like a dream. This opening up to work together provided us with mutual support so that we didn't feel overwhelmed and no longer felt left alone to sink or swim. We created a village, a small one. Though teaming was occasionally dysfunctional in some ways among the larger group of all adults in the program, each still coming from one's own more individualized experience and practices, the teaming was absolutely protective for our students. Under Sizer's wise leadership and his Principles, we all just naturally agreed, without discussion, that the development of good learning was our goal. We knew the aim, and it wasn't crowd control. Within this common, never really stated among us, mission, things worked. We all strove to help students learn. And because everyone focused on learning, students were engaged, with discipline problems now gone. We were supported in our effort to lift up our students mainly through just the program's structure that allowed us to work well and work together, despite a few fractious times.

If we'd had specific learning Standards that would publicly show we were successful, would we have welcomed them? Absolutely. No question. We'd have wanted others to see that our students learned, and for students to see they'd learned. Publicly released data with published test score results, which arrived a decade later, would no doubt have not only saved the program from elimination, but would have meant the program with its concepts and practices could have moved to the larger school and to other schools. Not even the severest critics can kill a program that shows formerly marginalized students learning well. Instead, without data evidence of success, the program was eliminated, by a remote new superintendent.

Ted Sizer's Coalition of Essential Schools Ten Common Principles

1. The school should focus on helping adolescents learn to use their minds well.

2. The school's goals shall be simple: that each student master a limited number of essential skills and areas of knowledge. "Less is more" should dominate.

3. The school's goals should apply to all students.

4. Teaching and learning should be personalized to the maximum feasible extent. No teacher should have direct responsibility for more than eighty students ... decisions about the use of students' and teachers' time and the choice of teaching materials must be unreservedly placed in the hands of the principal and staff.

5. The governing practical metaphor of the school should be student-as-worker.

6. The diploma shall be awarded upon a successful demonstration of mastery—an "Exhibition" that may be jointly administered by the faculty and higher authorities. The diploma is awarded when earned.

7. The tone of the school should explicitly and self-consciously stress values of unanxious expectation of trust and of decency, parents are essential collaborators.

8. Principal and teachers perceive themselves as generalists first, specialists second.

9. Ultimate administrative and budget targets should include substantial time for collective planning by teachers, competitive salaries for staff and an ultimate per-pupil cost, not [to] exceed those at traditional schools by more than ten percent.

10. Principle 10 was added in 1997: Democracy and Equity: The school should demonstrate non-discriminatory and inclusive policies, practices, and pedagogies. It should model democratic practices that involve all who are directly affected by the school. The school should honor diversity and build on the strength of its communities, deliberately and explicitly challenging all forms of inequity.

CHAPTER NINE

The Coleman Report: Demographics Matter

Sizer's influence was widespread, a national presence with 1,000 schools official members of the Coalition of Essential Schools, to teach "essential," pared down learning with guides, and new use of time, and conditions. The organization's annual national conferences were enthusiastically attended by teachers from everywhere, with conference attendance costs partially funded by Citi-Bank. Other major funders included the Annenberg Foundation and over $18 million from the Gates Foundation. Traditional ways of working were disrupted with new energy and conversations launching changes in concepts, structure and practice, including for us at Hope.

Top Coalition leaders were invited to Bill Clinton's White House in 1994 for the signing of the Elementary and Secondary Education Act (ESEA), which now newly required common high-level learning standards for every state, along with a test to assess success. Washington, DC was well aware of Sizer's ideas, his movement known and valued. And both his presence and his concepts of education equity and new ways of working permeated Brown University. His courses attracted over 100 students, with classes held in an auditorium. Breaking university tradition, he refused to simply lecture. Students chafed as he put the onus on them to confer about issues. With "student as worker" one of his Principles, his final course project wasn't just an example of simply feeding learning back to the teacher in the form of a test or paper. He demonstrated his Principle of public exhibition of learning in part by having some of his Brown students create a new vision of education and present their model to local school boards.

As another example of reaching out to promote new thinking on public education, Sizer brought Johns Hopkins University sociologist James Coleman to Brown to speak at an evening event. Coleman had conducted the large-scale research required in the 1964 Civil Rights Act to study the effects of school on learning. His report, titled "Equality of Education Opportunity," 1966, was always referred to as "The Coleman Report." Coleman surveyed over 600,000 students in 4,000 schools in multiple states to see what most influenced their experience in school. His mission was to find out what factors made a difference in the level of student achievement.

With Sizer's prominence in the community, the large, centrally located Sayles Hall was filled with university and community members eager to hear Coleman speak. Though university departments are often competitive for status and funding, Sizer was an equalizer, respected by all. Dark paintings of previous university presidents—all older white men—lined the walls, looking down on a varied community, a mix Sizer delighted in. As I looked around the packed hall, I saw young, fresh-faced students, gray-haired professors, other educators, and campus neighbors.

Sizer's star power commanded attention at this get-together for a prominent speaker. Bright and youthful-looking, he smiled broadly as he introduced Coleman. One sensed their mutual admiration as they worked from different angles, but with the same level of impact on education. Coleman's Washington-based study of the effects of school on student learning and Sizer's efforts to influence educators at the national level reflected different but linked perspectives. While Coleman was a numbers guy, a data-oriented quantitative investigator, Sizer was a qualitative researcher, interested in people and stories. Both saw the same effect of schooling on educational inequity, the way it sorted who would succeed and who wouldn't. At this moment, these two scholars and innovators pulled back the curtain on unfairness and the need for change nationally.

The Coleman study looked at varied "inputs" in school, such as teacher salaries and level of education, amount of technology, and parent involvement, and matched these with "outcomes" in the form of student achievement. Coleman found the one factor that correlated with student performance was parent demographics. Sizer's way of phrasing this finding was "Tell me a parent's level of income and I'll tell you the student's SAT score." Based on my limited view from my own classroom, I was initially baffled by Sizer's simple summary. He was at a different level of thinking I hadn't yet reached. I just had students in front of me that I had to teach, and colleagues with their own views, a limited perspective.

I did later understand why on this night both Sizer and Coleman claimed it was demographics that most affected academic achievement. Their common observation was that school wasn't making a difference. Accident of birth had the most impact on school success. Sizer was saying things had to change to overcome the limits on opportunity imposed by socio-economic conditions. Certainly, some students could break out of these constraints on their own, often with parental support or the help of at least one great teacher. But it was Coleman's large-scale research that brought to light the need to bring equity more fully to education. Sizer, long-immersed in research and observation, was taking the next giant step to change thinking, structure, and practices to be able to extend a helping hand to those previously marginalized. Achieving this kind of change at this time seemed like moving a mountain.

As a teacher, sitting there before these big-picture thinker giants, I thought that Coleman, with his numbers and data orientation, and Sizer, with his classroom observations, were disparate. I was surprised to see them so obviously connecting, smiling at each other. I marveled at this professional congeniality, which was so lacking at my school where people seemed to think so differently, with little if any time nor the necessary conditions to confer on what seemed our varied views. How could Sizer like a numbers guy? How could Coleman like just an ideas guy? But though I missed it at this time, cocooned in classroom work, I later understood that one's finding supported the other's. Coleman collected and analyzed the numbers, while Sizer had done the in-school observations of qualitative analysis, sitting in classrooms. It took more study on my part—actually returning to graduate studies—for this realization to hit me. School had to change in order to help more students. Sizer was a determined leader in the charge to accomplish this change. It would take decades to work through how to turn the ship around.

A vivid scene I witnessed years later fit the theory presented at Coleman's talk. We may have made great strides, but one small incident reminded me how even with a gradual shift over the years, we haven't yet won the battle. Working as a curriculum director in a city adjacent to Boston, I observed the lingering inequity after a high school graduation in a low-income, congested, big-city racially diverse community,

High school graduation is always a delight. The superintendent here spoke at this joyous warm June evening celebratory event, lauding the high school and the district's accomplishments. He praised graduating seniors for their "Everett Edge." Life and school hadn't been easy for these graduates sitting proudly before him. Their grit had gotten them through. They'd stayed with it. Their persistence and drive, learned in the packed classrooms of their over-crowded, 2,000-student high school, not in a smaller, softer, easier, more personal world, would propel them through life, the superintendent proclaimed. The names of the graduating students read by the principal were multi-national; there were kids from everywhere, and they'd made it through. The graduating students and their parents and teachers were elated.

But as I walked to my car after the ceremony, I happened to turn my head and saw a family that had been watching from the other side of a fence. A slight young man's body language, his fingers clinging to the chain link fence he'd climbed to get a better view, was clear—he was left out of this ceremony. He'd come to watch, but he wasn't graduating. His Haitian-looking mother had brought his small siblings along to view the event he was excluded from. My eyes locked with the mother's. I didn't know the specific conditions that had held him back, but from their dress, I assumed poverty, pervasive in this community of overcrowded multi-family houses, was surely one. Language too may well have been a barrier. Even now, after many hard changes in schools, with huge improvements made steadily and slowly over time, now in 2016, long after Coleman's talk in the late 1980's, I saw we were still leaving too many behind. This scene for me put a human face on the big-picture issue Sizer and Coleman, each in his own way, illuminated: While making strides, we hadn't overcome all the barriers. We have to continue to try.

CHAPTER TEN

Dream Work and Fireworks

While making the change from old school ways to new modes that we were just trying to figure out as we went along, unintended consequences that were mostly—not always—good proliferated. Since the structure set out for us worked so well, and we had some freedom to explore other new modes, we felt inspired to take some risks. No longer trapped in the sense that no one cared, with optimism we took a step beyond the normal in our new program, now called "Hope Essential," a hopeful title for a better way of doing school that worked.

In my lengthier English classes, teaching was a dream. Now with longer-time class, I had the chance to read and for us to discuss literature in class, knowing homework reading was risky: some would complete it, not all. Then, either they or I, most often it was the students, would bring up a point for discussion. In this way I ensured the full class would participate together, though those who devoured books could read ahead on their own, which actually didn't create any problems. With time for in-class reading, discussion centered on ideas.

My colleague John thrived on ideas, with his teaching of history bordering on a Marxist perspective that students clung to, instead of a dreary chronological slog through dates, names, and wars. Our students loved his presentations, which sparked their thinking. This conceptual approach not only carried over easily into English, but spurred engagement of every class member, regardless of skill level.

Our students delighted in coming up with an idea, or expanding on another's. Students with weaker skills too became engaged in discussions, which propelled their learning. No longer did class not speak to them. Discipline problems vanished as students were engaged.

Stimulated by John in his classes, with John always enjoying hearing what the students had to say, they knew their ideas were welcome. In my own classes, I'd chart students' points on the board, then ask students to write on either a specific question I saw coming from discussions, or on any of the topics a student raised. Providing options helped. With both John and me eager to hear their thinking, this dialogue that came from the students drove our classes. It wasn't us pouring ideas into students' heads. It was the give and take of ideas that propelled the work. The longer class period allowed time to read, think, discuss, and then immediately write, while ideas, opinions, and others' comments were fresh in their heads. Writing in class on in-the-moment ideas nicely improved writing alone at home away from the thoughts generated in class, and which I knew could be hit or miss in being accomplished. Not every household provided conditions that supported good writing. I'd visited a few students' homes and saw crowded apartments, a centrally located blaring TV, family expectations such as monitoring younger siblings. The in-class writing (in a silent classroom, everyone writing) improved as our discussions stimulated ideas.

Since John and I just wanted to foster thinking, not looking for right or wrong answers, a student could take his or her own stance on an issue, encouraging self-expression. Thinking on paper empowered each student to develop ideas and established what later research confirmed: Researcher Doug Reeves' "90/90/90" large-scale national study showed that in school districts with ninety percent students of color, ninety percent low-income, and ninety percent "Proficient" or above on state tests, one of the few common factors leading to student success was frequent writing with timely feedback. Out the window now for us was students' hastily drafted essay, if we received it at all, then the red-inked marked-up paper with a grade slapped on, returned, tossed in the closest waste basket, those carefully written teacher comments lost.

In one class, I expected too much. I forced a stretch by asking students to write a poem on the brutal murder of fourteen-year-old Emmett Till, who'd done nothing but whistle at a white woman while visiting a relative in the South. Discussions were going so well that I believed an emotional response to this incident would easily trigger a poem. But we hadn't been reading poetry, or writing poems. Puzzled, our shared students turned to John, instead of me, for advice on how to go about creating a response in a poetic format. Though surprised they didn't ask me, I didn't mind, and found it amusing that he had to think of an answer. What John made up on the spot probably worked as well as anything I could have come up with to get them started. Their poems bled with emotion. John helped out when needed.

But in a different less smoothly collaborative activity, to my dismay, John told our students that in essay writing they should first write a sentence, then a paragraph, then the whole essay. I told him, "No, they need to draft out their ideas first." Since writing is thinking, I asked students to get their ideas on paper, then shape them for the reader, a skill later enshrined in national Standards. I'm not sure John understood: A brief comment doesn't always accomplish a change in how one thinks. Lengthier, more substantive conversation succeeds more often to help make a turn in practice. While I was glad that I'd hastily attempted to correct what John had counseled for writing, I realized we were all still pretty much thinking from our own discipline's strictures and couldn't easily move a point into another subject area's understandings. Which is why ongoing conversation across subject areas is so important. Making connections across subjects helps when teaching all students, in place of chopped up different subject area content, because it provides continuity and greater depth for students, to retain learning. Now we had the conditions that better supported learning, the wind in the sail.

One thing I just happened to do made a surprising difference. In stating the opinions that motivated their writing, students were at times inventive with their thoughts, sentences, wording. I was finding excellent writing and insights that I would then read aloud in class. I varied whose work I selected to share with the class. Sometimes I would read just one good sentence, or a striking title. I was oblivious to the impact this would have, just choosing writing I liked. I'd read sentences, or a phrase that stood out to me. I later realized that when students heard the type of strong, opinionated writing I valued, with strong voice, they listened intently, then began to compete to hear their work, blushing in pride and smiling shyly when they recognized it was their own words I was reading. Years later these model pieces, called "exemplars," became pieces posted on state websites for standards learning. Having such exemplary writing as models is valuable, but it's different, with greater impact, when it comes from one's own classroom. For my classes, reading good writing aloud as models just happened naturally, with the goal effective self-expression. It was fun to read students' writing, as I could see they were trying to get my attention. I no longer faced the deadly old-school chore of marking up in that uninviting red ink a pile of dreary writing, only to have it quickly tossed out, with errors never corrected. With students working to engage the reader, I was in turn interested in what they had to say, and I no longer felt reading students' writing was a burden. Having the chance to get to know my students better through discussions and through their writing and in our lengthier classes was a boon. We felt ownership, and of all, not just some.

Another benefit was with a team of teachers dedicated to connecting with now more motivated students, in our new structure, no longer did I have to stand in the hallway during the class time break, under the pretense of monitoring behavior, in theory to stop fights that might erupt. That purely management task vanished. No one was starting a fight, or only now and then in jest, in lively kid manner. This meant that I was able to use the brief time between classes to breathe, pull my thoughts together, and prepare for the second round *of the same class*. When the bell rang at the end of the break, the most cooperative students immediately returned to the class, and the others followed. There was no need for us to herd them in. We were teachers, not the back-to-class police.

Closer connection with parents brought better two-way communication. With Sizer's list of Principles for guidance, and "parents as partners" one of our guides, I learned the hard way to include parents. In earlier years, very few parents came in for Parent Night, to confer with a teacher. Not all wanted to hear about one's child's deficiencies, may not have felt good about visiting a school where as a student him- or herself one might not have been successful. With travel also an issue, it made sense that parents didn't show up, since it would have taken two busses to get across town in the dark, possibly with no one at home to watch over younger children, and many parents either working nights or exhausted after a day on the job. Maintaining the ritual of holding "parent night," an old school tradition, at one time fitting for our nearby area parents, later this felt strange, as often we waited alone in classrooms with no one coming in to speak with us, no longer neighbors, making a school visit easy. Yet the empty building with no parents on parent night continued on, a pro forma continuance of old-school tradition that no longer worked. We saw and conferred with parents often in the Essential School program, on the phone or in person, very helpful.

Now, with parent backing and Sizer's mantra for parents to be included in the loop, Hope changed in this area too. But we'd been supplied with no tips on how to confer with parents. Inexperienced with parent meetings, when I accidently badly overstepped in an after-school meeting with a parent whose son was especially challenging, she instantly became offended, outraged. There was no way I could have known to be especially careful with this mother, obviously perplexed herself on how to constrain her son, I should have been much more diplomatic in our meeting. Instead of being careful, I jumped right to my concern. Poor move. Never a good choice. I hadn't yet learned to always start with the positive. The angry parent stormed out, and livid, over to a downtown central office superior to complain about me.

As it turned out, she met with Joe, who'd earlier been Hope principal. He told this parent, "If you have an issue with Mrs. Scheidler, you should speak to Mrs. Scheidler." I was astounded by such support from a big city higher-up, and surprised that he protected me, turning the parent back to me, instead of the administrator chastising me. I greatly appreciated this backing from the central office. As a former teacher himself, Joe understood student challenges. He also probably knew I wasn't a slacker, just interested in student cooperation. His response also may have been in support of the Sizer program, wanting to help.

I never saw this parent again. We teachers didn't view ourselves as parents saw us—in a power role. I'd known at least a couple teachers who left teaching because of one challenging parent, whom the teacher hadn't been prepared to meet with. I'd overstepped with my student's parent. Caught off-guard, I didn't show empathy. But I did work more thoughtfully with her son. And I was careful in later parent meetings.

Communicating on Fraught Issues Is Hard

But with things in general working so well with our students, and the chance to learn on the job, one issue in our roles as teachers in this new setting was explosive. Good, productive communication among ourselves as a group was not fostered by leaders, and none of us were used to civil conversation on tough issues. Challenges arose. Once we stepped on a land mine.

One morning, Lee, the math teacher on the first team to start up the program, walked into my classroom and asked me to sign a union "grievance" petition. A grievance is a formal union complaint, a big deal because it goes right over the principal's head and straight to the teachers union leadership, who then pursue the case. Union grievances, while at times over-used, often settle an issue in which teachers feel discussion won't solve a problem. This can be a good path to a needed resolution. I'd never signed one of these before. Others had signed lots. Often union grievances were charges that an administrator had broken a teachers' union contract rule, but not dealt with in conversation but confrontation. A teacher grievance is widely circulated.

Lee, now walking into my classroom, briefly explained to me the situation. Apparently he felt this couldn't be handled directly with the program leader. What Lee said in explaining made little sense to me, but I liked and trusted him; he handed me a pen, so I signed. It took about two seconds. I didn't think about this brief interaction again.

Fireworks ensued.

At the heart of the issue was a study period that the Essential School program head, Steven, had unilaterally added to the schedule without communicating with the teachers or the university liaisons. This addition required teachers to monitor students' study time, a supervisory job unrelated to developing learning. It was a common old-school study period. Supposedly helping students by sitting and watching them study—though if it were math, I'd be no help—was a waste of time in my view and pulled us away from a planning period that allowed grade-level teacher teams to meet. The school day teacher meeting time, a Sizer Principle, had been a victory for teachers that required union approval. It was no small accomplishment.

This union agreement was a breakthrough for the union to approve this new use of time to provide teachers time to meet to confer on issues. Anything coming from the powerful protective union was a big deal, sacred.

Time for teachers to confer has always been a sought-after break in the teaching machine that can help solve problems, develop mutual support, and create collegiality, even collaboration. Time to confer together during the school day was unheard of at the time, and wasn't attained in Hope's larger more traditional school until decades later, and then not for teachers who shared the same students. The fact that we in the Essential School program would be able to confer with our teacher team was potent, helpful to exchange information on our common students.

Sizer's chief schools liaison had worked directly with the union president, the all-powerful, no-nonsense, tough woman idolized by many, to guarantee that this valuable use of time was carved out of the intense school day. Lee, as a member of the program planning committee and first teaching team, knew of the union approval for teacher planning time. Although Steven's decision to switch the planning period to a study hall period showed his keen interest in helping students academically, teacher responsibility for study supervision instead of teacher conferring time was an old-school task at odds with professional collaborative time. It had been a tough sell to gain this union approval.

The team I was on, since we'd come in the second year, just accepted the study period supervision as one of our many new responsibilities, until Lee had appeared and personally asked us to sign his grievance petition. Lee had that kind of influence. But by joining the others in signing, we went over Steven's head to restore the planning time. It made sense to monitor students studying. But Steven had made this assignment on his own. So in having each of us sign the grievance, we subverted an administrative decision. Steven, though he still taught one class and forcefully promoted our program, had overstepped. Lee openly challenged his authority.

I was in the middle of teaching a class when I heard Steven explode across the hallway. He was in a meeting with the first year's team. A student, standing in the corridor, for whom curse words were hardly novel, opened his eyes wide, and said in astonishment, "Oh, is Mr. Johnson allowed to swear?!"

Lee was normally able to communicate easily with others, even in disagreement. Resorting to a formal—and more confrontational—union grievance wasn't like him. But he'd felt it necessary to go that route. Sadly, we hadn't yet developed Sizer's Principle of "conversation" as the basis for teachers working with program leaders and others to resolve issues. Instead, our "discussion" was nil. Ideally, we would have had an open meeting to clarify the various views in civil discourse, but we hadn't even come close to that mode of working together. Confrontation and going over the head of a leader, rather than collaboration, was more the norm, not unsurprising with teachers long used to solitary work, only able to turn to a formal grievance instead of conversation. Steven hadn't checked with teachers on this study time duty.

Later, many publications flourished on how leaders and teachers can work collaboratively to resolve issues, publishing in articles and books clear guidelines on how to conduct what became known as "difficult conversations." The better words to use, to soften a challenge, are printed. These guides provide a life jacket for drowning swimmers, saving either side from potential disaster. A wise administrator knows to approach a change cautiously. At the time, we at Hope Essential became known as fractious. It wasn't entirely our fault. We were thrown together without that lifeline. But as new ways of working, of turning school around, met with differing opinions, I suspect we at Hope weren't the only group to clash on issues, unprepared for those confrontations, as school began to change. Now such differences seem inevitable, predictable, though at the time unexpected as the lid was raised on the old way of strict control and old rules.

When Steven later stormed into my classroom to confront me on my signing the grievance petition, I hastily improvised: "If a teacher asks us to sign a petition, we do it." While this was not entirely true—because under normal conditions I would understand the issue and choose whether to agree to adversity by signing or not—my stance left Steven speechless. It was a position he could understand, more than if I'd admitted just being in a fog and trusting a colleague with a good reputation. I hadn't realized I'd offended Steven. I only later learned he was the one who'd on his own made the schedule for study duty. To his credit, Steven—always efficient—immediately cancelled the study period, freeing us teachers to meet. He knew the Principles.

Our students were used to sudden changes without explanation. They were immediately rescheduled from the study period into other classes in the regular school program. Since this development no doubt caused consternation among teachers in the old-school mode, we in Hope Essential once again weren't making friends outside the program. Yet with the union leader's protection for our program—carefully cultivated by Sizer's representative—no teacher in the regular program dared file a complaint for new students suddenly entering their classes. Without question—I didn't have to ask—many were annoyed with student increase. I empathized. But they didn't have a chance against the power of this new program. Conversation was absent, and unaddressed concerns built up. With communication between the regular school program and the Hope

Essential program absent, steam built up, later exploding, a sense of unfairness no doubt leading to its demise.

I had mixed feelings about the loss of the study period when one less than high-achieving student who constantly socialized sighed to me, "I was just beginning to use that time." I told him, "You're right. You were just beginning that." He looked at me, surprised I'd noticed. It was hard not to.

Yet, astonishingly to me, as a testament to how involved and committed our students began to feel, how invested in learning, they carved out their own study group time.

Helping All Kids Works

Having a racial and learning-level mix of students together in a class made teaching interesting. We all sailed along, together. No parents of higher achieving students complained. I paid close attention to the more advanced students' written work for improvement, expecting more of them. The struggling students were lifted by stimulating class discussions, and became writers.

One student who shows the success of mixed-achievement-level classes is Buddy. Buddy received extra tutoring help under Title 1, a longstanding federal program that provides extra help for students in poverty-level schools whose literacy skills test below a certain level. Buddy was sometimes pulled out of my class for this supplementary tutoring. His positive, caring, focused Title I teacher helped him develop skills that prevented him from becoming discouraged in a class that included higher-achieving students. But all students in the class were respectful of Buddy when he spoke.

While Buddy's reading and writing skills were less well developed, he'd learned to listen carefully, possibly picking up this skill from his supportive Title I teacher. He caught on to ideas and energetically participated in class discussions by supporting an opinion with his own view. The more privileged students, who were beginning to transfer in from the city's exam school, along with others who were enrolling for a more racially and demographically integrated program, learned a lot from listening to Buddy. These students benefitted from being in class with a student who struggled in ways they hadn't seen when locked in the cocoon of an exam school or one with a homogeneous everyone-alike grouping in tracked classes. The more privileged listened to Buddy's views. He was always eager to participate, and contributed thoughtful comments. His heartfelt contributions also motivated others with understanding concepts. He'd pick up on what I or a fellow student said and elaborate on it, adding to our discussions of history, a text, values, ideas. He frequently hit the nail on the head with his comments, and his positivity lifted the class. It was a joy to have Buddy included. I believe he gained confidence in having his views accepted in class.

Another example of innovation in the program illustrated two of Sizer's Principles: that learning should be personalized and "exhibited." Two students in the school's superb dance program, a life-saving creative self-expression outlet, chose to demonstrate their understanding of *Macbeth* by choreographing and performing a dance based on the play rather than taking a written test. Naturally, there was contention: Should doing what was easy for these inventive students who loved dance supplant the writing required of others? But these two students wrote plenty of other pieces, and their *Macbeth* performance gave them practice in connecting their academic study with their art. Their dance, though a controversially different form of presenting their knowledge, demonstrated understanding of the challenging play, personalizing learning, Sizer's term. Later, researchers led by theorist Howard Gardner promoted "multiple intelligences" to help students learn by using alternative means such as art and performance. So many of Sizer's ideas preceded and stimulated new thinking that later gained national attention.

As part of the struggle to find ways to work with varied students, I made a discovery that worked with a particularly challenging one. Thomas was constantly disruptive—hyperactive and incessantly social. In another school, where educators less impacted by a multitude of challenges could be more watchful, Thomas most likely would have been given a diagnosis of Attention Deficit Hyperactivity Disorder

(ADHD) and better served by a special education teacher trained in this disorder. But at this time, Thomas was stuck with just me.

When my class was in the computer lab writing their own original myths, based on the Greek myths that were my connection to my co-teacher John's western civilization course, I sat next to Thomas so that the other students could work undistracted. In an experimental, just-try-anything-and-see-if-it-works approach that had become a habit for me, I asked him to tell me a myth. Spontaneity within a context can help. As I typed his exact words into the computer, he focused intensely. Thomas saw his own words on the screen. I delighted in what he dictated. His myth was powerful, precise, and beautifully expressed. Inventive, it contained a unique moral. It was the strongest of all the students' work, and I read it aloud to the class. Thomas quieted down, for a time, exuding some confidence.

In another situation, I found myself acting once again as a renegade. I recognized that two very bright students, Kristin and Ethan, needed a challenge. So I created an Advanced Placement course for them. We would meet together outside of class, just the three of us, to go over practice tests. Kristin and I marveled as Ethan, brilliant, would give a correct answer. "It says it right here!" he'd state, pounding the page, as Kristin and I were in a fog on where it was he saw that answer. Both did well on the AP exam. I hadn't asked for permission from anyone to pick up this extra work, nor did I let anyone know I was doing it, but it seemed to me to fit the Principles. I didn't recall the guides stating that advanced students should be held back.

A few years later, the head of guidance was helping students with college acceptance and approached me about getting AP course credit for these students who were clearly exceptional. The credit would mean these students could skip a freshman college course on the same subject, saving them money. I don't recall how it was that I'd arranged on my own, not going through the Guidance office, for these students to take an AP course, and I didn't have a separate course, just some supplemental tutoring. The head counselor seemed surprised I'd done this additional work. But he didn't admonish me. I'd overstepped, but I believe he understood it was helpful for students. Such extra effort isn't uncommon among educators. Many take such steps for individuals. I felt the Sizer program empowered us to push farther, but working with Kristen and Ethan might have been what I'd do anyway, since helping a young person is its own reward. Only teachers know the special delight, the personal and professional reward, that comes from going above and beyond, even if it's only with one student. Certainly the movement Sizer launched gave permission to push farther.

Many students blossomed in Hope Essential. As more able students mixed with less accomplished classmates to bring up the class level, new long-term plans also emerged. Many began to think beyond graduation. With mixed-achievement-level classes boosting ambition, one less academically oriented student, broadly smiling, confidently told me she was staying an extra year in high school in order to be able to go to the state university. A strong transition program there worked well for incoming college students like her who needed extra help to move into college-level courses. One bright but reluctant, long-haired young man did leave school, but returned two years later, returning to Hope Essential.

We became a dropout prevention program, an island within the school, though, sadly, not loved by the regular program staff, and certainly not always peaceful. We weren't exchanging successes and challenges back and forth across the line between ourselves and the regular school teachers. And with contentiousness a problem, no one suggested creating another program such as ours in the regular school. What we were achieving touched the hearts of parents and students and brought many successes. But small victories with individual students don't hit the newspapers, are always just a teacher's own cherished sense of accomplishment. Sadly, we became better known for not working well together than for how we were helping students.

I Lose a Student

One genuine success was that old-school discipline problems for the most part disappeared. At Hope Essential we had the obverse of the traditional approach in which discipline was often a top-down squelching of behavior, which only tended to generate more bad conduct in reaction to a system that seemed not to care. Under that system, recidivism was a problem. The common punishment of suspension from school didn't correct unwanted behavior. The student only missed more classes, fell farther behind, and felt more like an outcast. By showing respect, listening, and encouraging kids to strive for higher level work, we were finding students more cooperative. As we created an atmosphere of learning in which the more academically focused students helped others, the culture within our program shifted from disconnection to connection, making students' experience more positive. Everyone learned.

But in one instance, I made an especially bad call. An event that haunts me still was with Jared, who crashed through the cracks. Most students didn't mind sharing classes with all the same peers, but Jared alone objected to the fact that he was always with the same classmates. Jared mentioned to me several times he wanted to leave Hope Essential and transfer into the regular school. It was a mystery to me that he objected to this one aspect of the program, of always being in class with the same students, and I begged him to stay. But then one day he disappeared, dropping out of our classes with no communication from the guidance office, possibly no counseling, as harried, overburdened counselors just accepted a student's request. I should have taken more time to confer with Jared to determine whether it might have been that he had a problem with a particular student in our group. Stopping to take that kind of time can change everything.

The next year I was running upstairs, late to a parent meeting in Steven's office, risking admonishment, because I knew we all wanted to connect with parents, when Jared called up to me from the stairwell below. He asked if he could come back to our program. He pleaded. Shakily he told me he'd just been expelled for fighting. Getting into a fight and being kicked out of school didn't sound like the Jared I knew. Standing on the stairs, looking down at him, I was torn. Fearful of Steven's wrath if I was late to the parent meeting, I asked Jared to see me later. Bad call. I never saw him again.

It was and is heartbreaking that Jared needed me as an advocate, and I let him down. I still see his scared, pained face. Being on time to a meeting to avoid the anger of a superior overrode helping a student in distress. Later, thinking about the situation, I realized that one student had been annoying Jared, and this teasing happened in every class. When I spoke with his mother about the issue, she rightfully yelled over the phone, "Move their seats!" I hadn't paid sufficient attention to this one detail, given the many other big and small issues I had to deal with daily. Once again, I learned.

Would Jared have gotten into a fight while in Hope Essential? Not likely, but possible. Would his discipline problem have been treated differently? Definitely.

There were other students who broke my heart. Charity, bright and eager to learn, always chose to sit right up front in class. Her comments were gems. Her poise and presence set her apart. On her own, she had read all of Alice Walker's short stories and novels. One day she told me was retaking the SAT test. She wanted to attend the historically Black women's college, Spelman, sister school of Morehouse College, the historically Black men's college in Atlanta. Her face lit up when she learned that Alice Walker had attended Spelman.

I should have helped Charity prepare for the SAT test, which was then heavy on vocabulary, with no context provided for the words tested, a test question that was later recognized as discriminatory. Even with all the words Charity picked up from her extensive reading, we would have needed to spend time learning Latin roots and prefixes, plus other skills that she couldn't easily acquire in her neighborhood. Sadly, her SAT score was not high enough for her to qualify for a scholarship, so she was unable to attend Spelman. I regret that I didn't drop other things to work with her. She chose another college, one close to Spelman geographically. I only hope that her intelligence, determination, and poise moved her along in life.

Kwame was a success story. He went on to Morehouse College, an environment that created national leaders, including Dr. Martin Luther King, Jr. and other prominent Black figures, such as King's aide and civil rights strategist, Atlanta Mayor Andrew Young.

Kwame would walk languidly into my class right at the bell to start class, move to the center of the room, and then stroll to the back of the room for his seat, from where he could survey the scene and quietly dominate. A basketball star, tall and lanky, he moved with an athlete's ease, a young Michael Jordan. I could count on Kwame to complete a point I wanted made. He was one of those students who transformed a class. He'd often have the final word on an issue. I didn't mind. Every student listened when Kwame spoke. The way my co-teacher John and I made sure our classes were culturally relevant, not common for the period, was Kwame's consuming interest. He read avidly.

Kwame was allowed to soar especially in one of our projects. John and I were asked to join a Brown research project studying the effects of computer learning. This project was a benefit for our students, who gained access to wider reading. We'd research and create readings related to our courses and put them into an online template to tailor readings for our classes. Students would read online selected pieces, instead of teacher lecture, in line with the program guide of active student learning.

One morning Patrick, a Brown anthropologist studying us, made an unannounced visit to check on me and my class. I was relieved that every student was engaged in reading the text I'd assigned on the library computers. Everyone except for Kwame, that is. I noticed that instead of reading about Langston Hughes, for that day's assignment, he'd located material I'd developed on prize fighter Muhammed Ali, who had taken a public stance against the Vietnam War. Kwame studied the text and photos I'd culled. I knew he was intrigued with the boxer's political actions and I also knew he would eventually get back to the assigned reading.

In an earlier time, I'd have to prod students to focus on certain reading. But now we got to know our charges better. As they were all drawn to the online readings, Kwame, as always, was a few steps ahead. It was hard to constrain, and limit material for a bright star. Kwame took it upon himself to personalize learning, and dig deeper on his own.

Kwame brought the class level up. When I showed a brief film that encapsulated the theme of a unit we were working on, then asked a question, Kwame just stated, "That's it!" He nailed the point I was looking to make. I just asked him to elaborate, which he did well. With his intelligence, quiet drive, and confidence, I have no doubt he has succeeded in life. I hope his success was fostered by our work together. Letting Kwame learn double the amount was important. In mixed classes, it's not hard to let some excel, however and whenever, including with on-the-spot unplanned personalization.

Other Successes, College as a Goal, Gratifying Unintended Consequences

Other pleasant surprises emerged too. Early one morning before classes I looked into the school library. Essential School students were intently working together at tables. They'd taken two city buses across town in the cold and dark in order to meet before school. They were sharing ideas, helping each other in study groups they'd formed on their own. While previously students would create physical altercations, with friends avidly watching, now heads were down and students were reading, quietly conferring, preparing for class. This early morning study time replaced the study period Lee had confronted the program head about. We teachers would never have thought to ask students to come in for early morning work. It would have been hard to entice them, and who knew what trouble we'd be accused of in asking students to come in early. Generating their own time to get together allowed these students to share ideas and process their learning by helping one another.

After-school work also blossomed. At the end of another school day, instead of running out the door as quickly as possible, as I'd done previously, I took a walk down our program's long corridor, the hallways normally empty after the final bell. Now students were still in classrooms, meeting with teachers or an advisor for a mentoring session or an after-hours chess club, conferring on class work with a teacher, or working together with peers. Since some found home too distracting for homework, the comfort of a protective group and some extra one-on-one help was welcome. I marveled that day at how much our school had changed. Students voluntarily staying late was school working, at last.

With each teacher contributing in his or her own way, Hope Essential sailed along fairly well, with some rocking the boat, yet still moving forward. Instead of what might have felt like demeaning "training" on irrelevant topics arranged by remote administrators, we'd been given broad Principles and trusted to determine what was needed. Each of us figured out our own way to do what was expected, conferring with one another individually rather than in pre-planned meetings. No one preached at us, or if they had, we hadn't listened, though we could have used some on-going instruction on collaboration instead of our lone ranger, independent let's-do-it-my-way approach.

It seems to have occurred to no one to provide professional development on how teachers accustomed to working in isolation could work together to meet new expectations. Instead, we were left to sink or swim. We were charging forward to do as well as we could. Always, it was helping students as the goal, and we did often feed off each other's successes.

Things were not perfect. How could they be, with teachers coming from a set tight system that fostered individualistic thinking and students with varied needs and multiple issues? School is people-centered, and people are different. But despite imperfection, it was an environment infused with learning. This essential value permeated our work. Students performed well because we expected them to. This endeavor was what we'd all originally signed up for. It was our sense of duty to our students that led the way. Whatever the downsides, students benefited well from teachers dedicated to help their own group of students, and having collegial support, however less than ideal, for what was otherwise a too discouraging independent journey.

CHAPTER ELEVEN

Leadership, and Winds of Change

The right leader for the job makes all the difference. A good leader is both competent and likable. But when the leader is less than effective, another must step up to make things work. The right leaders could have changed the trajectory of our school, even, perhaps, that of other schools.

Over several years, there were four different Essential School program leaders at Hope (including one substitute teacher in an interim position), with both successes and challenges constant. At the same time, similar reform initiatives were expanding all around the country, so we at Hope were left to our own particular joys and dilemmas. Sizer, who had set up our program and had often visited us, was now in demand everywhere. He couldn't watch over our one small program, beam his bright light toward us. It wasn't long before our potentially even stronger program, with its critics louder than its advocates and those of us exploring new possibilities, engaging more students, was shut down, with both large and small successes overlooked. Where were those wise and courageous leaders who could calm seas and promote the positives to others? Fighting against the tide, and against critics, is hard.

Steven, whose courage and drive were crucial to launching the Essential School program, had understandable ambitions to move on to a higher paying school principalship. After his departure, the math teacher Lee, of the first year's team, picked up some of Steven's tasks to help out in the interim. We were happy to see Lee sitting in that now friendlier office.

Lee was smart and relaxed, sanguine, always helpful, never hurtful. He had the sense of humor needed for an adventurous role. With his laid-back manner and intelligence, he earned our program teachers' respect. He'd been here from the decades earlier "riot" disruption, understanding the protest, understood the Sizer concepts, and enjoyed helping kids. He was also a good listener, while also knowing where school had to move. He created a sense of tranquility for us and fostered professional interaction. We felt his support. Lee was a great teacher and was good with students. They liked him and his sense of humor.

Lee chaired the math department, where he was respected. He'd formed a learning community in his department as he and his fellow math teachers gathered in the morning before classes to discuss math issues in the comfortable, collegial office. Under his leadership, Hope's math department, including both regular program and Essential School teachers, won a district award from a national grant-funded program that sought to change math teaching for urban students. Only a few urban districts nationally were awarded funding for a project of effective professional development. This new training turned math teaching around. Under this long-term program, not a one-shot flash-in-the-plan quick in and then gone program, Hope teachers, along with all the district math teachers, were paid to attend summer institutes that presented innovative teaching methods with follow-up sessions. Teachers were inspired to become better teachers and learned new teaching methods, tossing out the old textbook that no longer worked. This was the effective professional development needed to make a change in thinking and practice.

This well developed program designed for urban schools succeeded in creating for teachers new methods to help all students understand math by going beyond simple, surface explanations that merely enabled students to mindlessly do a problem with superficial math algorithms soon forgotten. The active learning mode taught and that teachers implemented produced math understanding, not the traditional memorization of algorithms. From these effective means provided to present information, teachers were inspired and armed to help urban students grasp math concepts. During the relaxed, paid summer institute, teachers viewed the film "Stand and Deliver," a true story in which "dropout-prone Hispanic students" learned calculus from actor Jaime Escalante so successfully that investigators accused the students of cheating on national tests. Through this immersion in fresh thinking about why and how to teach math differently, the Hope teachers acquired skills to bring this new way of learning to the classroom. Concepts and specific practices changed how math was taught, with the full school department group included in the professional development. Conversation on the learning permeated the math teacher group. Lee ensured that the district new learning was accomplished within the school. Hope's math teachers won a district prize for implementation.

Under Lee's leadership, teachers began teaching innovatively, no longer tied to a simple but less than effective textbook. An incentive too was that each Hope math teacher received one's own welcomed class set of the latest costly new calculators. They put numbers on each calculator. They were their own to use, and made sure not one left the classroom. The gift of a valued resource to support the learning was new, and greatly appreciated. Talking with these teachers, I saw how well versed they were in the need to change their methods and exactly how they could now approach their work differently. Within their department they'd all had the same training in the new practices, and conferred with each other on them across the chasm between the Essential School and regular program teachers, all meeting in the safe confines of the neutral space of the small math office.

Sadly, though, this strikingly successful change wasn't recognized in the rest of the school. Lee prepared an explanation of what his department was doing to present to the full faculty but this was eliminated when the principal declared there wasn't enough time for this. Hope's full math department—both Essential School and regular program—attended a special dinner meeting of all district math teachers, at which they received an award for best implementation, while the project wasn't acknowledged within the school.

In the brief period after Steven moved on and there was a leadership vacuum, Lee picked up the slack. Tech savvy, he manned the office computer and walked into our classrooms to deliver the day's student absence list. This valued morning attendance report gave us the names of students who were legitimately out of school, so that we could compare it with our class attendance to see if a student was cutting our class, rampant behavior in the regular program, but actually irrelevant for us, because no one cut our classes. But the absence list as a means to note class cutting was a longtime expected tradition perceived to work. It was just a meaningless pro forma traditional task. Due to the many absences in the larger school population, this list often arrived late in the day, with secretaries feverishly typing the long list of absentees, and teachers receiving it when it was too late to catch students who'd cut classes. The paper pile of students reported not to be in class but not on the legitimately absent list must have been enormous. Steven had been outstanding in getting the absent from school list to us promptly. This gave us a sense a leader cared when delivered early in the day when it might make sense. But the difference was that Lee calmly handed it to us in an adult-to-adult fashion. Such personal touches helped smooth relationships, showed mutual respect. Steven's officious dropping the list on our desk then running off to deliver the next one was efficient, but impersonal.

Eventually, a new program head was named, chosen by superiors, a remote selection process we teachers weren't informed of. Different from Lee, Suzanne, the first English teacher in the program, was presumably selected by the university representative and school administrator committee. While Lee exuded calm and competence, Suzanne, though good with students, only fostered division. In reaction, a member of the Hope Essential group—a math teacher—created a union rule that in the future, the program leader selection process would have to include an Essential School teacher. This rule was written into the union contract, but the damage had been done.

Given a choice, we would have selected Lee in a rare instance of full consensus. Lee showed us he could bring us together.

Suzanne proved to be the wrong person for the position. The next couple years, during which she fostered only anxiety and contention, were painful. While our grade level teams worked nicely, no one wanted to attend full program meetings. Communication and collaboration among the full group simply didn't happen. Lee would have used discussion and cooperation to calm turbulent seas. Also, because he'd been at Hope for many years, he knew most of the regular program teachers and would have been able to talk with them constructively, if even to schmooze. Suzanne had arrived at the school later and didn't mix with veteran staff. We'd missed the opportunity for the kind of "conversation among folks"—between the new program and regular program teachers—that Sizer knew was key to productive change. Things could have taken a different turn with Lee's awareness of the schism and his ability to reach out to colleagues. We didn't even have that conversation well in the full program.

I have no doubt that if Lee had been tapped as Essential School program head at this point—the right leader at the right time—it would have changed the program's dynamic and trajectory and that of the school as a whole. Our approach could have had a chance to spread school-wide. The outside-of-school "others"—the university representatives and district superiors who didn't know Hope culture and personalities or the school's history—kept selecting the wrong person. The gap between us teachers and those with power was rarely bridged. While Sizer's Principles called for "a tone of decency and trust," which worked in our classrooms, this tone was absent among teachers, in large part because it was not fostered by the program head. Leadership matters. A cloak of good will can embrace all when each is respected and treated supportively; dismissal generates anger and resentment. Our next new principal John Short easily won everyone's trust.

Complicating life at Hope, in an already complicated moment, was the drama surrounding the position of principal. We were used to principal turnover. Richard had had the vision to entice Sizer to our school. Now, in late September, he left for a downtown quiet central office job, after helping a new superintendent win his position. Having set up Hope Essential, Richard had contributed much to Hope. He deserved a break from the trials of an urban school and independent-minded teachers. But with Richard moving on up, a new principal would be chosen, and those in charge of selecting Hope's leaders were notorious for mishandling this decision.

An Effective School Leader

After Richard left as principal, his second in command, John Short, took the reins until a new principal was selected. As a young, energetic assistant principal, John performed the position's discipline duties quietly and supremely well. It was a job I always wondered why anyone would want, seeking out culprits, trying to herd miscreants into class and get them to behave there. John was on it. A small streak of movement, he swept through the large building and took action with disruptive students. With his open, friendly, no-nonsense demeanor and problem-solving approach, John quickly won faculty respect. He was a good-hearted, straightforward soul effectively doing his job, not favoring any faction, just wanting to support teachers and maintain discipline. Moving into the interim principal position, John gained everyone's admiration, a tough medal to win. We could rely on him for both discipline backup and smart, steady, fair-minded leadership.

In his new role as acting principal, John continued to move briskly around the four-floor building. He chatted easily with all teachers. While displaying accessibility, he was also collecting information. When he stopped to talk with me briefly one day (I happened to be standing in the corridor during the class break), I mentioned that—now, having transferred out of the Essential School program—one of my students, Pedro, had told me that in gym class a gun fell out of a student's pocket when he tossed a basketball, and that the student had just picked it up and put it back in his pocket. John stood up straight, looked directly at me, and said, "This is my job." He was off and moving, fulfilling his responsibility to keep school safe.

Using the clever ways of a canny administrator, John drew from varied sources the information he needed on this issue of a gun in school. Within a couple days, he called me and my student into his office. Pedro seemed petrified. Who wanted to be in the principal's office? What retaliation for being a snitch was he in danger of? But John just quietly probed. Skillfully, subtly, using indirect methods, he interrogated Pedro and determined the name of the student who had the gun without Pedro having to say it. The interview was brief and composed. John had investigated, and all he needed was verification of the name. Unlike previously, when a visit to the principal generated worry about what one would be castigated for, with John it was now just a meeting to calmly resolve an issue. By acting in this way, he kept school functioning smoothly, complaints squashed.

Later, a new teacher, Deb, who'd been in a situation where it appeared a student had a gun, attended early morning teacher meetings on school discipline led by the school's union representative, who loved to stir up trouble. Deb was shaken by the gun incident, and told me that as a single parent she feared that if something happened to her, her son would be an orphan. She soon disappeared from Hope. It was the way the early morning union meetings stirred up concern about discipline problems that had fostered Deb's distress. I'd advised her to not attend those rabble-rallying meetings.

But as school head earlier, John brought peace and support to the entire Hope faculty, no small feat. Even the union-oriented teachers, normally critical, trusted him. Morale soared. The permanent position, however, went to a more eloquent candidate who performed well in interviews but turned out to lack John's professional people skills. If teachers had had a full vote, we would have chosen John. But the top district management selected Gordon, understandably favoring an African-American leader for a largely African-American student population. John became principal at another school, lost to Hope, where he was sorely needed. Gordon lasted only as long as it took for the union-oriented teachers to oust him due to rumors that he wasn't handling discipline problems well. It was sad to see teachers so easily led to gang up on Gordon. The outcome was unfortunate, since Gordon was Hope's first African-American principal. He'd had empathy for students who needed someone on their side.

Gordon quickly lost faculty support—and his job. Often a renegade, I'd supported him and questioned what to me seemed unfair charges. I didn't approve of mob-like tactics of teachers who met and criticized this new principal's actions. I sensed racism. I too was soon out the door, choosing to move on. Factions are more easily spotted and dealt with in smaller schools and school systems, and when identified early and addressed, sometimes can be dispelled, though not always. It can be easy to stir up rancor, with tenured teachers safe.

Hope Essential Changes Its Essence

In other turmoil, with Gordon new, Suzanne, the new Hope Essential leader, stated at the start of a meeting that we as a group should be in charge and make our own decisions about the program. She called on us to unite against Gordon. This was like telling meandering cats to line up. Someone in the room that morning went directly to Gordon. It wasn't me. I never cared for this kind of sniper sleaziness. Suzanne was immediately moved out of the building.

At that point, a relatively new teacher became Hope Essential's program head. I sensed that Sizer's ambitious Principles had become watered down, the synergy fizzled. Clashes along the way helped ensure the program's demise. I felt bad too that Hope Essential was now siphoning off the higher-achieving students from the regular school program, never Sizer's intent. And I regretted abandoning the full school, feeling that I should be helping the traditional program too. So I chose to move back to the regular program. It was hard to re-adjust to just fifty-minute classes.

Back in the old teaching structure, to my amazement, a couple of teachers there recommended that the only sharp, engaged, outspoken student in one of my classes—a class leader who made the group teachable—move into the Essential School program. Celeste was the sole student in my regular program class who understood the material. She helped others understand. Celeste led and held the class together. She kept the focus on learning and was the one student I could rely on to make class work. I was livid that other teachers said Celeste should be in the Essential School program, when she was so needed in the traditional program.

The interim Hope Essential program head (it had now weathered several leaders in just a few years), a new interim substitute teacher now acting program head called Celeste at home to recruit her. She was gone from my class in the middle of the week. Since it wasn't Sizer's intention to recruit the better students out of the regular program, I complained, more than once, and not quietly, to Shirley, our guidance department head. Poor Shirley could only respond, "It won't happen again."

But with Celeste gone, I still had two wonderful, outstanding students, though in another class, the brilliant Idania and Nueva, close friends. Thoughtful, outspoken Idania could easily have been pulled into the Essential School program, but she told me she wanted to stay and help the regular school. We were like-minded in our sense of fairness. It was sad to see the school so divided. These two bright lights dominated my class, inspiring their peers. We needed more like them in the regular program.

In response to the inequity between the school's two components, some staff later sought to break the full school into smaller programs, in theory a fairer system. But no one had the clout that Sizer had had, nor the wisdom to work at multiple levels to create more smaller programs, and protect these smaller units from oblivious upper echelon district administrators. A few teachers attempted to hold meetings to discuss pulling together a similar kind of smaller program. But these efforts, lacking Sizer's vision and influence, didn't aim as high as the Essential School program at its best. New upper level administrators, who lacked understanding of what had been established earlier and its initial enormous impact, quashed the effort to create other small programs to be able to work better with students.

A next superintendent, strangely named Tom Brady, on arrival shut down the Essential School program. I suspect he heard only negative views of Hope Essential, not what was working so well.

It's always easier to eliminate than to correct or improve. The gulf between a school and a remote central office in a large district makes good choices difficult for those working in school, and students.

But I have no doubt that if we'd had state tests to report the learning that was happening, Hope Essential would have survived. Administrators would have leapt to institute the program in the rest of the school, and Hope would have moved forward. But lack of good two-way communication between the program and other constituents reigned. The "house divided" nature of the school cast a dark shadow over Hope Essential. The once bright, hopeful, too-brief program, with no data to demonstrate success, and many eager to complain about it, died amid the silence. No one had the voice—or data—to come to the Sizer program's defense. It wasn't long too that Sizer himself decided to step back from heading his highly successful national organization. In answer to the question of whether a program can survive without its charismatic leader, the answer in this case was no. But there's no question Sizer's concepts lived on.

Department Head, At Last

While many on the faculty lit into the new principal Gordon, I found him easy to talk with on a professional level, intelligent, and observant. He would step into a classroom and quickly, astutely, assess what was going on. The comments he shared with me were exactly right on the money. Among his other duties, he monitored the school cafeteria during lunch and talked with students who felt an affinity with him as a Black principal.

A city reporter who hung out at Hope saw that I was a supporter of Gordon. I considered it inappropriate for some teachers to attack a new principal, especially when I suspected that previous principals had been guilty of similar behavior Gordan was charged with in regard to discipline, given how hard it was to determine the initiator or the target of student skirmishes. So with journalists and photographers visiting frequently, I appeared in newspaper articles which the anti-Gordon group disseminated. The media doesn't always get school stories straight, and news editors seem to love to promote ruckus, disturbances, contention. Some teachers stopped talking to me. Others told me they were afraid to speak up on Gordon's behalf or report on the leader of the anti-principal faction. For some reason, I didn't mind being perceived as a renegade, a role not foreign to me. Without trying, I seemed to often end up on the other side of an issue.

Meanwhile, Janice, the teacher from another school who'd been brought in as English department head, soon left. Gordon asked me whether I wanted to be head of the English department or head of the Essential School program. I chose the safer position of English department chair, a position I'd long coveted and been rejected for twice. I was also half-thinking that if I were ever able to move on, this more traditional position would help on my résumé, a good assumption, as it turned out.

I didn't stay long in that once highly coveted position, that one step up one could have as a teacher. It was fun to work with Gordon, and I felt cut out for this kind of leadership role. But with the fractious faculty and my new thoughts on education, along with an advanced degree that was valued in schools, I now made other plans.

CHAPTER TWELVE

Back to School for Me

School was in my blood. My mother was an elementary teacher. She loved books, was always reading. Two aunts had attended Teachers College, Columbia University, and started their own school. Another aunt taught kindergarten in her home, while another taught at Michigan State. Education was a family value.

We moved to another state when I was young, for a better position for my father. When my formidable new fourth grade teacher, Miss Sutton, who appeared ominously huge to me at the time, looked at the all A's I'd earned at my previous school in an affluent community outside New York City, she smirked, "They graded easy there." Shy in her dominating presence and eager to please, I smiled, "Yes." But I was now determined to show Miss Sutton. She worked us hard, and I rose to her level, and beyond.

Teachers often feel students don't remember them. But a teacher can strike a chord that inspires us long after we've left their class. One who diminishes pupils can also push a student forward. Miss Sutton set me on the path to becoming high school valedictorian and being accepted at the one college I applied to.

During the years I taught at Hope, I added a degree from the Harvard Graduate School of Education to my Brown Master's degree in teaching. When Janice, a candidate from another city school, was anointed head of the English department, I was crushed. I decided to seek a different route. One hot summer day as I was mindlessly swimming laps, a thought came to me, "Go for it!" I decided to get a doctorate.

I'd earlier attended a presentation by Boston University professors on their weekend doctoral program. Their doctorate in education was designed for educators who had an additional graduate degree beyond a Master's, a perfect fit for me. Many of my graduate student friends at Brown had never finished their dissertation. I decided while swimming I'd complete that capstone requirement. I sailed quickly through the BU program. This program for practicing educators had rolling admissions. I applied in July, started in September, and finished in a few years by doubling up on courses and commuting in to Boston for classes while still teaching full-time.

A force propelling me was that Sizer's project continued to raise questions for me, unanswered questions always stewing in my brain. While Sizer's outline of briefly stated Principles encapsulated a guide, I felt I had only a surface understanding of the Principles and how they applied to our work at Hope. I wanted to know the full scope of his thinking—his rationale for what he recommended. Also, why were we teachers at times crashing into each other? I was eager to deepen my understanding of big-picture education ideas, beyond my limited classroom view. The Boston University program clarified my thinking. It was the key that unlocked the mystery.

To grasp the thinking that shook our small world at Hope, I needed to acquire insights from research. The doctoral program allowed me to explore school reform concepts of the era, lifting a heavy burden from my battered brain. From extensive readings and wide-ranging courses, I gained a broader view, including coming to see how different teachers assess the same situation in different ways. And my belief that all students should get the education they deserve, goaded by Sizer's Principles, with none allowed to fail, was validated though my readings. Now instead of seeing recalcitrant students as just annoying, I understood the job was to help them, whoever they were. Graduate school was therapy in that I no longer had to try to figure things out on my own. Immersion in academic study also catapulted me into a new world of a move to fundamental school change on a larger scale. I was soon to be at the epicenter of that change, rocked on tempestuous waves, on a larger scale.

"Demographics Is Destiny" Debunked

I and my teaching colleagues at Hope had only known that we were unhappy with students who interfered with our classes and disrupted our teaching. It wasn't until I read education research in my graduate studies that I fully understood how better schools help all students learn, not just some. I was awed to read of a parochial school especially dedicated to more struggling students that increased class size for higher achieving students and put all their best teachers in smaller classes of students less privileged by demographic circumstances. I'd always relied a lot on my more advanced students, or those especially engaged in a topic, to lead the way in classes. But I now better understood that all students need and deserve better attention. Demographics needn't determine destiny. I now saw better that the whole point is that school can make a difference. Propelled by a determination to understand and immersed in findings and examples of how schools could do better, I finally grasped equity on a deeper level. I was able to place our struggles and different views at Hope in broader context. While I'd heard the talk of the Coleman Report, I'd been picking up just bits and pieces of the national discussion. Now I began to comprehend the issues more fully.

I saw how Sizer simply yet importantly made education research concepts accessible, by conveying school studies findings to educators in a respectful way, and by speaking directly with people, in addition to his publishing. He was a Frederick Douglass for educators. With Hope Essential, I'd moved into a mode of teaching I didn't fully understand, but now, absorbed in research studies, articles, and books, I grasped Sizer's vision more clearly. One shouldn't have to get a doctorate to comprehend one's work, but I did finally catch up. I was privileged to be able to study education change. The trick would be carrying this to others.

Finding a dissertation project was easy. At lively, never-a-dull-moment Hope High School, I had a wealth of material at my fingertips. I interviewed colleagues, across the battle lines, to include those not part of Hope Essential, and worked through varied statements to make sense of all I was hearing. Without a transcription device to turn statements into writing, I listened and re-listened to audio interviews and typed the exact words people said in interviews, thereby memorizing words and capturing thoughts of others. This moved me to new understandings with this one task, valuable insights as I next jumped into a whole new role with many new personalities and beliefs.

In my graduate study readings I was especially struck with the work of UCLA researcher Jeannie Oakes, author of *Keeping Track: How Schools Structure Inequality* (1985), who reported that it's only students in top-track courses who learn the particular skills, understandings, and terminology needed for success in college. I knew those students, the privileged ones who moved on to higher education and fine careers, and I knew the ones whom school overlooked. Research reports crystallized my understanding as I matched theory with my own experience. Moving to a higher level of thinking prepared me well for the challenges of my next step.

Teacher Empowerment: A Compelling Concept and Quandary

Another specific interest I had in my look at studies was the concept of empowerment, an issue for me personally in my teaching. I loved working as I wished, not as others might want me to, unless I saw good reason to change what I was doing. With no assistance at the time as we stepped into a new job, we teachers were left to figure things out on our own. Once we'd done that hard adjustment, why change, plus it's hard to make a change. I liked figuring out strategies and connecting with students in my own way. But I also began to see that Sizer and his assistants also had struggled with the issue of empowerment in guiding educators to more strictly follow Coalition Principles. Issues of, Can teachers lecture in a recommended "student as worker" environment? What constitutes "using one's mind well"? Can using one's mind well be demonstrated by a teacher promoting learning through full, engaging class discussion, as John and I were doing? If "all students" is the guide, is AP allowed? Should educators be dictated to, simply motivated, or left on their own to solve problems? Sizer had used carrot motivation well, inspiring and empowering teachers without critiquing them. But sometimes correction, judiciously applied, is needed, and especially when success is going to be tested. Sometimes teachers are right on the mark. Other times scrutiny and assistance is needed. It seemed to me that at Hope, there was a plea for teacher empowerment, but this was skewed by whoever the leader was at the time.

I was intrigued by Harvard sociologist Chris Argyris' extensive writing on worker empowerment. I devoured several of his books on organizational change based on his potent 1970s and '80s studies. Argyris reports that industry assembly-line workers are the best people to solve an efficiency problem when and because they're empowered to make that solution work. If the workers themselves decide what needs to happen, instead of being told what to do, they make sure their solution works. When outside managers try to impose a solution, Argyris notes, it often fails, since those excluded from the decision may not adopt outsiders' dictates, and the advice may not be appropriate for a solution. Workers knew best what to do, because it was their job and they knew the work, was the thinking. The workers are closest to the problem. Argyris cites examples. It turns out this may or may not apply to schools, which are more complex than a machine. As new ways of schools working came on the scene, this outside force propelling change wasn't always appreciated. I was to find lots of resisters in my next new role, as the federal government dropped required new Standards with a test on educators. Sizer had relied on teachers latching on to his concepts. But it was hard to light a fire of educators racing to integrate new areas that would be tested into their teaching, resented as "top-down," and also not easy to change one's work to accommodate an outside force. Lee's math teaching revolution transformed teaching but this had been dependent on outside experts to light the spark and train teachers in how to work differently. The long-term professional development worked. The nation now was moving toward a law that required a change in thinking and practice. Figuring out to make this work was to be a long rocky journey I was about to join.

The concept of worker empowerment was compelling. I loved reading about workers empowered to create their own ways to make a system work. But allowing workers to use their knowledge to improve assembly-line efficiency is not necessarily transferable to the complex situation of schools, where the kid gloves of a sensitive Ted Sizer are required, and clear goals harder to articulate. And a lot depends on who the workers are—in this case, educators—with their own talent and skill, their understanding of the goal, as well as the right type of guidance.

Empowerment can go awry. I'd seen empowerment going in an anti-school leader direction at Hope, where union-oriented teachers schooled in antagonistic worker-management more confrontational mode garnered followers to drive out someone I viewed as a good principal. It's possible the principal under siege had a better handle on what would be best for students, but the teacher group, with their own concerns, felt, and became, powerful enough to remove him. To me, the result didn't move the school forward, but simply generated contentiousness not conducive to a smooth environment. Years later a more expansive, empathic next Black principal Matt was adored by teachers, quickly smoothing rough seas, with students, and faculty, a different leader and influence.

Often teachers have insights and approaches that make things work better, and it's good for them to be empowered. Sometimes the right leadership fosters change, but not always. I liked Stanford professor Larry Cuban's observation that making school improvement happen must be like repairing a fine Swiss watch, not using a hammer. Finding the right touch for the particular people is what brings success. A leader who's run out in one environment—and I was to see many—is just right for another.

In the Essential School program, we'd pretty much proved that just putting teachers in charge might succeed in some areas, since we all had high expectations and each worked hard for our students, but collaborating with each other on the larger scale, outside our small teams, wasn't one of those areas. Sometimes pulling people together works well, problems solved, not always. No one stepped in to train us in the skill of collaboration. In our unique situation, worker empowerment went off the tracks with regard to the larger group effort, given our multiple views.

At one point in the Essential School program a fellow teacher, a rule-follower type, came to my classroom to give me an agenda for our advisory period. I believed the advisory time agenda should come from what students said. My team-teacher John and I both felt we were doing what was best for those we advised. Others assumed what they were doing was right, but it wasn't our way. How to teach well varied too, and was individualistic. We weren't like assembly-line workers with that clear goal of working together to solve a simple problem of efficiency. It took years for common learning as the specific goal to clarify the work, as educators learned new ways to help all students. I've seen many self-empowered teachers excellent in classrooms, and a self-empowered leader set up a barrier to moving a school forward.

In spite of this one knotty issue of empowerment, with when and why, my doctoral studies answered many of the questions I had when entering the program. The foggy glasses dropped from my eyes. My vision cleared. I'd joined a small, driven cohort of teachers and school administrators who wanted to move quickly through the program. We met with the Boston University department chair in charge of our program. The truly type-A assistant principal in our group asked him if we could take both the quantitative and qualitative research courses—very different research modes—concurrently during the summer to speed up our progress. He just scratched his head and said, "Well, no one's ever done that before." We did it. I received my doctorate the following spring, after just three intense years. Only one other in our group joined me in graduating, and she'd taken a year off from teaching. I was in a hurry. I was self-empowered to move on.

PART TWO

New Federal Law for Student Learning Is Unwelcome

CHAPTER THIRTEEN

Moving On: Crossing the State Line

Having completed my doctorate, I loved the rapport I developed with the new Hope principal. Gordon cared about learning. He loved calling me "Dr. Scheidler." I enjoyed the chance as English department chair to bring together regular program and Essential School teachers, transcending boundaries. And at long last I had an office and a phone. But this once dreamed-of position was only a steppingstone.

Part of the reason I moved back to the regular school program was my interest in equity, as the Essential School program excelled with students while others in the school floundered. I wanted to work with the part of the school left behind by the more favored program. Another reason to move to the traditional school program was that the initial high expectations of the pioneering Essential School program became watered down, as new teachers moved into the program but didn't get the same information on the Principles that we earlier teachers were provided. Sizer's second book, *Horace's School*, called for a tweedy-attired guy in a building who could explain and coach, on an on-going basis, a key role never possible to implement, in part due to the always challenging issue of funding, and less attention to continued learning. And now as Sizer's program expanded, he was in demand on the national stage. And Sizer's Brown consultants, funded by grants, in what they called the "soft money palace" of the Coalition of Essential Schools' short-term all-grants funding, departed for more stable positions. Without those watchful observers, Principles dissolved; old-school work seeped in. There was no one to explain, remind and effectively counsel on using the Principles as guides. The third head of Hope Essential was not a visionary, and as one fairly new to the school uninterested in connecting with the regular program teachers or top echelon administrators outside the program's insular cocoon. The program was just treading water, no longer heralded, beginning a slow demise as the shine of a new venture wore off. Without the political capital of a Sizer to protect the program, it was vulnerable. I too felt vulnerable, due to my alliance with Gordon, whom others opposed. I was beginning to think it might be time to make another move, one not within the school.

It was hard to leave. Life at Hope High School still had its attractions, if only in the sense that there was rarely a dull moment. Also, I lived just a couple minutes' drive from the school, just down the street. That would soon change, dramatically. Inertia kept me here for a bit longer. Since I lived within walking distance of the school, it was fun to easily attend basketball and baseball games, evening student performances, nighttime parent-teacher conferences. But despite the advantages of proximity, I was also eager to move on. I was soon to leap into a bigger adventure. A neighboring state was making major changes to public education that very much appealed to me. I jumped ship.

Where Did Standards Come From?

Coming from the changes of Sizer's program to be able to better work with all students, and having my eyes opened in my graduate studies readings, for me, when Massachusetts early on picked up the mantle of state testing, this caught my attention. I was eager to join that transformation of public education, unaware of pitfalls.

The harsh turn to standards with the test had been bubbling in Washington, DC for some time. Discussion of the need to improve US schools had begun under President Reagan in the 1980s, partly in response to the reality that the country was falling behind Japan, whose rapidly rising economy was threatening to surpass ours. Japan was churning out cheaper and better autos, threatening the US automotive industry. Everyone was buying Japanese-made cars. Also, taking technology invented in the US, Japan was number one in the US, selling Japanese-made Sony TVs and video recorders, which everyone bought. Japanese businessmen turned US-written books into globally popular films. They bought Rockefeller Center. No longer was the label "Made in Japan" a sign of shoddiness, but of excellence. Coupled with this economic threat during the Reagan years, a 1983 national report on education titled "A Nation at Risk" condemned the quality of US education. These researchers accused schools of creating the memorable "a rising tide of mediocrity." There was a sense that we as a nation needed to do better. Education had to improve.

In response to many calls for school improvement, at a 1989 national governors' conference in Charlottesville, Virginia, the nation's governors voted to have the federal government enact a law for education accountability and equity. The new law required states to create specific skills for students to acquire, called "standards," along with a test in English and math to assess this learning. Without the test, the law would be meaningless—common higher level learning would be just a suggestion, not a requirement, easily ignored. No longer would teaching be individualistic and random. And a test on the standards was for all students. The 1993 federal legislation opened up an opportunity for me to take on new challenges. New law gave rise to concern from educators and parents. But I was used to protest against change. I wanted to join this effort for a different way for school to work to better help all.

When governors forced the federal government to bring in accountability in the form of a law, sanctioned in the mid-1990s, this major change hit the nation's schools like a tornado, distracting and demoralizing in initiating a shift no one in schools wished for. But I saw this move as a next step from Sizer's movement. Every school would now have to show what their students were learning. It wasn't a voluntary sign-up-if-you-wish change, as Sizer inspired. For me Sizer's Principles were a precursor to these new higher expectations for every student. But a difference was that it was the unique elements of the Essential School program at Hope with its change in use of time, teacher roles, and guiding Principles that allowed us to better engage all students, and creating teams that provided support for teachers that helped learning soar. As pioneers, guinea pigs, we'd limped along, striving, our progress hardly streamlined, but with both students and teachers benefitting. Adding a test that would show learning would be the icing on the cake. Others didn't have that perspective.

A Breakthrough Law Hits Schools

The summer after a year of bringing together Essential School and regular program teachers as head of the English department for the full school, I found myself relaxing on a warm beach as my friends took a leisurely walk along the sand as I read through the *1993 Massachusetts Education Reform Act*, not normally a beach read. The legislation early on set out the law for standards for learning, and required a test to assess success. I loved this new plan. It was exciting to read.

Since I'd been driving in to Boston for graduate school, I now felt more in tune with education in that state than in my home state of Rhode Island, where I'd only ever been a teacher, and only at one school. After reading the Massachusetts act, I began to apply for the school system curriculum director positions that proliferated across the state line. Suddenly districts formerly with supposed tight budgets newly found the funds to hire people to oversee this new initiative. Naively, I jumped at the opportunity to lead. Little did I expect the joys and hazards to come, as I met with teachers spooked by the new law.

When I read the Massachusetts Department of Education documents, I smiled at the Sizer terms I saw there: "exhibitions of learning," "all students," While some viewed requiring a test as a negative move, I saw it as a way to establish the needed proof of learning. It took many years for schools to adapt to the specific changes that would show that proof. Many teachers simply re-thought their courses and on their own achieved high test results. Over time, more jumped on that train. I leaped into the struggle. Others weren't as well prepared as I was, and this "trigger document" law caused heartache. For most educators, the turn to a state test was a blow. Those in economically disadvantaged school systems were especially wary of the test. Those in more affluent towns feared that their teaching would be constrained, and parents there worried that learning would be "dumbed down." For most, the new requirement was a zinger out of the blue, not well explained to teachers or administrators. Documents were issued, but few were prepared for this leap. No longer would teachers have full independence in what they taught and how. But Massachusetts, under its longest serving and determined Commissioner of Education, coming from the US Department of Education, and a believer in this effort, steadfastly urged district leaders forward. This state rose to the top nationally on varied tests. It wasn't until well into the two thousands that Rhode Island, with different conditions, adopted the Massachusetts specific state standards and test. Acceptance there was much slower.

Early on, I asked one Massachusetts principal what would be done to accomplish the mandated change. He calmly said, "We'll schedule classes differently. The lower-level students will be moved into the next course level up." I was startled that he believed a simple schedule change alone would create better learning and help all. The shift to serving all students well would be much more complex. Having teachers re-learn ingrained approaches to their jobs was only half the problem. It was the new concept of helping all students learn the same areas, and with the test, that was the scary part, with the longtime belief system that some couldn't learn. But fairly quickly the state found ways to address that mindset, by bringing strategies that helped more struggling students. Other states fell behind.

When I was hired as a district curriculum director and Assistant Superintendent (both titles same job, different salary levels) to head up the change to accountability, my new job now meant working in many different schools and school systems. We heads of the shift weren't always loved. Curriculum directors and other administrators moved around. But I was ready. I'd been at Hope over a quarter-century. Massachusetts was speeding ahead with school improvement, and I was eager to participate. Stasis, even when hit by exploding land mines, for me was boring. I was used to the liveliness of change from just our one small but lively and ambitious Essential School program. I'd been one of those for whom there were new expectations. So I believed I was prepared for the next step up. Little did I know the bumps ahead.

One disconcerting piece of new law that struck me, and others, was now principals would no longer have tenure, as a way to force administrators out if new expectations weren't met. Now, on paper, they'd be held responsible for better learning, not just school management. But in reality, accomplishing this task of improving the quality of learning was shifted to the new teaching and learning district heads (now my job), and would not be a simple task. The legislation stipulated that Massachusetts would create "Curriculum Frameworks"—documents in each subject area with specific learning described—though only English and math would be tested for accountability ratings. Helping with this was a job a principal would find hard to do while managing a building, and required a deep love of learning to take on the new expectations.

Now that the Education Reform Act of 1993 accountability meant sharpening educational goals by testing to see if students were learning basic concepts, the issue was, Did we want students graduating who hadn't mastered reading, writing, and math? The goal was clear; how to get there wasn't. I had discovered through my graduate work that empowerment is a compelling idea, but I also learned from Hope that empowerment is a tricky concept for achieving school improvement. Empowering can take educators down a path that may not lead to the concrete knowledge needed for college and life. Providing schools with specific learning goals and then allowing them to find ways to achieve those goals was a good idea. But trying to lead some and empower others who were on the right track was a tight rope walk, risky, with no simple answers. That sleeping giant was good only with the right goal, and best ways to get there. Now with standards to learn at least the goal was clearer.

The trickiest skill in attempting to introduce standards learning to educators was when to step in and when to stay away. I knew well that as a teacher I didn't like being told what to do. Who does?

I wanted to figure things out for myself. Many educators did this on their own, possibly to avoid being told what they should do. But there were times when stepping in was needed. Calculating this, and correcting, isn't easy.

We had an unexpected disappointment early on. In a small, relatively affluent, all-white suburb where I served as Assistant Superintendent for teaching and learning after leaving Hope, two fine teachers missed the boat. When I observed a team-taught middle school US History class, I saw exactly what one would want to see: Students were meeting in small groups to discuss issues, the two teachers moving around the class to monitor discussion, everyone was engaged and on task, the room exuding energy. Students appeared to be learning. I had mentioned the standards to these two teachers, assuming they were sharp enough to incorporate material that would be tested. But then their state test reports were a disaster. When I met with the superintendent, he looked at the results and accurately noted, "These scores pulled down that school and the district."

When I asked one of the teachers about a test question students had done especially poorly on, she looked at the question, turned white, and said, "We don't teach that." I realized I'd assumed these devoted teachers would have looked at the standards for their subject and folded them into their course. There was one student in the class with a perfect score on the test. She clearly knew a lot of the material tested, but she'd learned it from her mother, a US history buff. If the class as a whole, which was so engaged with their teachers' dynamic pedagogy, had received instruction in the areas to be tested, they too would have done well. These teachers were empowered to be good teachers, but their good work wasn't borne out in reported scores. They missed the mark. It was sad that they hadn't looked at the areas to be tested. I realized then that guidance helps steer good work, though this may not be apparent until it's too late. And seeing where guidance is needed and how to address the need can be a delicate matter.

Later I walked into another district's central office and saw the superintendent reading out the history standards to a large room full of teachers. He'd taught history himself and wanted to see strong understanding of the subject. Proud of his own area, he wasn't shy about sharing his expectations with his staff.

In a small low-income town where I later worked, I encountered another example that challenged the application of Argyris' conclusions when related to empowering educators. For a couple years there was a federal requirement to use Title 1 federal funds—only allowed used for neediest struggling students—for after-school tutoring to improve test scores. The teachers here in this district wanted to be able to do the tutoring themselves, not bring in outside consultants, concerned that they didn't know the students, so I worked on getting state approval for this approach. To comply, I often drove through dense traffic into Boston to locate the right person at the Department of Education offices where school administrators attended meetings to learn the specific guidelines for a school to use its own teachers as tutors. The grant was complex, and I spent many hours and days working on the specifics required in the grant application for our teachers to tutor.

After finally gaining grant approval, however, a bright-light shining middle school math teacher, a nearby Mount Holyoke College graduate, whom I was hoping I could count on to help make this tutor program work, suddenly left for knee replacement surgery. I wasn't expecting this. I'd hoped to rely on her to lead the math teacher tutors in the right direction. This hoped-for leader was gone for well over six weeks, the full period of the tutoring project. She'd had the math background to lift and focus the group's efforts. Another teacher, who lacked the first one's superior understanding, took charge of the project and succeeded in sabotaging it. This one only wanted to see how the tutors could use the time expeditiously, instead of focusing on the needed skill development that would improve the school's low test scores. It was teacher empowerment gone awry. Since I was brand-new here, I hadn't dared step in.

But I wasn't alone in disappointment. National studies of this Title I-funded experimental tutoring expectation showed that my program wasn't the only one that failed to increase learning. It was heartbreaking to try and fail. But the studies on this project showed that empowering teachers to tutor on their own can improve learning only when goals and practices align with what's needed and complement what's taught in classrooms, not unrelated or random, as our program had been. Additional attention to learning alone in tutoring doesn't boost achievement. It depends on how that time is used. I hadn't spent the time and effort needed to help the tutors spell out what specifically to teach. And I knew how combining supplemental work with what teachers were already doing would be unwanted intrusion into classroom practice. It could be a bag of worms I'd have stepped into, with teachers not anxious to reveal what they teach, especially to a new administrator. This is just one of the failures that accompanied accountability, but the law remained hard and unrelenting, and, in my mind, a good thing, as we strive to do better. Stumbling along the way was better than not trying, as long as we learned

Holding Feet to the Fire: Public Test Score Reports

As incentive for every district to teach the standards, the 1993 Massachusetts Education Reform law stipulated that test score reports on how well each school was doing on the test would be posted on the state Department of Education web site. From the beginning, posted test results were broken down by racial group, poverty level, second-language status, and learning disability, to ensure attention to these formerly marginalized students. This state used colorful, easy to read charts. Asian-American students were off the charts, always scoring well beyond middle class white students. Closing the achievement gap for all groups was always a goal, so categorizing scores in this way was helpful, though often painful for educators to see. Initially, posted scores only verified the gap between higher-income, all-white suburban districts and urban and low-income districts. So it was exciting to see when a traditionally underperforming group made gains. Posted data showed when people were paying attention. I constantly scoured, still scour, district and school test results, and delved into reasons behind a shift above or below the norm. I wanted to know why the change, how it happened, what was done differently. I was an assessment fiend, because I knew good scores meant better learning. I became like author Kingsley Amis' "crap detector," in *Lucky Jim*, with the main character feeling he should be sent into his university's get-together events to determine how boring they were, hyper-sensitive to tedium. I was sensitive to who was going along a good path and who wasn't. I did find that always there was a reason for the decline or improvement, and I wanted to know why.

While I initially cringed to see the racial buckets that students were placed in, easily accessed on the charts posted on the Department of Education web site, I soon recognized them as helpful categories to determine who was doing well and where help was needed. When language-learner students scored well, with their normal language issue, I could see a district's efforts with second language learners was working especially well. In Marblehead, a small affluent community located on the ocean, with four yacht clubs and luxurious water view homes, the excellent METCO Program (Metropolitan Council for Educational Opportunity) brought in Black students from Boston who chose to attend school outside the city. Marblehead was the first school system in the state to adopt the METCO program. In this suburban setting, I saw in the English scores that the African-American students did as well as the more privileged white students in nearly all of the English areas tested, but did poorly on straight-forward vocabulary word meaning questions. The principal wasn't surprised. He told me, "Studies report that students in families who have access to reading at home—newspapers, magazines, books—show better vocabulary." I urged teachers here to provide instruction on how to use context clues to improve vocabulary (English Standard number 4), and to define more challenging words in class. It was good to see urban students intermingling here, and learning well. Overall, the gulf between poor and wealthier districts later shifted with both surprising downturns and encouraging successes. Having the test score information that so many disliked, fearing bad reports, was a gold mine of data we could use for improved learning. Some educators scrutinized their own scores avidly; others didn't want to look.

At first the wealthy all-white suburban communities with well-educated parents scored high on tests, and urban districts scored poorly, but over time, testing led to big breakthroughs, showing students learned more.

"Naysayers" Can Be Powerful

Accountability in Massachusetts hit a brick wall in one particular area. With schools' overall test results reported, it was initially—and remains—hard to convert individual teachers who refuse to integrate Standards learning into their teaching, or are simply stuck with not knowing how to.

Teachers are protected by tenure, in Massachusetts called "professional teaching status." As a tenured teacher, one can undermine a principal, those who lost protective tenure with the 1993 law. And many curriculum directors, who never had this tenure protection, were easily ousted as a result of teacher complaints. We had to walk on eggs. Lack of cooperation from a recalcitrant teacher especially hurts small districts, since one outspoken negative influence on others has more impact. It's hard for another more optimistic teacher to counter negative influence. And the force of a teachers union can easily hold back progress: Teachers unions support teachers. They're a blessing protecting teachers from perceived unfairness, and for ensuring that teachers get decent, if not well-paid, salaries. But with something like administrators requiring time for professional development, when many educators may have more responsibilities that make that hard, this can prevent moving forward with better help for students. At one point when I asked teachers to stay after school to review a state test where scores were poor, I was summoned to meet with the union head. I changed that time.

A school district's status is based on how well each school is doing, but a single teacher's score isn't made public in the state reports. But if, as I observed in a well-off community, one science teacher had lower scores than her colleagues, this brings down the overall science score for the school. A school can't require better test scores.

Also, exceeding expectations occurs. I visited a fifth grade teacher whose science scores were second to the top in the state of all 1,500 elementary schools. I learned that in this wealthy community that she'd majored in science in college and took advantage of state-sponsored professional development in the science areas tested. Her top scores raised the science scores for her district. She was the only science teacher in this small school with two other elementary schools, so these were her scores. No one had asked her to "teach to the test." I spent time in her classroom and met her students. They learned science well, and loved science. Though it's the school and the district scores that are made public, principals know whose scores are high, whose were not so high, because they receive this information; principals know where students are assigned. Yet there's not always a lot they can do to change things. When one principal moved a teacher out of her grade level due to poor scores that were inappropriate for her students, that teacher never stopped complaining, protected by tenure. At the other extreme, when one skilled elementary teacher in another school disregarded the school's curriculum and purchased her own books to use in her classes, and taught in her own way, her principal—knowledgeable in literacy development—allowed her to work independently. This teacher's reading scores were always sterling.

Trying to change an uncooperative teacher can be a hurdle. One school-based curriculum leader wrote to me in my online course, "I wish I had one ounce of the confidence of that (recalcitrant) teacher," who openly opposed moving forward. Because it takes a great deal of time and attention to try to move, or remove, a challenging teacher, out of self-preservation, principals often just look the other way. As a result, it falls on the shoulders of district curriculum directors to keep an eye on district scores and try to address areas that need improvement. A principal knows that he or she can be easily sabotaged by a disaffected staff member, and acts accordingly. I wasn't so savvy. It can be hard to see where trouble lurks.

Though I saw accountability as the basis for school improvement, helping all students with common learning, I, and others, felt battered with regard to one tested area. Statewide, during the 2001 *No Child Left Behind* era of the George W. Bush administration, eighty-five percent of middle schools in Massachusetts scored below proficient in math among special education students. This became the Achilles heel for principals and for curriculum directors. When just one school in the school system performs poorly in one subject area, and the full district is therefore rated below proficient, that one blot is troubling.

When at last this dreary math area problem was resolved, I suspect it wasn't so much that teaching had changed, or students suddenly learned more. It's more likely that superintendents complained, and changes were made to the test or to the scoring calculation.

CHAPTER FOURTEEN

National Mandate Isn't Welcome

Testing English and math standards for accountability rocked educators' world. It was as if the sky was falling. I saw the distress in teacher panic. It was mainly the "all students" expectation that was hard to grasp.

My state of Massachusetts, as nationally, found it a struggle to make the quantum leap change, but we all stuck with it, more or less, persisting, with each school system in Massachusetts now hiring a head of teaching and learning to head up the change. And gradually, over time, not without distress, on the whole the state moved to accept, though not love, this change.

Massachusetts moved to tops in student achievement nationally, with care taken to make the effort to include all students. In contrast, my home state of Rhode Island, with state commissioners of education coming and going, and lacking the same firm, consistent, and responsive state leadership on standards learning, never reached that same success. My former once proud school Hope's ranking, with 85% low income students, one-third multilingual learners and one-third special education students, hit bottom, quickly moved to state takeover status, and remained stuck there. It wasn't until a new Rhode Island Commissioner in 2019, coming from New York state, which embraced standards learning, Dominican herself, bilingual, who knew all students could do better, took the reins to move the state's schools forward that attention was paid to standards learning, despite persistent teacher union opposition, not uncommon nationally. New York was among the first states to produce a standards-integrated full curriculum, posted on the internet, which others hastily adopted, even though the New York curriculum didn't fit well for other school districts.

As I moved across the state line to become director of curriculum in my first new job in a small district, it didn't help my credibility when information from the state on one tested area served to pull the rug out from under me. When I told Dave, the high school English department head, exactly what the writing question was to be on the first high school test, Dave commanded his English teachers to sweep their desks clean and teach this one writing skill. A state Department of Education official told me that was exactly the right thing to do. So it didn't build a lot of trust when on test day students looked at the writing question and were surprised to see that the writing question was totally different, a much easier question. Apparently the state leaders had changed their minds and made a switch. Dave and I didn't have the conversation on this change, because this issue was too painful. Still, with all the bumps in the road, overall, we complied, if haltingly. It was state law.

Despite the challenges, Massachusetts held fast on testing. Initially the groups of students expected to have the most difficulty with the test, special education students and second language learners, were spared from being tested, a huge relief to many. At that early time of the mid-nineties, these two groups were not included in testing because many believed these groups couldn't learn so well. That changed. After the first few years of testing, with broad discussion, the state decided to test all students, including those with weak English language skills or having a learning disability. The move to inclusion was a painful and extremely helpful move, now with high level expectations for all. At a social occasion, apart from school, I happened to talk with a strong special ed teacher. She was distraught and planned on leaving teaching when her high demographic school system adopted a new elementary math program she believed her students would never be able to learn from, shattering for her, as happened with many.

As an incentive for students to take the test seriously, but a teacher concern, Massachusetts required passing the high school test for graduation. This helped ensure paying attention to the standards for these lower-achieving students, immensely helping them. The test at tenth grade as a graduation requirement allowed a couple more years to make up the learning deficit, providing several briefer re-takes over the next two years. Modifications included that special ed students with a reading disability were allowed to have a teacher read the test to them, and a special ed teacher and student could create a portfolio of work that demonstrates standards learning, as an alternative to the sit-down test.

Now with all included in the test, educators hastened to find new ways to help especially lower-achieving students. Students who formerly weren't expected to learn to read and write now learned, if only at a more limited level. Teachers of these traditionally lower performing students were heroes, if not test-loving. Eventually, the state also provided more new ways of developing learning for struggling students that became accepted in schools, though this took some time to happen.

Over time, in small and steady steps, the state made some minor corrections on the test, in response to criticism, as protest against the test never let up. Still, educators and schools complied. Every year students learned more, and though no one really liked the pressure, most teachers eventually accepted the way the test forced them to develop better approaches. Helpful changes in how schools worked—new pedagogy right for students, teacher collaboration on instruction and helping more challenging students—resulted in more widespread common learning. A new phrase early on became common, of teaching as a "Guide on the side," rather than the "Sage on the stage," though those "sages" lecturing didn't disappear altogether. Collaboration blossomed. Now educators found ways to work together because more was expected of them, and individuals couldn't always do the job on their own.

Expectations tightened in the George W. Bush presidency. Outside of schools, while among policy makers and officials, there was a strong sense that public education needed to do a better job of serving all students well, and the test enforced this, inside schools, the response was different. The devastating loss of educator independence hit hard, but it was the 2001 *No Child Left Behind* Act (NCLB), passed with full bipartisan congressional approval during the George W. Bush presidency, that was a sledgehammer hitting educators' world. The Bush administration set a stringent goal. NCLB called for all students to attain proficiency on state tests by 2014. This harsher expectation setting out a target date was different from the voluntary engagement of a group excited about doing better of Sizer's era.

NCLB's stricter expectations turned schools around. It was a pivotal moment in US education. Commonly criticized, this version of the education act forced a permanent change in thinking and practice. Under this 2014 timeline pressure, new ways to help struggling students were created. An example of working differently that was state-promoted is "tiered learning," in which more struggling students are taught a skill in class, then also in small groups, and if still needed, one-on-one teaching, for more lasting impact. Providing more time to learn a skill such as in this way became more accepted, in part because it came from the state level.

With the break-through NCLB moment of high expectations sifting into school, new victories arose. A special education director in one school system where I worked, knowing the special ed law, acquired a lawyer and arranged for a one-on-one tutor for her special ed daughter who the school informed the parent was not capable of learning to read. With a tutor three times a week for just fifteen minutes, the child learned to break the code to learn to read.

A reading specialist in another district too had been informed her daughter wouldn't be able to learn to read. Mary Ann worked individually with her daughter, one-on-one, first starting with letter-sound connections, rhyming words, and gradually moving up the ladder of reading ability to become a fluent reader. With new belief in student capability, breaking old norms, now more learned.

While not every student reached proficiency under NCLB, most got closer. No longer could a student be written off. Principals helped, mainly in the area of class attendance, because accountability required data, including attendance data and percentage of students taking the test. Schools that had earlier shunted less academically attuned students aside now insisted that all students attend class, no longer slipping through the cracks, leaving teachers to figure out how to work with students who formerly escaped class, reaching out more, stretching capability. With rising federal expectations, now all teachers were expected to teach well, and this helped raise the school level. Urban schools now cracked down on students escaping to roam the halls, because each was tested. Hallway monitors now walked the corridors of urban schools, the get-into-class police. Still, working hard to get frequently absent students in class, especially on test day, was hard to achieve. Why come in to take a test they knew they'd fail? But now racial groups, special education students and students new to English learned better to read, write, and do math. While not all achieved the Proficient level on the test, the fact that many who had previously struggled grew in learning was an exciting accomplishment. An incentive in Massachusetts was those scoring at a higher level receive free state college tuition, helping to make college possible now for many.

One special education teacher I worked with had a student transfer into her class in the midst of his senior year from Connecticut, which at the time had different standards and test. This otherwise cheerful, can-do, upbeat teacher Sarah, seeing her new student was a weak reader, walked into the principal's office, exasperated, and told him, on helping this student with the test that year for graduation, "I'm not doing this." But Sarah knew the special ed law that poor readers could have a teacher read the test to a student, if this was written into the student's special ed plan. At test time, she cleared her week. Sarah had her paraprofessional take over her class, while she read the test to the student. He passed. He wasn't not smart, just a weak reader. Sarah ran again to the principal and delightedly announced, "I'm doing it again!"

I later saw this student in the school cafeteria line. Tall and handsome, African-American, speaking quietly and proudly, he nodded as I congratulated him. He told me he was taking a course in another town to fulfill graduation requirements. His girlfriend was driving him there to the night course. I saw Sarah at graduation. She was beaming. It's hard to imagine a reward that would be more satisfying. Just his movie star good looks would not have helped this student sufficiently in his next steps. With skills and confidence, and a high school diploma, he now had a better chance in life.

Creating Robots Out of Free Spirits

At the beginning of testing, I was Assistant Superintendent for Curriculum and Instruction in a small, all-white, semi-rural Boston suburb, with cows and a few working farms. Here the new superintendent, many parents, and the school committee all wanted better schools. Since pretty much everyone at the leadership level wanted to improve, I didn't really notice NCLB's abrupt new expectation of every student proficient by 2014. As we moved to standards learning here, teachers jokingly, I liked to believe at the time, claimed I was creating Stepford Wives, with each of them a programmed robot, denied their precious independence. But the new standards expectations have always maintained it's what's taught and learned, not *how* it's taught, that's important. And in a small town, one can keep an eye on each teacher. Teachers could choose *how* they taught, a nice empowerment, if only a small concession. Soon we were humming. We made a shift here to pretty much embrace standards learning as the guide. An impetus was in quickly seeing the test scores move up. With teachers' recommendation I purchased a full new kindergarten through fifth grade math program that worked well because it aligned with what was tested. These teachers knew their earlier program wasn't working, so pushback was minimal. We won a state prize for one of ten districts statewide that was "most improved."

But then I began working in a city closer to Boston, where the middle school fell under the "Needing Improvement" label. A dark cloud hovered over the district, once proud of its schools. NCLB made us all here feel bad. With test scores reported out by needs, race, and economic category, our special education students weren't making the mark. I brought in a superb math consultant, Grace, who'd helped the special ed teachers with math in my previous district, but without success here. We wracked our brains on how to lift that cloud. When I complained to Debbie Meier, Harlem principal extraordinaire and a close friend of Ted Sizer's, at a national conference in San Francisco, she commented to me non-judgmentally as I complained about this one disheartening issue, "Well, yours is the type of school system NCLB aims for." Overall, many students here did well, but not all. It was that one group that was the thorn. Part of me knew Meier was right. But it was tough to be under the gun and not find the key to better performance. That dark cloud haunted me. I could empathize with more challenged districts.

A difference between the math standards and English was math instruction tends to rely on the school system's math textbook. The district selects a math text program and that content was what's taught. The new math learning was different from the English standards and test, because the English skills can be taught with any book. Unfortunately, it took a while for education publishers to catch up with what the math test tested, leaving teachers in the lurch. It was the proliferation of varied standards and tests nationally that made it hard for a math program to fit all states. When earlier, at the start of standards, I asked one math teacher to spell out what he taught over a year, he xeroxed his math book's table of contents and handed it to me. It didn't match the test.

It wasn't until standards and tests became more common nationally, not until 2015, that math textbook publishers started to better address how to teach in the new way needed for the test, a breakthrough. Math teachers finally had material they could use that were aligned with what's tested. And the new materials helped enormously to bring more teachers to the way of learning that developed understanding of math concepts. Finally, a major turn in math development hit nationally.

Common *National* Standards and Test Are New

Standards became not unique to states, but more common nationally, with Common Core State Standards introduced in 2010. Within months, they were adopted by 45 states and the District of Columbia. With Standards now moving to more national guides, this now meant a teacher could do an internet search on teaching a common Standard and find multiple good ways to develop this, a huge help. But there was the usual unsettled reaction to new Standards.

It was in yet another discombobulating move, beneficial to students and initially an annoyance for teachers, that national Standards hit, unexpected and unwanted, as always. As always, Massachusetts fairly quickly made the turn.

With seemingly endless movement in always taking a next new step up, it was the National Governors Association and the Council of Chief State School Officers (the Commissioners of Education in each state) who initiated development of a set of stronger common Standards, called *Common Core State Standards*. While many blamed Obama for this change, he didn't develop these new Standards. Now we moved from the small "s" "standards," which are the varied standards of different states, to what was hoped to be the same Standards nationally, with the capital "S," for Common Core Standards, again a good move.

Though individuals were blamed for these next new Standards, they were developed by committees of experts knowledgeable in each subject area and based on the longtime standards of the National Council of Teachers of English and the National Council of Teachers of Mathematics. Microsoft's Bill Gates had to announce publicly multiple times that he had not himself created these next Standards, only funded their development.

While those in classrooms felt just when students were beginning to do well with learning their own state's standards, many wondered, why change? But it was exactly because many were now accomplishing the learning that it was a good time to raise the bar. Even I, who liked the idea of standards, and at the time of the shift in a high performing district, felt the weight of new national Standards an unwelcome burden. It felt like just when we were beginning to get it right, the goal post moved. And again, it was not appreciated at the time by educators, but was a needed next step toward more ambitious work. Massachusetts wisely took a gradual path to the change to new Standards. As it turned out, the new Standards were similar to this state's earlier standards.

A new test to assess the learning of these now national Standards was designed, also rocking the boat. Still experiencing PTSD from NCLB (which some called "No Child Left" or "No Principal Left"), educators didn't welcome a new test. And since it was intended to push for higher expectations, the new test proved harder.

Pushing the Envelope with PARCC

In Massachusetts, the new Standards were gradually over a few years moved into the test, and integrated in starting with earlier grade levels. The reality of a harder test was seen when in 2019 the new more difficult PARCC test (Partnership for Assessment of Readiness for College and Careers) reached high school, with a more complex writing question. In 2019 the tenth grade English scores in higher-income districts took a sudden nosedive, with tenth grade English teachers apparently not paying close attention to the new writing expectation. In response, teachers now scurried to pay closer attention to the new fine points of writing, a good thing. On the next test those scores spiked up, with scores moving back up by as much as 30 points, proving that what teachers do in classrooms in seen in the data. And that next test after 2019, in 2021, tested learning of the Covid-19 school shutdown period, when mostly nationally scores took a dive, illustrating where there's a will there's a way. Pride in their good test scores in high demographic districts, and possibly a nudge from higher-ups, encouraged teachers to attend more to what was tested, even during remote learning.

NCLB Languishes, Obama Makes Welcome Changes

Required congressional re-authorization of NCLB, due to expire in 2014, languished during the Obama administration, due to the unpopularity of both the president and the law. With educators working hard to help each student learn what was expected, but many not reaching the Proficient level, teacher stress was high, pushback heavy. The Obama administration then provided relief, softening the goal of attaining proficiency to switch to simply showing progress, termed "annual 'growth." The official name of the Obama era version of the federal education act also changed to the more positive Every Student Succeeds Act (ESSA) in 2015, with this next new version of the accountability act title hard to twist into a pejorative.

Obama's Secretary of Education Arne Duncan, former head of the Chicago Public Schools, used what he calls "bare-knuckle politicking" to wrench ESSA approval from a now divided congress. Obama also presciently altered the law to allow state choice of what standards and test to use, protecting it from accusations of federal overreach, and making it safe from the next president, as well as appearing more democratic. But cleverly, Obama offered states financial enticement to adopt Common Core and its accompanying test, PARCC. So with a financial incentive, with states and school systems always needing more funds, initially 40 states adopted PARCC, and also states moved to PARCC but called the test by the state's own name, as Massachusetts did, to avoid the appearance of federal government control. I signed up the school system I was working with at the time to accept the new funding. Though called "state Standards," Common Core became closer to national standards with widespread adoption.

Scores Rise, then Fall

The global pandemic changed everything.

Harvard Graduate School of Education dean of students and education researcher Martin West stated in a 2022 national zoom presentation, "We've had the greatest decline in student achievement in US history. We have to develop strategies for this."

As slowly, over the years, test scores rose, and a harder test arrives, thereby boosting learning, then nationally state test scores dropped sharply with the 2020 pandemic school shutdown. The demographic learning gap only increased with less advantaged districts, as seen in test reports. A well respected National Assessment for Educational Progress (NAEP) post-pandemic research report shows that the national average reveals a drop of 19 percentage points in grades 4 and 8 in math and reading since 2019. Other reports state student learning as seen in tests is set back by over a decade. Suburban schools had drops in test scores, then many were able to bring scores back up to close to pre-pandemic level, while urban scores remained flat, low.

US Secretary of Education Betsy de Vos agreed to have testing cancelled in 2020. With this reprieve, many, especially those in urban schools, during the pandemic period of school closure, pleaded to have the state test dropped permanently. But by eliminating the test, one wouldn't know how urban schools fared relative to suburban schools. And the goal of higher level learning would disappear without the challenge of testing. A new superintendent adjacent to Boston, under the shadow of the state Department of Education, posted on the district web site that she was proudly joining with the state's other twelve large urban districts to call for no testing for urban students, a post quickly removed. But even with urban superintendents pleading for no testing permanently, and urban teachers especially crying for the test to be dropped or modified for some students, beyond that 2020 year—some calling testing a form of "white supremacy"—Massachusetts, and nationally, states stood fast and administered the common national test in 2021, because it was the law. This 2021 test allowed educators and the public to see where losses and gains had occurred during the Covid-19 period, mostly revealing learning loss that would take years to overcome.

A Commissioner of Education Makes a Difference

Overall, in general, with successes and setbacks, my role in Massachusetts' response to standards and testing was both challenging and rewarding. It was key that the respected, ambitious Commissioner of Education for over a decade (before his untimely death) met with us district teaching and learning leaders, to urge us to carry out the statewide drive to perform in our own schools, with the result of Massachusetts heralded as a top-achieving state nationally. A 2020 longitudinal study by Harvard and Brown researchers, "Lifting All Boats?" (with a title from an earlier education report) on how Massachusetts state tests over the past twenty-five years have improved learning, states:

> "Massachusetts now sits at the top of the nation in test scores, and states across the country have sought to emulate the Commonwealth's education system. . . Educational attainments have risen substantially over the past two decades." (*LIFTING ALL BOATS? Accomplishments and Challenges from 20 Years of Education Reform in Massachusetts*, Richard Murnane, John Paypay, et al., June 2020).

This 1990's to 2020 assessment documented by researchers reports there remains an achievement gap. But this research doesn't take into account that the more challenging PARCC test hit all schools. It's hard to compare 1990s learning with 2019 when the test got harder over the years. In the first 1995 test and for years after, students were asked to write just a simple formulaic paragraph, setting back by years good writing instruction that used the writing process of drafting then refining, for instead minimal competence. The 2015 tested Standards call for re-instituting the writing process. The simple formula of earlier tests, called a "hamburger" format, which many teachers adopted for the test, of introduction, text evidence, and conclusion, though helpful for more struggling writers, now went out the window with more complex writing called for on the 2015 test. Nationally, many perform better with now the harder test, as achievement rises, including in urban schools. It's the small stories of successes at the teacher by teacher, school by school, district by district level that give us hope.

With the gradual return to in-class school after the 2020 and later years shutdown and partial shutdown, teachers find learning loss and also inappropriate behaviors, with students having spent a couple formative years not under in-school and in-class rules and expectations. A ninth grade teacher comments in 2023, "We felt like we were teaching seventh graders last year."

Hope High School, still recovering from the Covid years, in 2022 has on the English state test 60% of students in the "Not Meeting Expectations" category, 25% "Partially Meeting Expectations," for 85% below proficient, and only 14% of students "Meeting Expectations," with none in the "Exceeding Expectations" category. The school's math scores aren't reported because the percentage of students below proficient is 95% or higher. Educators in urban districts would have a much better chance for success if their schools had what we'd had in Hope's Sizer program: Teacher teams sharing the same students for ownership, school-day time for these teachers to meet, long-block classes, teachers as advisors, parents as partners, but also professional development in goal-oriented and culturally appropriate pedagogical methods, using learning guides for areas tested, and also leaders who inspire, explain, and model collaboration. Some of these pieces are happening, and some pieces use the terminology, such as "professional learning communities," or PLCs, teachers meeting, and "advisories," but not the full better practice beyond the words. It's the full shift from the old assembly-line worker role with many classes a day, many students, teacher isolation, limited conversation between educators and district leaders that's needed, and would be a dream especially for urban schools. To bridge the ever-widening achievement gap, dramatic change to provide better support for educators is direly needed.

CHAPTER FIFTEEN

Correcting Myths: It's not "Standardized"

Myths and misinformation on the state test abound. What's commonly termed in a disparaging manner the inappropriate term "standardized" test to refer to the state test, is instead in education terms a "criterion-referenced" type of test—setting out what's to be learned, then testing for it. A standardized test is different, a national test that comes out of the blue in theory to test what students know, then label that student. These are the earlier Iowa tests, the old IQ test, now no longer in vogue. Today these old tests to capture a snapshot of learning are considered unfair, because we now know more about how students can learn, not get pegged at a certain level. The state test is a test used to bring up learning. We know what's going to be tested; it's not a mystery. We broke through the barrier of keeping some students down in tracked courses when the state test came along to help guide students in basic good learning, the standards.

If students already know the basic skills tested, the teacher may go on to other skills and understandings. If students aren't proficient in the basic skills tested, they must learn them, with understanding developed in such a way that the student learns. Why would we not want all students to learn to read, discuss, write and understand math well, before graduating? The test encourages this, to move the skills and understandings along.

The SAT—once called the Scholastic Aptitude Test—changed its name in 1993 to the Scholastic Assessment Test, acknowledging that it didn't test for innate intelligence, only to check for where a student was in learning at that point, and acknowledging that a student could become what seemed "more intelligent."

For equity, the SAT in 2005 dropped altogether its heavy vocabulary knowledge question section that was sets of analogies, word associations that only students of greater privilege, and broad, challenging, and varied reading would know. The College Board organization, which produces the SAT, finally recognized that the analogies, which were purely vocabulary knowledge, were biased toward certain socio-economic groups. It was learning developed in those upper track classes. The tested higher level vocabulary words would have stumped many intelligent students who were not provided these words from home lives or in school, resulting in a lower score. An earlier otherwise intelligent student was branded not so intelligent by the SAT because the vocabulary analogies test section would have been puzzling. Those old SAT analogies sections would have been doable for students who had read Dickens, George Eliot, studied Latin.

Now that we understand that knowing limited and only more common words doesn't mean one isn't intelligent, and that intelligence is malleable, can be developed, the state test tests ability to decipher word meaning from context, now one of the main state Standards nationally. This skill of using context clues to understand vocabulary meaning that's tested helps develop intelligence and reading comprehension, not the earlier negative slap in the face for not knowing a word. When students don't know a word, with Standards learning, teaching the skill of figuring out word meaning from what's stated on the page opens the door to expanded learning, allowing the caged bird to fly, not keeping one down. With use of context clues as a skill to be taught, the student taking the state test can simply look back at the reading passage on the test to see what a word most likely means, from the context of the passage. No longer is a reading passage way over a student's head. How to understand a word is a skill taught and tested, thereby expanding reading ability.

Correcting Myths: It's not "Standardized"

'Advanced Placement teachers have long known well this concept of using a test to guide learning. Their own subject's AP test is at their fingertips online, as the state test is. AP teachers learn quickly what's tested, keep up with any changes, attend AP conferences to learn how to do better, and develop this learning as well as possible with their students. AP teachers must submit their course syllabus to the College Board for approval, to make sure it suits the test. Students' AP scores are sent directly to the teacher. The AP teacher is eager to study his or her students' scores and work to improve the scores, out of personal pride. The test is no surprise to the students; they've been prepared for this. If parents knew AP courses teach for the test, they'd demand for more of this, with a high score on the AP test appearing on transcripts for college application and helping with financial aid, and exempting students from a college level course on the same subject.

Because AP teachers know active student learning works best, I've only ever seen lively, engaging AP classes, with students working in small groups as the teacher moves around to check their discussions. An AP class is alive. Standards learning only brings what we've long had for these more privileged students who are accepted into AP courses.

Lawyers too study for the bar exam, motivated by the chance to practice law. College graduates study for the graduate school admissions tests, working on the practice tests easily available. SAT prep courses abound.

Regarding the criticism that the state test is "punitive," it's only when the Standards aren't learned well that it's a painful, punishing test. State test scores aren't seen by colleges, as these are only intended to assess a school, and only published, and without names, on the state's department of education web site. So in this sense the test isn't punitive, only assessing, for the intended benefit of providing information. Also, the state test scores are not "high-stakes," which the SAT and AP tests are for a student. And it's only in part multiple choice questions—for ease of scoring with large numbers of students—with half of the test score on writing ability, not simply filling in a bubble. The terms "high-stakes standardized bubble test" is manufactured by the media and promoted through word of mouth by critics. Taking the test and seeing how students do helps right the ship.

Next New Common Core Standards Are Chilling

Raising the bar is unsettling, and beneficial. By the early two-thousands, we'd come a long way in working on bringing all students up to a new level of learning. Now it was time to raise that bar. But when in 2011 piles of documents spelling out the new Common Core State Standards were dropped on my office floor, my heart sank, and I was in a small wealthy, well-educated suburban community. Learning here was easy. But even I, who loved having standards, wasn't ready for new Standards.

At the end of the school year, after a meeting, the high school assistant principal picked up stacks of the new Common Core curriculum documents (labeled "Massachusetts Standards"), from my office floor where they'd been dropped by a delivery service, never touched. "I'll put these in the department heads' mailboxes," he cheerily stated, believing this was helpful. My heart was in my throat, knowing well how unwelcome the sight of new Standards would be for department heads. It took me months to open those booklets. As an example of how others too felt about new Standards, when a curriculum director friend asked a teacher at this time about the new math document, the teacher said, "Is that the blue one or the green one?" That new booklet was possibly never opened. Even Department of Education officials joked at our meetings that the shrink-wrapped thin plastic covers on standards documents were never punctured by many. When I did brace myself to take a look, I loved the 2010-2011 Standards.

The new test on the Common Core, PARCC, implemented five years after the Standards came out, after presumably giving people a chance to review the Standards, was more challenging. PARCC is a good high level test. But it's challenging for many students, but so was the first state test at that earlier time, and students grew in learning as a result, with PARCC the next step up for its time. Now students needed a further push.

Significantly, and helpfully for students, in 2015 the SAT started testing the 2010 Common Core Standards. With the 2010 Standards finally the SAT Standards, now at long last when teachers taught the Common Core Standards, this helps prepare students for the SAT. School work helps with SAT prep work, no longer having the SAT test different areas that could reflect home environment. If the teacher chooses to teach these Common Core areas, he or she helps with college acceptance. As I sat in a school conference room and heard an SAT representative state what was now newly tested, my heart sang.

Common Core Sweeps the Country

Common Core became national, initially adopted by most states, good for students who move around the country, and now making available a multitude of online resources to support the teaching. Soon these next new Standards and test became familiar throughout Massachusetts and the country. Now North Dakota and Montana, Pennsylvania, New Hampshire, and many other states, had the same Standards as Massachusetts. It was simply easier for a state to just adopt Common Core and the test than re-invent the wheel, with adoption aided by federal financial incentives, so that these became nationally accepted.

Initially, almost all states adopted Common Core, then many pulled away due to school and public pushback. States that pulled back from the harder test diminished learning. But many if not most states changed the name of their tests and Standards to the state's name. When revolt hit, due to resistance to unwelcome outside top-down interference and fear of the test, the Massachusetts Commissioner of Education just stated, "They're 'Massachusetts Standards.'" Those who checked saw they were identical to Common Core. Only the cover title page with the state's name was different. People bought this; they adjusted, and educators appreciated and benefited from online national supports and educator-developed teaching plans on common skills now national, easily accessed online, a huge help to bringing Standards to classrooms. When these Standards years later hit Rhode

Island, Department of Education officials said Rhode Island's new Standards were just those of neighboring Massachusetts. The PARCC test in both states is more challenging, but it's a good test.

While state adoption went fairly smoothly, bringing the Standards to classrooms is another story. Eventually, in Massachusetts teachers appreciated Standards learning because now students coming into one's classroom for a new school year have more common learning than in earlier days. There was no longer the widely disparate knowledge of different teachers the previous year. Students had a leg up for the new year's class. A student is sunk when the teacher doesn't teach the Standards, because the leap becomes harder, a stretch.

Seeing that one's own students did well on the test warms the heart. Also, a benefit is that new teachers like having Standards as a guide. When the 2020 pandemic shut down school, the Standards were a good guide to bring needed learning back. With many teachers leaving teaching due to the chaos of school and health concerns during the coronavirus pandemic of 2020, new replacement teachers had support with what to teach by following the Standards learning. The looming test helped spur the learning.

CHAPTER SIXTEEN

A Wise Commissioner of Education

Concerns about the test were and are rampant. It was the state leader who made testing work. Massachusetts had a courageous, determined Commissioner of Education during the time of the shift to accountability. A former elementary school teacher himself, with a Harvard doctorate in education, and coming directly from the US Department of Education in the George W. Bush presidency, which pushed NCLB, Mitchell Chester understood this move to change as a positive force. And he had the political skill to steer the state through stormy waters. The state's Secretary of Education, now Harvard professor, Paul Reveille, noted on his passing, "Mitchell was a rock-solid, centered leader with a great gyroscope that kept him balanced, yet relentlessly focused on equity, evidence of what's best for children and pursuit for a path with integrity."

Under Chester's guidance, Massachusetts achievement rose to tops nationally on varied assessments. Chester was the longest serving chief state school official in the country, serving from 2008 until his death in office in 2017, at the too early age of 65. Committed to pushing learning forward for all students, he was one of the greats.

As I and other district teaching and learning coordinators sat in sprawling hotel conference rooms, Chester always admonished us that we needed to do more, always only about still pushing forward. When it was politically not possible to base teacher evaluation on test scores, as the Obama administration attempted to do, a move less than popular, Chester presented to us curriculum oversight administrators data and charts showing how we were not doing as well as we should. He asked, "How can so many teachers be rated so high when our students' test scores are so low?" A rhetorical question, urging "We can do better."

With his charts and graphs posted on enormous screens at our meetings, Chester compared Massachusetts scores with those of the tests of the National Assessment of Educational Progress, but he didn't compare us with other states. He was not interested in asking, "How are we doing in relation to Montana, or New Jersey?" We district leaders believed we were behind everyone else, and the Commissioner charged us to work harder to improve.

Chester was also just a nice, approachable guy, informed, intelligent, and politically adept at insisting on ever higher expectations for educators and the ever more challenging state test. He was always working against the grain, looking to boost learning. He believed firmly in accountability as the path to better learning for every student. Chester spurred us district leaders forward, even as we confronted pushback in our own school systems. He was the engine that drove us in the varied school systems to keep pushing for better work.

Chester's persistence paid off early on, when the state required every educator to continue their professional development, not simply rely on earlier courses we'd taken to be licensed for our positions, in order to constantly maintain currency with thinking in the field of education. Somehow he early in the accountability system gained the state teacher union approval for all educators—teachers and administrators—required to enroll in a set amount of hours of professional development every year. In a next step years later, to promote educators learning how to work well with more struggling students, the state required that every educator, including principals, take a certain number of hours of professional development on working with multilingual learners, even for those in districts that had few if any students new to the country with limited English. While teachers thought it strange to be required to learn about working with a type of student they didn't have many of in their district, everyone complied, as it was a requirement to learn new ways of working. In contrast to Massachusetts' educators' acceptance of such requirements for continued learning, in neighboring Rhode Island, required professional development became a major point of contention objected to by the union, which always worked to protect teachers' time, as Massachusetts educators continued to learn, despite this additional burden.

The Commissioner just never stopped pushing harder, using the test as a measure of learning. While everyone in Massachusetts—superintendents, educators, students, parents—complained about the test, all went along with expectations, the next step up, not without grumbling. And no one complained about the Commissioner. Compliance—though always fragile—was successful, and raised the bar, lifting the full state.

It's always been helpful that Massachusetts had its own test, MCAS, though similar to that of other states. Student achievement success was due to the gradual but relentless move to the more difficult later national PARCC test. When in earlier years fourth grade English Language Arts scores suddenly dropped statewide, educators were concerned. What was wrong with our teaching? Reading specialists around the state got together and analyzed the fourth grade reading passages. They provided data to show the Department of Education people that the reading passages on the test were above fourth grade level. The next year, scores went up. It wasn't that fourth graders suddenly learned to read so much better, but that the test was modified in response to valid criticism. Those reading passages changed. Officials at the Department of Education had listened, and corrected the test.

Similarly, one year, while scrutinizing the high school English test with teachers in an upper-income community who tended to dismiss the test and needed to pay more attention to what was tested so it would reflect their good work, we saw a three-page, complex passage from a Shakespeare play no one ever taught. Even those of us who loved Shakespeare were confounded. It wasn't that students didn't know the skill tested using this passage; many were just stymied by the archaic dense language. The passage made no sense to us in our small group reviewing the test, though one recognized the passage and the play it was from.

I then regularly over the year asked these teachers under my supervision if they were teaching Shakespeare in its original text to every student, not the readily available simplified version, most likely annoying these good teachers. The next year I had to laugh as I saw the question on that skill now was instead on a Bob Dylan song. I didn't see Shakespeare tested ever again. Our students, in a high demographic small community, weren't alone in their inability to read at that level that had been on the test. It wasn't a fair test of the skill it was designed to assess. It would have been fun for me to sit in on that discussion at the top state echelon on whether to continue to include Shakespeare, with some not wanting to let go of this traditional sacred reading. But dropping Shakespeare was a concession to districts where the level of reading would be too challenging. This was an example of overstepping with the inscrutable passage, then pulling back. When I later moved to a district adjacent to Boston, I was happy Shakespeare was gone.

A key quality for success was that Commissioner Chester was out and about, around the large state, speaking and listening, visible. Never self-isolating, he listened to complaints and made good decisions for school improvement, backing off on an issue if a concern was valid, otherwise holding firm. I loved too that he never missed a scheduled presentation open to all at the Harvard Graduate School of Education, his alma mater. Groups of Department of Education experts followed him here also, as he spoke to students, professors, alumni, community people.

The Test is Too Long, It Takes Too Long to Get Results, The Move from Paper to Computers is Unsettling

A main criticism is educators nationally argue that it takes too long to receive test scores, with testing in the spring and not getting full results till later, in late August or September. While results from multiple-choice questions, which are machine-scored, can be, and are, quickly sent to districts, it takes time for groups of educators from around the state to read and assess the student writing that's on the test. Actual people read and assess the writing, trained on using a rubric to assess, a longtime practice on national tests, not machine-scored. To score writing appropriately, this takes some time, so districts don't get their full final score results until the start of the new school year.

But in receiving test results later, do educators really want to see test results at the end of the school year, when everyone's brain is fried? When districts receive the spring results in the fall, educators are fresher, more open to seeing how they can improve, from a more optimistic fresh perspective than right after a year's work, when all are exhausted, drained. That summer off is essential and restorative. Seeing one's students' test scores at the start of a new year helps guide that year's work. Plus, taking the time to assess writing well is essential for fair assessment.

In response to the common concern that the test takes too long (at times a cover for resisting the test altogether), charged with "interfering" with other teaching, Massachusetts eliminated one writing question. But this cut made the test less valid and put too much emphasis on one piece of writing. In this case, an attempt to address the widespread criticism of taking too much time won out over having a more valid test. State ownership of the test helps to quell concerns, but the outcome is not always the best. Chester was always alert to critics, accommodating where possible.

An element of the "taking too long" issue is also the claim that teaching the tested areas takes too much class time that teachers could otherwise use to focus on other material, presumably more important work. But deciding what's "more important" can be chaotic and individualistic, not easy to settle on agreement. It's not totally clear what might be more important for students to know about math and English than the areas of learning reflected in the Standards. Wanting to teach "more important" material could be code for teacher preference, as opposed to skills dictated by the state, a form of imposition always an educator concern. This complaint of testing interrupting learning is why a steadfast commissioner needs to correct problems with the test and take slow but steady steps forward, while preserving teacher autonomy in *how* one teaches. But, most important, it's best to stop the locomotive of teaching to assess how well students are learning, near the end of the year, check the results, and modify, or celebrate, as needed.

From Paper and Pencil to Computer Hurdles, Changes Keep Coming

Another trauma was moving the test from pencil and paper to online. While this shift was fairly easy for the small, more privileged suburban districts where many students had their own home laptops, and for districts that had moved to "one-to-one" computer use, urban educators understandably worried that there wouldn't be a sufficient number of school computers, and that students wouldn't have the needed computer skills. To be able to take the test online, all students would have to learn specific tech skills, which was stressful, but beneficial at a time when the nation was moving in the direction of everyone needing to be tech savvy. Soon students caught on to the computer testing, more efficient for everyone. Now urban students caught up with digital skills their suburban counterparts already knew. Admirably, educators followed the new and ever more challenging expectations, while continuing to voice concerns. Moving to the online testing when every student needed to learn computer skills helped at least somewhat with the required remote learning of 2020.

Listening in the Face of Change

Commissioner Chester, because he believed in accountability, led smartly and smoothly through all of this, listening to critics, adjusting as needed, always seeking to ratchet up the results. It seemed that new harder expectations were always coming, and when states promoted new areas, it was students who benefited, hard on educators, working well for public education.

Chester did everything right. As state leader, he walked the tightrope carefully and cautiously. His wise decisions on hot issues were key during the time the Massachusetts State Legislature was deciding in 2010 whether to formally adopt the new Common Core State Standards, which, although not that different from the Massachusetts earlier standards when one took a look at them, were controversial, because few like new expectations, and many were suspicious of what was perceived as federal overreach. The move from the earlier Massachusetts standards was a small step in actuality, and, when the dust settled, beneficial in many ways, but once again fostered lively conversation. Few if any wanted more change.

A commissioner has a say in whether or not to adopt a policy, but it's the politicians who approve or vote it down. Chester had been involved in the development of national Standards. He led the national committee on the PARCC test design. Serving in the US Department of Education, he had helped devise a policy tough for many to accept, NCLB. During this time of rising expectations around the more demanding Common Core, Chester was widely visible and forceful, speaking informatively to administrators and educators at statewide meetings.

During the contentious debate over whether to move to the unwelcome Common Core in 2010, I chose to attend one of the statewide open meetings that the beleaguered but patient commissioner held at a nearby state university. I feared I'd never be able to find the right building on the unfamiliar campus. As it turned out, it was hard to miss.

Flashing lights from a teachers union truck alerted us to the site. Arriving at the university, I was instantly greeted by a huge flatbed truck with a large neon sign with bright yellow lights flashing "No New Standards." Top state teachers union leaders were following the commissioner around the state with their truck, vigorously flaunting their stance. As I walked into the huge state university meeting hall, people I didn't know smiled and greeted me warmly. I'm sure they were union representatives, possibly thinking I was a teacher, not the evil administrator on the side of standards that I was.

While resistance reigned outside, inside, this meeting was tightly controlled. Seated at a long table flanked by his aides, the commissioner listened to each speaker, to my surprise while eating pizza—probably his only meal of the day. Attendees had to submit comments in advance for approval to speak. Individuals, mostly district leaders, were called on and many just used the occasion to sing their own district's praises. Finally, the commissioner managed to leave the building, probably through a back door in order to avoid the army of union protesters and make his way to the next meeting. He showed up, listened, and moved on.

Now Massachusetts made a surprise careful decision, not charging forward, but also not stepping back on whether to adopt the national Common Core Standards and its harder test. Within a couple of days, the state legislature approved the Common Core State Standards. The union had made their point. But I suspect the skirmish was actually won by legislator lobbyists who understood the value of common national expectations. The commissioner knew well whose ear he'd primarily have to reach. By doing his listening tour, he allowed the union with its truck to make a statement in opposition, and for others to be heard. Then he made his decision to move ahead. His big-picture view moved the state ahead.

Not So Fast: Pulling Back from PARCC

Even in my high-scoring, high-income town at this pivotal time when states were making the decision to move to the national Standards or retain their own, even I wasn't eager for a new test. Too much else was going on, as it always is in school systems. Where would I get the energy to fight this new next battle on a new test? Since Commissioner Chester had chaired the national committee overseeing the development of the test on the new Standards, I assumed that a few years later we'd adopt the test he'd been working on, PARCC.

But just one day before the state legislature was to approve PARCC, a *Boston Globe* front-page article reported on a study showing that according to early research, scores on PARCC didn't correlate with students' success in college. For me, this was head-spinning: With many other factors that influence success in college, including finances, diligence, mindset, poor college fit, social life, and a multitude of barriers, how could good public school learning—kindergarten through high school—not help with college success?

In response to this well-publicized critical news report on a single study that led to legislators hearing complaints from constituents, the Department of Education pulled back from instituting PARCC at that time. The commissioner, sensitive to political pressure and public opinion, knew one can only push so far. Dropping the PARCC test at this time was a huge relief for urban districts. I was sad at the time that we missed out on the higher level test, but when I then moved to an urban district, I was hugely relieved.

The state instead took a slow and circuitous path to full adoption of PARCC. Implementation was incremental: First just a few PARCC questions were integrated into MCAS, now called MCAS 2.0. Then the next year everyone took the PARCC test, with MCAS now called the "legacy" test. By taking these slower steps to move to PARCC, it was gradually accepted in schools. And when fully implemented, it wasn't called PARCC, just still called MCAS. When Rhode Island adopted the Massachusetts test, it was the full new Standards and harder PARCC test that hit the state, sending educators reeling.

Slow and Steady Steps Forward

In my role as Massachusetts curriculum director, I stepped back and studied the new Standards and test, and I provided workshops for teachers to look at and confer on the new questions. Unfortunately, state presentations didn't address exactly what the new Standards were. I suspect there was an optimistic expectation that groups of teachers would form in schools and districts to study the new Standards and figure out how to work these into their courses. I didn't see this happening much. I still today teach integrating Standards into teaching in my online courses, especially needed post-pandemic.

Wealthier districts in addition to urban schools complained about PARCC. Some were discreet about it, but one superintendent in a more privileged community confidently announced they weren't going to pay attention to state tests. In 2012 all the schools in this lily-white district were Level 1 on the state ranking system—tops. But in 2018, with a reprieve from paying attention to the test, only 45% of students—less than half—scored at Proficient and above. Between 2015 and 2018, 70% of students in this privileged small district scored Advanced in English, but in 2019, with the PARCC test, only 17% achieved Advanced. I couldn't fathom why a good school system wouldn't want top state test scores, to reflect the high-quality teaching and learning going on there. When scores nose-dived even more in 2021, after the pandemic year shutdown, the new superintendent urged teachers to teach their subject's Standards. They complied.

When districts like this one choose to free teachers from providing learning in tested areas, huge score drops make it seem that the schools aren't doing so well. As a parent, I'd be worried to see my child performing more poorly than the state average. While no doubt many were delighted that they didn't have to pay attention to the tested areas, and parents saw tests as annoying, it was hard for me to understand why district leaders and educators wouldn't want to help more students acquire the important skills of the test, especially since this would have been fairly easy to accomplish in a higher-income district.

Boston, on the other hand, has the traditionally underperforming groups typical of large urban districts and the kind of diversity that makes high-level learning a challenge, with 42%—close to half—Latino students, 30% African-American, 63% "Economically Disadvantaged," 78% "High Needs," 29% multilingual learners, and 21% special education. Nevertheless, in 2021, post-pandemic, it earned the accountability rating of "Substantial Progress Toward Targets." This means teachers are working hard to bring students along. Sadly, earlier, a new superintendent was hired in large part due to the fact that she was anti-test. From Tennessee, with a doctorate from the University of Memphis, and having served in Tennessee from 2004 to 2007, she missed the major shift to if not embracing, at least paying attention to, the Standards that Massachusetts adopted. She'd missed the big push this state had urged. This superintendent was soon replaced by a local superintendent.

The pandemic setback had the effect of pushing everyone back in learning, as it was clear to classroom teachers pretty much everywhere that missing out on in-class face to face teaching left students far behind where they were before the pandemic shut down school. National and state data confirmed this.

CHAPTER SEVENTEEN

Superstar Urban Teachers

As state tests became more just a part of school, no longer novel, the urban school teacher Ben was a superstar. An example of a prized teacher who year after year helps his low-income, racially diverse students to earn top test scores, reflecting high level learning, Ben teaches seventh grade, then opts to work with the same students in eighth grade. I found his classes always lively, interesting, with everyone engaged. Each December he transforms his classroom for students to act out "A Christmas Carol" on a stage, costumed in period attire and wigs, which they love, and changing genders with different clothes, for the fun of it. For his other classes, this same stage set becomes Anne Frank's cramped attic quarters. Ben told me this set was a chore to arrange, but I saw the students loved having their classroom become a stage setting. It was worth the effort.

Also, when I described to teachers how classroom libraries can develop reading comprehension, fluency, and vocabulary by providing easy access to books for independent reading, Ben told me he'd been using a classroom library for years, acquiring no-cost books from his town's libraries when they cleaned out their collections. His students also delighted in small group creative work. Ben was always at least one step ahead with best practice. One day when I stopped in to see his class, students were moving around the room to meet individually first with one group then another, performing to expectations, and then rotating on to a different activity. Ben observed, however, "But you have to review the test with them," to get good state scores that reflect his high level active learning success. Ben made sure his students aced their test scores. It was the dynamic class activity instilling learning, all promoting literacy development, that produce top scores.

In this same district, I got into trouble with the teachers union when I asked the tenth grade teachers to meet after school several times to discuss strategies they were using to prepare for MCAS. Since two of the teachers were new to the grade level, and one new to teaching altogether, these after-school sessions on ways to develop the learning tested were helpful. Apparently in response to a complaint from one of the teachers, I was summoned to meet with the school union representative on asking teachers to stay after school. Following a tip from the principal, I moved the meetings to the school day, scrutinizing the teachers' schedules to find times they all could meet. Then an administrator saw us meeting during the school day and I was called into the principal's office and asked to explain. Frustrated, annoyed that I was summoned to the principal's office for helping to prepare students with strategies to learn skills, I just told the principal we were done meeting. Then on the day of the test, my phone lit up with congratulatory, celebratory messages from teachers who'd monitored the test. Michael, in his first year of teaching, had received accolades from his students. The testing monitors all reported to me that the students raved, "He really helped us prepare for the test!"

When I congratulated Michael, he told me how much his students hated practicing for MCAS. His writing work meant they had to learn how to shape their writing in a certain way, following common criteria that helped organize what they had to say. Though the students had complained constantly, hating this drudgery, they were thrilled when at test time they said they knew exactly what to do. I was pleased that my having called the teacher group together, challenging as it was, had provided impetus for this teacher to provide tedious but helpful instruction that paid off. Michael was proud that his students had done well on the test. Under some stress and student whining, but with a good outcome, they learned how to write better, and appreciated becoming familiar with the type of writing expected of them.

Seeing how much they'd learned developed confidence, in Michael, as well as with the students who saw they knew an important skill.

Great teachers such as the Ben and Michael pick up the gauntlet and bring more students along. We just need to create better conditions to give more educators everywhere a chance to inspire and improve their students' learning. Michael on his own figured out what to teach and how, and was rewarded. Ben chose different ways and reveled in academic success too. Prior to testing, a lone teacher, with few paths or honored positions beyond the daily class work had little incentive to work more carefully and skillfully. It seemed few cared. Now with testing an educator can enjoy seeing success in one's students' learning, and gain recognition. Ben was known in the district for his always top scores. Michael, as a first year teacher working with struggling students, beamed that he'd been awarded success in figuring out how to help, and winning.

PART THREE

Moving On, District Leadership for Change:

Successes, and Challenges

CHAPTER EIGHTEEN

A New Position of Curriculum Director

When accountability was dropped on schools, opening up new curriculum positions, I seized the opportunity to jump from the classroom directly into a district central office position. I first landed in Scottsdale, in the less highly populated central part of the state, away from big city exchange of ideas. It was a more settled environment. However, this time of major change to oversee teaching and learning to comply with the required shift was right for me, but a surprise for others in schools, those happy with how school had worked for decades. My role was exciting, while also lively, and bumpy. In my own mind, I was helping to convey state and federal law. I should have known from my own experience that changing people's minds isn't easy. But, on the whole, teachers I met here in my first job as an administrator were cooperative, at least in my presence, and principals supported me, understanding it wasn't my decision to change their lives. My presence allowed principals to step back from the cascade of bullets in bringing news no one wanted to know about.

The now looming test for everyone, especially in my new community of Scottsdale, pulled back a curtain on what was earlier considered a good school system, with two-thirds middle-class white students. Teachers loved these students; rapport was easy. But this small district had its own unique issues, with many recent arrivals from Puerto Rico with limited English language ability, flying directly from San Juan to the Scottsdale airport to join family, escaping poverty conditions in their homeland. With this new population, educators couldn't count on home support from families who were just looking for inexpensive housing and wondering where the next meal would come from, with the added burden of a language barrier. In a community more biased toward middle-class white students and somewhat resentful of non-English-speaking newcomers, testing all students was a time bomb just waiting to go off. That test would reveal the gulf in learning, and the need to reach out. But that inclusion wasn't desired at any level, from the all-white school board, middle class townspeople, or schools folks. People I worked with here, however, were nice to me, a newcomer, friendly, easy to work with, a nice way to launch a career attempting to foster the change no one wanted to see. Writing off a certain group would no longer work.

No One Likes Being Told What to Do

Coming to here directly from classroom teaching, I was just happy to have a new job. It didn't occur to me I'd be seen as the evil bearer of bad news. I didn't realize I was walking into a role that put me in the position of Sizer's assistants who'd attempted to coach me and my fellow teachers at Hope to move in directions we didn't always care to go, such as changing modes of teaching. But this mode of teaching was a comparatively small change I wasn't about to take on in Scottsdale. The Massachusetts bigger shift of testing all students would take years to adjust to. And the shift needed never did work here. I didn't even try to touch *how* one should teach. It was about what to teach, and to whom, a big enough area for me, especially at this earliest time. Years later, educators realized that active learning worked best, and help, from multiple sources, was provided.

However, it was good that I didn't fully understand from the teachers' view how unpopular my role as a district leader was. Being cautious would have made me reluctant to promote the change that I'd been hired to carry out. It was probably my naiveté that allowed me to work for change against others' wishes. And it was good that I didn't

A New Position of Curriculum Director

yet know what I shouldn't do, or even what I *should* do in my new position. The shift to turn teachers to standards understandings, and with all students, was new to all of us. Administrators and teachers did know that the state had published curriculum frameworks setting out learning expectations, and that tests were coming, soon. I was to just try to figure out how to find the switch, let alone turn the switch.

It took years for me to realize that the process was simple: Everyone affected needed to sit down together, see what the Standards were, and consider how they could be integrated into their work. I was able to do this later, as change hit statewide, and everyone knew well what was expected. But now, initially, getting people to that table wasn't even yet possible. The discussion of how to implement standards worked sometimes later. The bombardment of written documents and a looming test that no one yet knew the content of dropping on schools wasn't like Sizer's soft approach of cultivating interest, keeping things somewhat vague, and allowing people to voluntarily sign up when they were ready. Conforming to a test as yet unknown when I entered Scottsdale was different. It was a relief to everyone when later we actually saw what the test would look like. Now it was just that there was a law, coming from above, with standards and testing required by the state. And I was the messenger.

A Challenging School Population

As I started commuting in to Scottsdale, a small remote town amid curving back roads, I felt I was moving back in time. The single thriving business that once sustained the local economy had shut down. Unemployment reigned. At a Subway sandwich shop in town, I saw two older women, nicely dressed for a lunch out, ask about an ad for one dollar off a sandwich. They were told the ad didn't apply there. Disappointed, they left, poverty hitting me in the face.

And though surrounded by small, all-white towns, Scottsdale had a surprisingly high percentage of students of color. As Latino families flew from San Juan to join relatives, this brought in high numbers of multilingual learners, who don't do well on state tests in large part for the obvious reason that they don't know English. The schools here needed a lot of help for students who depended on teachers to learn, but the all-white school board's solution was to attempt to move the welfare assistance office out of town. The "newcomers" weren't welcome. I'd landed in a challenging spot.

Police Officers Pass Around Drugs

Uniformed police officers attended my first district administrators' meeting in Scottsdale, with their dark uniforms, glistening badges. My previous interactions with the police had been minimal—just a few speeding tickets—though always intimidating. To my amazement, these officers passed around small packets containing various drugs, the non-medicinal kind. Oblivious to what this exercise was about, I just handled the strange packet, looked at it, passed it on. I couldn't see how their purpose was related to my job.

But the police were letting us know that in the crowded low-income housing units of this small town, an active drug trade was thriving. Few schools are free of drug-related problems, though usually it isn't publicly known. Even elite private schools are not immune. In Scottsdale, due to poverty, drug use and dealing was big. Many young men turned to crime for day-to-day survival—basic food and rent—and many of them were enrolled in the schools. The police apparently, I later deduced, wanted school leaders to be aware of the criminal activity going on around us. For their part, the townspeople and town officials preferred simply to dismiss problematic students. No one had the answer of how to address the drug-dealing problem or turn students around, keep students in school and on task. Regular school attendance when a student wasn't yet fluent in the language, an outsider, wasn't at the top of young people's agenda. Survival was. Fast money was a lure. At this time, in this environment, teachers only saw miscreants as trouble-makers, as we'd earlier seen at Hope, now a problem for schools when every student learning was expected.

When I taught at Hope, I hadn't recognized the influence of the dark side of poverty in my classroom. No wonder many of my

A New Position of Curriculum Director

former students' attention was diverted. Although some city schools found ways to take a more open-minded, empathetic approach to such problems, I could recall a discussion in the principal's office of a student with drug issues. I offered some ideas on how this student could be helped, but the principal just looked at me and said, "We just get these students out of school." Expulsion was easier than helping. For me as an educator, the situation was more complicated, based on my wish to help students succeed. At that earlier time, students deemed unreachable were dismissed. It was federally required testing of all students that forced turning around this view and practice of dismissal.

My role now in Scottsdale was trying to help the tuned-out, marginalized students, including those who resorted to criminal activity, for solutions to their problems. Getting an education is a long path that some young people prefer to avoid in favor of a faster and livelier route to desperately needed money, quick cash. Immediacy was preferred. And it was often the brighter students who chose this potentially dangerous path. I wanted to help entice back to school those who'd stepped away from the help school can provide, for skills that would enable them to move on to brighter futures instead of depending on choices that just led to trouble. I'd seen in my own teaching that recalcitrant students can be turned around, but I also knew it was tricky to make happen. But now as an administrator away from the classroom, it was easy to forget how challenging it could be to engage students in academics when things such as basic survival and the appealing known danger in an otherwise bleak life were on their minds. With testing, and required to report the percentage of students tested under accountability, schools had to re-think erasing students.

A solution here in Scottsdale was that there were two school systems in the district. White middle-class students, who'd earlier been the predominant demographic, were valued. Students of color weren't welcome. The schools ran as if the "others" didn't exist. Teachers and administrators alike seemed to hold the view that the traditional tracking system—shoving students of color into low-level classes, denying them a better education—was appropriate, and that it worked just fine. For them, those "other" kids didn't count. The town-wide mentality was to serve the middle-class white students, who were more like them, and therefore easier to work with.

I was here when the first state test, which didn't count for accountability but was testing the test, but which reported both the percentage of students participating and how well they did in math and English, was an unwelcome report dropped on the district. No longer did the mostly content middle-class white teachers and students represent the full picture. Now everyone counted, and it wasn't pretty.

Invisible Students

I didn't see the Latino students in Scottsdale schools. They'd been placed in remote corners and even working in small closets, instead of included in mainstream classrooms. It's possible they weren't even physically present—registered, on the books, but not there—ghost students whom no one seemed interested in having in school. It can be easy for a teacher to feel that a disengaged student who may not know English well is just an annoyance. And it's hard to explain to a harried teacher that the job is to try to help every child succeed, especially when the system is set up otherwise. A student not welcome easily acts out inappropriately, hurting even more his acceptance in school. The many strategies now used today, after decades of requiring that all students are tested, weren't even dreamt of at this earlier time.

The ways poverty and race are connected to the failure to educate all students was never discussed in Scottsdale during my tenure here. The focus was always only on how to get these kids out. Although applying standards to all was now a statewide goal, we never conferred on how to better serve impoverished and different language fluency students to bring them into the world of education, to offer them a path to a better life. I couldn't even find these kids. The school system response had long been to turn a blind eye to this issue, call in the police, use disciplinary measures. The tests were a wake-up call no one wanted to hear. Coming from Hope

Essential's racially and socio-economically integrated classrooms, I felt I was in a time warp.

Although I held what I believed was an important district-wide position, I was assigned here to a basement elementary school room, while the superintendent and other district-wide staff had spacious offices in the centrally located town hall on the town's main street. But town administrators wanted the schools people out of their city hall building, not a good sign for the school system. So the school system itself was caught in the anti-newcomers view of town officials, who wanted to protect the past. But for me, in my small basement place of refuge, though cut off from central office thinking and discussion, it was good for me to be in an early-grades school, able to see teachers and hear what they were thinking, and away from the central office discriminatory discussion with school board members. However, within the school, I overheard such disconcerting things such as the normally calm school nurse vehemently complain that a child's lips were hardened, possibly because of limited heat at home, or dehydration. Usually a school nurse is more caring because she sees the effects of poverty as vulnerabilities rather than nuisances. It was the norm here in school culture to complain about those who were different.

With no one to promote inclusiveness, as Sizer had done, dismissive attitudes toward poverty-level students of color reigned. Anyone inattentive in class was just an annoyance. The administrative meeting with the police was the only time I saw evidence that the school was even aware of another student population besides the middle-class white students. With one-third of the district population Latino but invisible in classrooms or corridors, it had to be federal and state authorities to point out and enforce the expectation that all should be well-served.

In Scottsdale, those who taught multilingual students were a small group of bilingual Latino teachers. These dedicated and empathetic educators of color too were relegated to odd, otherwise-unused spaces, confirming their status. They knew it would be futile to ask for a real classroom. I felt terrible then when I arranged to meet with this group of teachers and then forgot about the meeting. I apologized profusely to one, but she smiled broadly and told me it was okay. I realized they'd been happy to meet together to discuss issues on their own. No one else had thought to include these outsider teachers in meetings. I'm sure the meeting I missed was more helpful for them without me, an outsider to the issues they knew so well.

The Effect of Test Scores in a Low Income District

The first accountability test, arriving here after I'd left, was a bomb dropped on the school system. The arrival of the first state test scores coincided with a downward spiral for the schools in Scottsdale. As school morale sagged, the number of Puerto Rican students over the years rose quickly to nearly two-thirds, as now test scores branded the district with a low rating. White parents pulled their children out of the district. Behavioral issues arise from unengaged students who are given too few ways to connect with school. With most teachers' attitude that if students weren't acting like their more academically inclined middle-class white counterparts, they could be written off, test scores showed school as a whole wasn't working as well as believed. Since nothing promoted inclusion, it was no wonder when the data on student level of learning and attendance numbers, and percentage taking the test, arrived, people felt helpless. To see in data where a school system stood in comparison to others in the state was not encouraging, spurring on new thinking, only disheartening. The myth of a good school was broken when only some did well, shattering long-held beliefs.

Later, with helpful state funding, the town was able to build a beautiful new combined middle school and high school building on the outskirts of town, where land was available. The downside was that almost all students had to take a bus to reach this building over rough, curving roads often icy in winter. Missing a bus creates problems. Any haven the school might offer was physically challenging for its marginalized young people to get to, not convenient, as well as psychologically remote. The location outside the town showed the schism between the white and non-white, poverty-level worlds. I'm certain there was no Latino representation on the building committee to call attention to the transportation problem, so school remained at the margins for more disadvantaged students, psychologically and physically.

This building placement was different in big city Everett, adjacent to Boston. This low-income, racially diverse, densely populated district where I later worked built a magnificent new high school for its over 2,000 students right in the town's center. The superintendent had the political capital to win voter support to replace a park, where many once ice skated in winters, with a striking new, centrally located five-floor building. Students could easily walk here from any part of town, and did, at any time, day or evening. I'd see students shooting hoops in the school gym—that escape-from-home outlet—at 8am on a Saturday when I attended weekend teacher meetings. In this district, school was also a convenient place to let off steam, release energy in sports. Making school inviting physically is a small step toward helping in the classroom. This beautiful new high school's upper floors also had magnificent views of the high towers of energetic, affluent downtown Boston, suggesting at least surface accessibility to wealth and economic security, a thriving hub, something those in Scottsdale could not see as a future. That new school there was off in the woods.

Surprises from Everywhere

Seeing the lay of the land here in Scottsdale, I shouldn't have been surprised by a school board decision. Located as I was away from the central office, I was caught off-guard by a sudden school board announcement that affected my work. School boards represent the town's side of a school system, with members often receiving complaints on issues from parents and other constituents. When we in the schools are immersed in school-oriented issues, it can be surprising for an education leader to hear concerns from a community member, coming out of left field, off the radar of one's own focus. Here now teacher professional development time for educators to confer on learning issues was sacrificed in one major blow to instead address concerns of town shopkeepers.

Parent and community members' perceptions don't always jive with inside schools views. The schism between community and parent concerns, and on the other side educator concerns, is enormous. I once received a phone call from a parent in a more privileged district who threatened to circulate a petition around town to have a teacher fired, one who had given his child what the parent considered an unjustified poor grade. He'd researched the teacher and had ammunition. This threat to fire a teacher, and because of one grade, shocked me. A superintendent in this same district later, who was resigning, wrote on the district web site when he resigned that he'd asked parents "not to walk into a teacher's class and tell them what to do," but that they continued to do this. Another superintendent told me that meeting with his school board was always an "out-of-body experience." For me, it was often hard to stay awake at evening school board meetings when the debated hot topic was where a new soccer field would be placed, not a whole lot of interest to me.

This difference of viewpoint can at times protect schools from interference from those outside school when a hot topic within school isn't of interest to outsiders. But town interests can catch educators off-guard. School leaders are consumed with issues such as student discipline problems, employee-management challenges, school policies, budgets, a disaffected teacher. The concerns school board members hear from parents include things like the amount of homework—too much or too little—or an individual student's disciplinary situation, often complaint about a teacher whom the parent feels is unfair. Others in the community voice complaints about rising property taxes or want to ban a valued book. When interviewing for a curriculum job in another district, the superintendent told me about a problem he was having with a company in town. All I could think of was, and why is this at all relevant to me? Another superintendent told me it was always strange to meet with his school board, confiding, "They don't like me and I don't like them," yet he continued to survive well there.

A school board hires and fires a superintendent, so most try hard to accommodate even unusual requests. But appeasing people who don't fully understand how schools work is a conundrum. In Scottsdale, the school board in a major decision that I'd had no clue of in advance summarily eliminated something important that affected my own work. It was town versus school, and the townspeople won. Business people, a political group school boards need on their side, won, over an important program education relies on.

Teacher Learning Time is Precious

The Scottsdale school board—all white—represented town views. So in hindsight, it shouldn't have surprised me when its members voted to eliminate the half-days off from school that teachers everywhere need for ongoing professional development, discussion and new learning. During the common "released time" away from teaching, teachers confer on educational issues. These few sessions halt the speeding locomotive of educators' schedules so they can stop and think and confer about learning—more important than ever with state learning requirements exploding on the scene. These meetings were particularly valuable to me as an opportunity for teachers to hear about new ideas, sharpen their skills, and learn from outside experts as well as from colleagues.

But Scottsdale shop owners complained that when school was closed on these half days, students leaving at noon came into their businesses and caused disruption. Actual theft wasn't mentioned publicly, but may have loomed as a concern. This complaint was all the school board needed to hear. To appease business owners, they voted unanimously to eliminate that valuable half-day professional development time. There was no discussion of the issue beyond the powerful school board, who opted to cut the released time altogether rather than try to find a way to protect it by seeking other possible solutions.

Since they're elected officials, school board members are partial to complaints from the community, which can make their decisions tough on schools. In a normal, ideal situation, a school board confers with the superintendent on an issue, and at least takes that viewpoint into consideration, often finding solutions that accommodate schools. The cancellation of the half-day professional development time—only three times a year—was simply issued as a statement at a televised school board meeting. With my out-of-the-loop office remote from the central office, I only heard about the decision to eliminate time that I was responsible for when I arrived at school the next morning, hearing from teachers who'd viewed the meeting on local cable TV. I was stunned. I'd been kept in the dark that canceling that time was an issue. That half-day time had been crucial to maintain currency in education, not back-sliding. In the more privileged school systems where I later worked, a school board would value whatever a superintendent argued for in relation to how teacher time was used. For them, education was valued. One high demographic district I later worked in had regular half-day Wednesdays, every week, for time for teachers to confer. No one complained.

Yet Another Surprise

To add to drama, another initiative I'd been working on for the superintendent faced a set-back. The superintendent asked me to search for a new elementary reading program, to be completed in one year. She stipulated that no one would pilot any programs with their classes, a normal process in adopting a new program, to test it with students. I could only imagine her concern would be teachers would disagree if they piloted different programs, a discussion to avoid, in some minds.

I immediately formed a teacher committee. We investigated, made school visits, and completed our work within the school year, selecting the reading program that had the most support for struggling students, such as "throw-away" books for study at home that could be tossed out and easily replaced if needed. The at-home books were perfect for the district, with this extra support. Based as I was in a separate building, without close communication, I didn't know at the time that the district didn't have the funds for that crucial additional take-home material.

A New Position of Curriculum Director

On the night we were to present our new reading program recommendation to the school board, the superintendent graciously invited our committee to her house for a relaxing, congenial dinner in advance of the meeting. Then at that evening's televised meeting, Susan, a young, blond, petite, sweet-looking teacher, set off an explosive by charging that the time teachers needed to learn how to use the new reading program was lost due to the school board's decision to eliminate the professional development half-days.

Susan was right, but I was horrified when she announced this at the on-camera board meeting, an open attack. Usually surface calm works best. And it was too late to remedy that mess. Those half-days were gone. Such a divisive issue is usually raised quietly behind the scenes, ideally timely, without criticizing board members in an open meeting. The superintendent was understandably embarrassed, livid that this shot was fired. I believe she felt it made her look bad that this disrespect for the school board had happened. She hinted that I was the one who arranged this criticism. I was somewhat used to being blamed for things I would never do, and the elimination of teacher time had taken the wind out of my sails. But I would never have arranged for a teacher to make such a bold complaint, to the school board, and on-camera. I was to learn, if I hadn't already, that lots of things that are expected as norms don't always happen in schools and school systems. Misunderstanding, miscommunication, and unfair criticism abound. Dysfunction is not uncommon.

The evening's initial pleasant celebration of our committee's success, based on intense reading program research completed with unanimous teacher support over the grade levels and across three elementary schools immediately soured. What was to be a celebratory announcement on the reading program adoption poked school board members in the eye, usually something to avoid, especially with their right to hire and fire. I could only speculate that it was the teachers' union—always eager to raise grievances—that had planned this admonishing of the school board in a confrontational way. Protected by tenure, angry teachers—whatever they were angry about—could make a stir.

I suspect Susan had been selected because she appeared demure, cooperative, not hostile. Instead of this criticism at the public meeting, she could have mentioned her concern about professional development time during our relaxed dinner with the superintendent, who as a skillful leader always aware of differing viewpoints, could have found a way to work something out. As a former elementary teacher herself, and earlier an elementary principal, the superintendent knew people needed support for classroom work, certainly for a full new program of studies. She would have been happy to find another way to provide teachers with training on the new reading program, an area she cared about and knew was important. She may well have felt the school board believed she'd staged this complaint herself. As a superintendent in a different community, she could have urged the school board to have discussions with the store owners about the early release from school problem.

If multiple sides were involved in the decision-making process, it would have taken some time and effort, but the few half-day school closures could have been changed to a full day, as many schools have, eliminating the problem of students going from the classroom into the town. Or the half-day could have been switched to the morning, with students arriving in the afternoon, not released into town as a group. But alternatives to shutting down the teacher training time weren't on the table. The decision to high-handedly eliminate professional development time showed how removed school boards can be from issues directly affecting teachers, too often a chasm. Some districts keep the union leader in the loop, hard as those conversations can be with the different perspectives.

When a problem is solved without discussion, revolt pops up. Issuing a decision without discussion is easy, but not a good solution. Avoiding conversation doesn't work. Morale drops, trust is broken, rebellion persists. And the problem always comes back to undermine what could instead have been a consensus, meeting the needs of all, not just one faction's demands. But it's hard to bring up a delicate issue and discuss it with those involved. It's easier to use a public forum to dictate a new policy. It's easy to condemn a decision on-camera, to avoid face-to-face conflict. Sizer was on the money when he urged the need for "conversation." But conversation on a controversial topic is hard. And school issues are always complicated, not simple to resolve well.

Teachers were able to figure out how to use the new reading program. But they had to do it on their own. It would have been much better to have had the school-day time free of students to openly discuss and have the ability to develop the early literacy well, especially for racially diverse students, with reading development a critical skill, a lost opportunity. Teachers would have felt more supported if they'd had released time to work. And it was sad that underlying the decision to eliminate the professional development time altogether was the attitude on race. Having low income students coming into town businesses en masse was to be avoided.

Money Makes a Difference

However, happily, I discovered a goldmine for the district, one that quickly found popularity with teachers. I loved writing grants for extra funding for professional development. Though the half-day time we'd had was canceled, I soon found I could obtain supplementary funding to pay teachers for curriculum presentations and discussions. So while not every teacher qualified for particular professional development, I could now at least work with some people. I was the money tree. I'd spend hours, weeks to write a state grant proposal, apply, win a big grant, and grant funds were protected by state requirements for how the funds could be used. I wrote the grant application for a specific use I saw, and I could control how the funds were spent. These state grants were all about learning. Especially in this low-salary school system, teachers were thrilled to get paid for extra professional development time.

Grant writing was a brutal grind—tedious, time-consuming, deadly boring to write out the required text—but well worth it. I churned out applications. Scottsdale, with its low-income, racially diverse, and multilingual students, had all the right qualifications and demographics for the state department of education to love funding us. I won teachers over by paying them for curriculum work. Whatever the topic, they signed up. However effective our meetings were, teachers were happy to get paid for just showing up. This new professional development time gave me a chance to open windows to new ideas.

Another Lost Opportunity

Yet snags held back progress. In one attempt at a different approach to scheduling, many high schools in the area were moving toward long-block classes. Since I'd had such a good experience with extended time classes as a teacher, I picked up the task of trying to bring the high school department heads on board. I knew from my own experience that lengthier class time meant a respite from the exhausting barrage of multiple too-brief classes and too many students all in one day. It meant time for a deeper connection, getting to know one's students better, as well as more time devoted to one subject—all of which enables teachers to reach otherwise disruptive students, by sustaining focus. But moving into uncharted waters isn't always desired. And I hadn't yet learned that what worked well for one school wouldn't necessarily work for another.

Like any step into the unknown, changing class schedules can be unnerving, new territory, scary. With lack of trust in administration a factor here, as in so many districts, teachers may have been skeptical this schedule change would be made to work. We'd had no choice in Hope Essential, just informed of the class time period. When one has no choice it can work better. Getting full faculty agreement can be hard.

Hoping to be helpful and achieve some progress, I obtained grant funds for the department heads to be paid to meet with me to discuss a move to long-block classes, an initiative popular locally, so people could visit neighboring districts to see how it worked. I brought in an outside expert to speak to the entire high school faculty on the topic. But my efforts bombed.

The popular version of such scheduling at the time in this area was to offer only semester-long courses with longer classes, a change from full-year courses with shorter classes. At Hope Essential, since our class days rotated over the school year, we had a full year of longer classes, rotating daily to fulfill the state-required hours of school day time. Our courses extended over the year. I did have some reservations about the semester courses lacking year-long continuity. With the model that was picked up in this local area a student would have, for example, long-block freshman English for the first semester, then English would be eliminated during the next semester and picked up again in the next school year. That was a long time to wait for a second semester course. Would students remember from one school year to the next?

Articles touting the joy and utility of this semester courses use of time flourished. Research data reported that even for a subject such as a foreign language, students who missed the spring semester still retained the skills by the next year's fall term, a concept that even in my hopeful view required a suspension of disbelief. I worried too about math learning continuity, a key area on state tests. We at times felt lucky if students remembered math sufficiently when the test was given the day after it was taught, let alone the far-off next semester.

One department chair in our meetings was Tim, the district music director. Fatally, I neglected to see how the semester courses might affect his music program. With accountability on math and English, music to me seemed nice but not crucial. The music program wasn't in my line of vision. I underestimated both Tim's devotion to his program and parents' great appreciation of his work. School music performances are hugely beneficial, and sometimes lifesaving for disengaged students, keeping them in school. Concerts enrich the school system and kids' lives. They bring joy. Parents delight in their own child's performance.

Tim was the high school band director in addition to his role as districtwide music director and class teacher. He was well loved by students and their parents. I hadn't known how popular he was in the community. He showed me that he had an office full of Christmas gifts from grateful parents—huge fruit baskets, you name it. Parents treasured his work with their children. As is common, the music groups at each school, even the younger children, performed at events year-round—evening holiday performances, graduation ceremonies, showing off their talents at any special school event.

Tim, always working above and beyond, also took his band kids out of state for performances and competitions. Students visited places they'd otherwise not go. They marched in the Washington, DC presidential inaugural parades for which bands had to be selected. Tim proudly told me that his students were routinely accepted at Boston's prestigious Berklee College of Music. Since I was focused on academic subjects, it didn't occur to me at the time that Tim's students needed year-long courses. Practicing marching, and the trombone, for just a semester, then missing it, wasn't sufficient. They needed the full school year to maintain proficiency. But Tim, normally not shy about giving his opinion, never mentioned this need in our meetings—he just stewed in silence.

Fearful of change, the faculty voted almost unanimously against moving to longer-block semester courses. Also, I learned that prior to the vote a parent attorney went to the superintendent to denounce the change. The lawyer was a band parent. Clearly, Tim felt the only way he could protect his program was to go directly to the top, outside our discussions. Superintendents tend to pay attention to lawyers.

The Conversation Solution

A high school in a different district succeeded in implementing long-block semester courses, but kept the music and foreign language courses year-round. This modified use of time happened because people got together, considered various needs, conferred in civil discourse, and looked "outside the box" for a way to accommodate reasonable needs. It took time in this district for discussion, and a course schedule specialist to work out the new schedule, but it was doable. Scottsdale seemed to have a pattern of preferring confrontation and going outside of normal channels.

Semester long-block classes also worked remarkably well in another district. A math change in low-income Monson, where I later worked, lifted the full school system. Tracy, a sharp, bold math department chair, was able to not only accomplish the change to long-block classes but profit from it with advanced math ability across the board. When ninth grade students finished the first semester long-block course, the equivalent of a year's math, she arranged on her own for students to move in the second semester of that year to the next level math course. So students didn't skip a semester of math, common elsewhere. Instead, they progressed to the next level. In two years, students completed four years' worth of math. It showed up in top state math scores.

In Tracy's school, kids became math stars. The intensive doubling up of courses, helped along by her tweaking the course content to more fully address state-tested areas, resulted in students scoring especially high on the state math test, a huge challenge that was a stumbling block for other districts. Since all students completed a double load of math before taking the tenth grade math test, the school's accountability rating soared. And this accomplishment occurred in a small, remote, low-income town with limited resources and a traditionally underperforming student population. That all students learned math especially well there was a result of Tracy's drive to make her vision work. Her bold initiative wasn't a problem for the school, because everyone loved having these solid test scores that would have been at best mediocre without the year-long continuity of intense math learning. No one complained that math got priority, and students benefited.

Downward Spirals are Tough to Halt

But Scottsdale was stuck. With its limited English language issues, poverty, racial disconnect, lack of two-way discussion on hard issues, and an all-white school board, not representative of the full town, it's not surprising that improved learning, especially for those who needed it most, was blocked. The schools could not rise to the challenge of state tests.

I informed the school board about national statistics on racial groups and the effects of poverty conditions in relation to the upcoming tests. No one said, "What can we do?" "How can we help?" Instead, off in my basement office, oblivious to harmful decisions such as the plan to eliminate the professional development days, I wondered what problem would sneak up on me next. The school board had fired the district business manager. We were the only district in the state without a business manager. The town side now oversaw school budgets. What accidental slip, or even just seeing a place to cut the budget, might make me next to go? Not knowing what unexpected incident might come along, I felt my position uncertain. I didn't have a big salary, but cutting costs is always a board's interest. I felt vulnerable.

So when low test scores arrived after I'd left the district, the schools' plight only worsened. The initially low scores only sank lower. By 2012, each Scottsdale school scored well below the state targets for growth in learning. In 2014 the district hit Level 4—one level up from the bottom, rated "Underperforming" and "Needs Intervention." By 2015 the school system hit bottom and has remained there as "Chronically Underperforming" and "Needs Substantial Intervention."

Scottsdale remains one of just three districts statewide called "Commissioner's Districts," required to annually submit a report to the state board of education for approval on how the district plans to change. Frequent leadership changes and pervasive low teacher morale raise seemingly insurmountable hurdles. Students who are racially and culturally different from their teachers, and not fluent English speakers, present challenges when concerns are not addressed early. The student population in the district moved from one-third Latino during my time there to over half in 2017. Research tells us it takes eight years for a non-English-speaking student to fully learn English, sorely challenging for students on tests that require them to read and understand complex high-level reading passages.

By 2018, three-quarters of Scottsdale's students' families were low-income. Relatively wealthier white families fled the district. A bus takes students from the town to the nearby all-white districts. The overall "high needs" student category in 2018 reached eighty percent, close to all students having various special needs. That year, with a strained budget, large personnel cuts were scheduled—though more, rather than fewer—educators were needed.

It's possible to bring up learning, and test results. In another small low income district, state experts stepped in, due to low performance. I saw online their scores suddenly jumped sharply. When I contacted the district's Title I teacher Ellen, she told me these state consultants initiated, at no cost, fourteen different practices in one year: Teacher data teams, teams working together targeting literacy and math student needs, and hearing from experts helped immensely. Ellen said it was an intense year but well worth it to see students doing so much better. I have no doubt that Ellen was the link who made this intervention work for children.

During my time here in Scottsdale I felt I'd accomplished a lot: I'd brought the curriculum frameworks and standards to be tested to teachers' attention. I'd created at the superintendent's request the teacher committee to select the new K – 5 reading program, accomplished within the year. I'd reported to the school board that Scottsdale had the high needs populations that correlated with low test scores, and I had drawn in considerable money through grants to bring in learning ideas. Still, much more was needed to help teachers boost achievement. But I felt my position was tenuous. I didn't feel I had the backing needed to make achievement for all happen here. I started looking around at jobs in other districts. Curriculum jobs were now plentiful. I jumped to another school system, tripling my salary. The teachers I'd worked with here had mainly been nice and cooperative, especially given that I was often the conveyer of bad news. Both teachers and administrators lauded me to the visiting search committee team from another district. One in the visiting group asked me, "Kay, do you walk on water?"

When I was awarded the new position, Tim, the music director, was the first to come up to me, smile broadly, shake my hand, and sincerely congratulate me, stating without irony, "Even good news travels fast here." It was sad that teachers felt so poorly about their schools. They were happy for me that I'd found a new spot. A teacher I barely knew told me with eyebrows raised that my new district would "Let me fly." And it would.

CHAPTER NINETEEN

Fairfield: Involved Parents, Loving Learning

Moving then from Scottsdale to Fairfield was like moving to another country. The two school systems couldn't have been more different.

In Fairfield I found the ingredients to make it ripe to improve schools, and in just a few years we accomplished this. Working with a superintendent as ambitious as I was for high quality student learning, we soon won here a state prize for one of ten high schools statewide, of over 360, for having the "most improved" test scores, and going from mediocre to tops in state rankings. We moved to rank seventh statewide in district test scores. *The Boston Globe* and *Boston Magazine* rankings of school systems by test scores, reporting good learning, meant young families eager for good schools flocked to the town. Fairfield was a perfect setting for me to push for better work, with lots of support behind me. The stars were aligned. School board members, the superintendent, and parents were ambitious for learning here. It seemed everyone wanted one's own child to go to Harvard. Parents and students loved the teachers, who were caring and ambitious. While my tenure here ended harshly, with principals plus others departing, still we had made a difference. The change we brought doesn't happen without cost, bodies strewn.

When I set out to drive from Scottsdale to Fairfield for my job interview, I followed the superintendent's directions to the central office, which he described as "a little white house with green shutters." The job I was exploring had a long title: Assistant Superintendent for Curriculum, Instruction, Assessment and Professional Development, a new position created here, as superintendents found they couldn't pick up the teaching and learning leadership now needed while also having their plates full with the many responsibilities of district leadership. This school system had the added responsibility to manage growth, with two new schools constructed during my brief tenure. The new superintendent here, Mike, had come from a "high performing," as in high demographic, district, and wanted to see that same strong learning happen here. He'd come from one of the top districts in the state, which administrators in other districts called the "W" districts, including Wellesley.

As I drove into this grassy, serene town, where pretty little houses and open space abounded, I managed to find the correct white building with green shutters of the district central office. The more cynical teachers here did refer to it as "the White House," implying dictatorial. Educators were about to see change they never asked for. New principals Mike hired for almost every school had higher expectations than those of the earlier sleepier era. Standards and the test helped move progress. Dissidents lurked.

The hiring committee was mainly principals. My interview for this new position seemed perfunctory, with softball questions. When one principal asked a question I wasn't clear on, another principal supplied the answer for me. I later realized that my résumé provided the right fit for this community, and the less I said in the interview, the better. I suspect this committee liked my many college degrees. Next thing I knew, I was meeting alone with the superintendent. I just allowed him to talk; superintendents like this meeting with a new person where they can expound on their education views, trusting an interview committee's recommendation. Then I met with the school board, again just *pro forma*. But when the school board chair asked me where I'd like to be in ten years, I probably shouldn't have said, "On a warm island somewhere." Then I clarified that I'd like to be right there, heading teaching and learning. I really didn't crave the more lucrative, higher-up next step up superintendent position with its many different demands, always in the spotlight, each move watched. I felt safer as a behind-the-scenes person working to help teachers improve, and to help the district to soar in learning. I wouldn't stay hidden for long in Fairfield.

Fairfield was a different world. At the time I arrived, the town was semi-rural, with some working farms, cows. This would quickly change, as McMansions sprung up in this town with lots of space, far from the crowded tenements of Scottsdale. Here were special conditions that soon allowed me to help propel the schools to the top in state rankings. With our scores high, the town then exploded with young families moving in, wanting the best for their children. Everyone focused on trying to do their best schoolwork. Fairfield was on an upward spiral, in contrast to Scottsdale, propelled in a different way by the community that didn't embrace all students.

My job was cut out for me, and I felt surrounded by support for improvement. It seemed the forces here were all on the same page. But resisters existed. Upon my arrival in Fairfield, I queried a high school department head about the upcoming state test. He smiled consolingly, if a bit patronizing. "Our students do well on tests," he assured me.

Not so well this time, I soon saw. In my first year, over half of the tenth grade students scored below Proficient in math on the first state test. I knew we had some work to do, especially in a community that paid so much attention to education.

Eighty parents served on the board of directors of the schools' parent group. This number grew. Parents and most community members only wanted to help. These school-loving parents had a large, well managed get-out-the-vote organization that ensured that every new school system budget increase was voted in by the community, supplying more money for more resources and energetic new young teachers. When I was asked to speak to the large parent group about what the schools were doing, the parents who approached me were afraid I'd be boring, so they helped me organize the presentation. We used the metaphor of architecture for school improvement, with new homes construction, new school buildings coming in. Parents and I agreed (along with the school board and superintendent) that along with new buildings we wanted to see better new schoolwork, a great education.

Earlier hidden in that basement office, now I was forced into prominence and gained the skill of speaking to the community. Parents and community members now wanted to see me, and hear from me. I could no longer hide.

When attendance at parent meetings later started to dwindle, parent group leaders asked me what a good topic to present on might be. I had a quick answer. Here, it seemed each parent felt one's own child was "gifted." Unfortunately, our longtime "gifted and talented" teacher, who had tested children and selected qualified students for her in-school program, retired. This retirement may have been related to pressure from many new parents who wanted to see their children in the so-called gifted program. But we couldn't find a good replacement who could come in with the same needed competence in the area. Also, pulling out only some certain children for "gifted" work—as elites—was no longer an educationally favored concept. Inclusion, not just pulling out higher achieving students, was the preferred education concept. Plus, this separation of tested students based on perceived intelligence, using certain tests, no longer worked for this community, since each parent believed one's child was special and warranted special teaching. So now, in losing the pull-out teacher, to work separately with some students, parents were pressuring schools to boost learning for one's very own special child by modifying classroom work. The code word term for "make my smart child smarter" was "differentiation," which meant, in parents' minds, pay attention to my child. Every school system has its challenges.

I brought teachers to the evening parent meeting to speak on this hot topic of "differentiating instruction," addressing a student's unique needs in the classroom. Having teachers speak helped, because otherwise I'd be alone facing a firing squad of ambitious parents. Sixty parents showed up, a full house. The teachers were terrific at explaining to parents what they were doing in classrooms to boost learning as appropriate for individuals. I suspect not every parent was assured, but we were getting this message out that we were trying. I stood behind the teachers as they spoke brightly, rightfully proud of their own work. Parents just listened, not openly confronting those who taught their children. I'd never seen a parent in Scottsdale. It was this welcome parent involvement that helped Fairfield schools raise in overall achievement, as happened with other similar school systems. It was unfortunate that Scottsdale didn't have the parents clamoring for better education that this district had.

This suburban town was just a forty-five-minute smooth highway commute into the high-paying, elite Boston area jobs, but with not much else besides school here to occupy stay-at-home moms, who didn't need to work themselves. So the town's social life centered on the schools. A dinner-dance school fundraiser event that started with just a dozen parents quickly blossomed into an all-but-required gala, raising needed additional large funds annually to support the schools. Parents were falling all over each other trying to help the schools.

The parent organization was well-organized, focused, with effective leaders. These parents worked supportively with the superintendent. Here, as parents had the extra time and interest in school for their children, and weren't cowed by an administrator, they met directly with the superintendent on issues. Scottsdale parents may not have felt welcome in this same role, possibly unsuccessful in school themselves. Fairfield parents ensured that principals' phones too lit up regularly with calls. I always felt that it was up to me to make sure we exceeded academic expectations—both parents' and the state's. I benefitted from this focus. Ever-watchful Fairfield parents knew what I was about, and appreciated my work that they saw reflected in public increasingly higher test results as a result of strong classroom work. Real estate agents here loved me.

A Super Superintendent

It was the Superintendent Mike who was the catalyst. With three Harvard degrees, including his doctorate in education, Mike had attended the elite Phillips Exeter Academy; he'd played football for Harvard. Mike believed in school. His only suggestion for me was that I wasn't "stepping into it" enough, pushing hard enough against earlier beliefs and practices. It was good I took some caution.

Mike was fun to work with. He urged me to make changes, which was fine with me. He valued high-level learning, as did I. He spoke of "Old Fairfield" (mediocre) and "New Fairfield" (in Mike's view, education-excellence centered), moving ahead under his leadership. We both focused on academic achievement. He showed me the yardstick he'd used in his earlier district, telling me this was what he used in his previous district to show news reporters to measure snow accumulation when the state was hit with a heavy snowfall. "Why are your schools open today, when others around the state are closed?" reporters asked. "Because it's Tuesday," Mike proudly grinned. Nothing would halt school. And because all of us administrators worked so hard, Mike would lighten the mood with emails including hokey jokes on Friday afternoons. We found this relaxing, lifting the weight of school problems as we moved into the weekend, a nice, sensitive touch.

While we school and district administrators knew we primarily had a supportive community for change to rachet up learning, others weren't as happy with changes. Despite a culture of so many working to raise the bar, an involved parental community that keeps school on its toes, and a school board eager to see learning improve, all with their own children in the schools, not everyone was on board with the push for new and better work. There were enough teachers of the "Old Fairfield" mindset who'd preferred the pre-Mike, laid-back, more independent *laissez-faire* way of school. Things had been fine here before, they believed.

The teachers union here, as always a strong support for teachers, backing teachers, always looking for better pay, a good thing, protecting them from being forced into overwork, including beyond the boundaries of the school day, and always having to present a face of opposition in order to be able to negotiate, fostered resentment of this new superintendent who to them seemed overinvolved in how school worked. The previous superintendent, ousted by the school board to move forward, had been easier to please. Union-management is always by definition contentious, in some school settings more than others. Mike, feeling mostly district-wide support, at times made waves as we sought improvement. He attempted to tone down Christmas celebrations, in respect for other religions, but when charged with being a bit of a grinch held a nice open meeting to discuss this issue. I was a new person with new teaching and learning oversight, a role that didn't exist before, though happening statewide, so I was most likely resented by some. I didn't hear of any dissention. We were protected in our bubble of the "white house."

And still, as with Scottsdale, I was a grant-writing machine, which endeared me to teachers. Since I'd been successful with acquiring state grants earlier, it was also easy to do the same in Fairfield. I gained some popularity by drawing in new funds for professional development, with teachers always happy to be paid for extra work. My supplementary grants funded curriculum work, classroom materials, and professional development, such as on the needed "differentiating instruction," to vary work to meet student needs in ways appropriate for the student, Sizer's "personalization."

Outside presenters funded by these supplementary grants helped teachers become current with state requirements and new teaching practices. The money poured in. When we brought in a costly new math program, I was able to bring in top national consultants to help teachers understand the material. I kept an eye on the state's competitive grant notifications, applied for everything, and won every grant, even the most competitive ones.

People noticed. One of the parent group's prominent leaders told the school board in an open public meeting that I earned my salary with bringing in grant funds. I don't know how he knew this, but I loved him for noting it and publicly speaking out. Without this additional funding, we couldn't have made the sharp turn to improve the quality of learning that Mike and this community, and I, wanted to see. Funding teachers for extra time to learn new skills also helped mollify resistance to change. When one teacher raved about a consultant she'd heard on the concept of "differentiating," I easily had the funds to bring this person in to work with teachers, which they enjoyed.

The district budget for my curriculum and professional development job was sufficient in Fairfield; Mike made sure of that. But since I could also bring in even more money to fund my many projects, I did. Why not? Attracted by extra pay, teachers learned in special sessions, such as the tested math areas. I set up a grant-funded tutoring program for students at the high school, and when I visited, I saw teachers working one-on-one with students. It was a happy, busy time. Popcorn and chocolate abounded at this after-school tutor session, purchased by the teachers to entice students to extra math learning. Everyone was having fun, and state scores soared, even in that always challenging area of math. By tutoring on the state standards, teachers were learning the math areas tested, to help improve math achievement.

In my annual evaluation, instead of a detailed long written evaluation citing my missteps, often the criticism supervisors feel they have to do, Mike simply listed three things: "Find a good secretary. Drive safely. Keep up the good work." He let me know right away if there was a brush fire I needed to put out, and I moved quickly to stamp that out.

The Tide Turns

Always looking to try something new to see if it would work, one January Saturday I held a full-day session for teachers to work on a common area of state-tested writing. Motivated by extra pay, over forty teachers showed up, ranging from elementary to upper grades high school teachers. It happened that we had a small TV in the school library where we could briefly collegially convene to watch a political event happening at the time. A light snowfall began outside, also creating a feeling of community. Inside, working in the warm, familiar library, energetic young elementary teachers presented their work on our project. Their enthusiasm brightened the more old-school, somewhat jaded veterans who were proud of their academic work, but less student-centered than wonderful new young elementary teachers can be, open to new ideas.

This Saturday workshop felt like a turning point. I pointed out the one main writing area tested, and we worked on it, as a group. Teachers came on board. We were making a change, together. After this one get-together, I felt a shift. The teachers who attended were more open to change, then helped persuade others. Teachers here understood the direction in which the state's system was moving, and understood the need to pay attention to the test. I still had to help with current teaching practices and paying attention to tested skills, but now I felt the turn was less of a chore, no longer the tough slog of Scottsdale, where minds were more set. The wheels now turned more easily. It was Mike's support of my work and parents' support of schools and administrators that made the whole cloth difference.

Parents loved seeing the published schools' test scores, ranked by score levels. Finally, I could do my job. Mike gave me free rein, never micromanaged. Because of his full support, I could help the schools make the turn to standards learning. When I saw we could or should move in a direction, I went for it. I was a heat-seeking missile, a well-programmed drone heading for a signature target. Some found me overzealous. One principal in particular chafed at what she considered my intrusion into what she considered her school. I caught on to this too late.

A New Project Helps Turn the Corner

I made sure that we were one of just twelve districts statewide to obtain an especially large professional development grant. I didn't know how well this grant project would work. It could never be predicted how effective a new project would be and how it would be received by teachers, but it looked good. An experienced teacher later told me it was the best professional development she'd ever had.

I hastily pulled together a team of middle school teachers from different subjects to attend this grant project's sessions with a well-known Cambridge-based consulting group. I met just briefly with these teachers in their school corridor, and apparently my enthusiasm motivated them, or they appreciated being tapped, and this small group signed on to the project. As it turned out, this was a grant for creating "webquests." Teachers would collect web sites for students to research a course topic, rather than having teachers talk at the class on the subject. This project was Sizer's "student as worker" concept, in which teachers create an environment for students to do the work learning to learn on their own, novel for this era.

With webquest professional development, these few teachers learned how to cull web sites of different levels of difficulty for varied students, thereby differentiating, meeting needs of more struggling students, and to allow higher achieving students to soar, even seeking out new sites on their own. This fit a need. Webquests promote reading and research skills, and ask students to condense material into a writing piece, all tested standards. We also now centered on technology use, which parents of this growing tech-oriented town were eager to see. And we were breaking through the constraints of separate subject areas. Collected internet sites could be on history or science, with the literacy skills of research, reading and writing.

In this project, teachers created a "rubric"—new at the time—to guide and assess learning, offering precise guides and feedback, instead of just slapping a seemingly subjective grade on a project. This full project brought the best of learning of this time, and lit a fire under teachers, because it was new and different. The project provided the tools to differentiate. It had students doing the work, Sizer's expectation, with the teacher acting as coach, observing and guiding.

The middle school teachers who'd signed on to this project idea "got" the fine professional development; they understood its value and loved it. Then, on their own, they trained more teachers. This grant project worked better than I could have imagined. It took on a life of its own. One late afternoon I was leaving a school after a meeting, and a teacher asked me to visit the computer lab. The room was filled with teachers, pizza, donuts, soft drinks—all that high-sugar stuff that keeps a teacher going later in the school day, normally *verboten* for the computer lab because it sticks up keyboards. Snacks fueled their work. Teachers were on their own training others to create webquests. Teachers were fixated on their screens, delightedly exclaiming to others when they located a web site that fit their own project. A relaxed yet intense aura pervaded the jam-packed lab, as teachers worked together to create their own webquests. Collaboration was satisfying to see, with teachers happily working together.

A small parent group disparaged this webquest project as only one technology application, and they wanted to see more. This parent criticism was annoying, especially because learning was getting turned around. I knew this project was an important one that included many of Sizer's Principles that were now permeating the education world as we upped learning. The guided research turned classwork over to the students to explore. It would be hard to explain the full impact or how it suited new thinking on how to develop learning to critical parents who have their own views of what school should be. Teachers were happy to adopt this new tool, so that was sufficient for me. I chose not to attempt to argue this to hypercritical parents, a wise move as it turned out. I later heard that over-explaining this kind of thing could backfire, as it had in another wealthy, high-performing district.

Heads rolled after a teacher and administrator group in another high demographic district of involved parents tried to explain a good, new, cross-subject-area project to the school board. Proud of their work, the administrators and teachers wanted to present it openly. One hypercritical prominent school board member attacked these presenters, arguing that their report's assessment was too subjective. He charged that they didn't have data to show their project was more successful work. This vocal criticism hit the newspapers. These school leaders who had presented were soon gone, from the power of one prominent critic, the project they'd worked so hard on killed. The downside of an involved community is that it can be tricky to explain to community people the value of a somewhat nuanced school initiative. Such communication explanation takes time and effort. Educators compile their own knowledge base and speak the same language. We can't be sure others understand. It takes special circumstances to be able to explain some conditions to those outside school, a fragile rope bridge shaky to cross.

It's also hard for one to know what feeds snipers who aren't in the open "conversation." The gap between education thinking and outside of school community thinking is often a gulf. This only got worse with new math approaches. A friend lost her curriculum job when favoring a new math program to which one school board member objected, I suspect not the only such instance in moving to new math. My friend was only supporting a math program earlier selected. It was the hard-to-explain new way of doing math, by discovery, instead of old-school math memorization. My friend as a new curriculum director hadn't known not everyone embraced that program. As new ways of working were introduced, in response to state and federal expectations, these were lively, and risky, times requiring careful conversation that few had the time for. I knew webquests constituted fine learning, and teachers did also. We left it at that.

Improving Math Is Dicey

Still, in Fairfield, I happened to be in the right place at the right time. With our soaring state test scores widely reported in newspapers and online, people paid attention to our schools. Word-of-mouth parent praise of our classrooms and teachers strengthened our reputation as a fine community in which to raise children. The incoming bright kids eager to learn, with watchful parents catching possible missteps, principals regularly communicating with parents, connecting well, helped change school for the better. When teachers saw that their own students' test scores were high, this boosted pride. We were riding on a wave of success.

I also paid attention to our one group of traditionally lower performers, special education students. When a school underserves a "subgroup," this test results number pulls down a school's state rating. And special education parents rightfully keep a close eye on school for their children's well-being. I knew helping students with a disability was an important area. In my last year in Fairfield, I brought in a good math consultant Grace, whom I'd discovered at a conference, to work only with our middle school special education teachers, costly, but well worth it. That year, the middle school special ed students excelled on the state test, moving out of the lower rating. The next year, after my departure, those scores dropped. Without continued close oversight, the school and district moved from a top-scoring level down to Level Two because of this subgroup, and remained there, pulling down the district rating.

While a big accomplishment overall, however, here was with math learning, and resulted in good state test scores, the adoption of a new way of learning math was a challenge for parents, for whom new terms in math and ways of working were a mystery. Two third grade teachers stepped into my office in the middle of July. They'd gone to a math conference and learned about a new program they felt we should adopt. I began to hear of other dissatisfaction with the current math program at different grade levels. When one strong fourth grade teacher told me that she was going to create her own math program, I knew I had to step in. We didn't need to reinvent the wheel.

Soon I was taking teachers to workshops on new math programs that matched what was tested on the state tests. I brought in teachers from other districts to talk about their experience with these new programs. This didn't inspire everyone. When one presenter described how hard she had to work on her own using a different math program, the teachers' union president and her friend made a show of standing up and walking out of the session. Still, I persisted.

Mike told me that a Boston University elementary math professor lived in town. I nabbed her to speak with our teachers—paying her well—and she did a fine job presenting the new approach to teaching math understanding. With my grant funds, I could spend the time and money in professional development to bring the message to all our elementary teachers that we were making a change with math. I had the luxury of two years to work on this, to get the message out and attempt to give teachers guidance on how math was to be developed in their classrooms. A teacher committee piloted two different programs and selected the new program, though one not my choice.

I knew we had to go with the teachers' choice, not mine. It worked. Somehow, we were working together on this major needed change improving and turning around math development.

In the districts that didn't take the time to go slowly with the process of involving teachers in a program purchase decision, those teachers get resentful of the "top-down" nature of the decision process. Having a new program handed to you without your input is not appreciated. These teachers often never relent in stating they'd had no choice in the selection. We hear about it forever. Hurt feelings interfere with how well a new program is embraced, and how enthusiastically (or not) it's used with students. In Fairfield now, teachers felt invested because some of their own whom they respected had tested out the different programs and agreed on one. The teachers selected the program that provided more teacher support, which turned out to be a wise selection since math ability varied among teachers.

This new program initiated a dramatic change in how teachers taught math in all three of our elementary schools. Starting with full teacher professional development, and first looking at the new math ideas, helped make this work. It helped that I wasn't an elementary math expert. Here good teachers moved things along and settled on the right decision for them at the time.

The Joys and Pain of Parent Involvement

Parents were not so enthralled. Accepting a totally different new full math program for kindergarten through fifth grade went fairly smoothly for teachers. Parents hated it.

As we made the change from old math ways and developed standards learning, children did well on state tests. In another district where a new, better math program was brought in, I saw (because I was always checking state test data) that math scores improved there in the first year of the program, right away. I don't recall noticing that immediate jump in Fairfield at the time. What I do remember was parents' reactions.

The great good thing about Fairfield was parent involvement. But now while it was right to just have teachers make the decision on which new program to adopt, we'd left our otherwise involved parents out of the loop. Looking back, we could have explained the rationale for the change to key parent leaders, who'd then disseminate information to others. I could also have included key parents in the discussion of selection of a different math program. Now parents complained, as they saw their children's math books and homework, incomprehensible to them. It wasn't the simpler math they themselves had learned in school.

At one parent meeting, a mother said she took one of the math program problems to a Harvard professor, and she reported to parents that the professor didn't understand it. As I listened to this, I thought, How could he? The farther away we get from the teacher in the classroom with the math book, the less anyone would understand. I didn't say this at the meeting. My ability to be speechless when hearing something that astounded me often left me in good stead. One of the qualities that helped me survive in moving school along was that I was tongue-tied when anyone said anything outrageous that was contrary to my own beliefs. Others claim deafness. "I just don't hear things like that," our successful principal Jane told me as she made a culture shift at the high school. The English department head had stated that all special education students should be moved to the administration office. Jane had a special needs child.

I saw I had to pay attention to parents learning the new math. Many were tripped up by the different terminology. "Ball-park estimation" is an example. This concept taught students how to round off numbers and estimate in one's head an anticipated number for a calculation. We do this in our heads for a restaurant bill, a grocery receipt. It's a real-world concept, good to know. The student uses this skill in checking one's problem-solving correctness, a great skill, but one not taught in earlier times.

But such new terms stymied parents who wanted to help their children at home. In addition, our program had children keeping math journals, to write about math. This was novel for parents too. They were lost on how to help. Home parent support can have its downside when parents don't understand new and different ways of learning to help their children. Fairfield parents were annoyed and frustrated. While we had parent assistance guides to distribute, these often got lost in the busyness of school, a crucial error.

I hired a pricey national consultant to help a large, dumbfounded parent group. I also brought in other consultants to speak at parent sessions. Principals were heroes of diplomacy. Now it was also the teachers, beginning to grasp the concepts and practice, who educated principals and parents to the math program. I did get better myself at working with angry parents and conferring with those who had concerns, not just ducking issues and counting on principals and teachers to help out. I would just listen, attempt to explain, and agree when possible. Letting an issue just ride itself out—safely ensconced in my own office, not out in the schools—also worked. I couldn't put out every fire alone.

But with major changes moving Fairfield schools forward, snipers lurked. Not everyone was in sync with the move from "Old Fairfield," where tradition reigned, to big changes, such as perplexing new math. The dismay at change was even beyond the elementary school math dilemma. Teachers spoke of how the previous older Irish-American high school principal would burst into song singing "Danny Boy" loudly in the building after school, savoring the resonance of the near-empty building, and creating a cheery, relaxed feeling among teachers still working late in their classrooms. That principal was not someone pushing on learning. Old Fairfield was good at just leaving people alone, valued by many. But Mike didn't seem to hear these other voices of those who longed for those good old days. Word that's passed on quietly to others, outside of the open conversation, at the time called "parking lot discussion," unfairly doesn't get to those in leadership positions, common not only during this period of intense change. With Fairfield the fastest-growing town in the state, as Mike proudly told me, now schools were full with students who were eager to learn and fun to teach. There were holdouts off in the corners.

In my years of working with Mike, we moved education to a new level. The schools were humming. By 2004, my final year here, now eighty-five percent of tenth graders scored Advanced and Proficient in English, only one percent Failing. In math at the high school, where earlier only half had attained Proficient, now three-quarters of students scored Advanced and Proficient, only three percent Failing. Scores slid down after I'd left.

Out-of-the-Blue Zinger

School, even with its twist and turns, its small number of critics, sailed along, until it didn't. Often, district leaders are slammed with an offense that's a cover for other concerns. One high-profile superintendent with the common issue of Food Services budget overrun (with cafeteria workers often giving a lunch to students who can't or don't pay) meets with the school board in a private session to explain the situation, in two-way, face to face discussion, and they reach an understanding. But another superintendent with the same charge of overspending in that area is summarily fired. Too often this parting of ways comes in an open school board meeting, unexpected, and humiliating when this happens in public and on camera, which is often. Whatever the stated cause, a disproportionate reaction is often a cover for concern on other issues not well expressed in a person-to-person way. For us, one spring a principal in a nearby town gave a graduation speech he'd found on the internet—a speech that turned out Mike too used, and was accused of plagiarism. That other principal was well-liked, and the speech wasn't an issue. With Mike, this same graduation speech was controversial.

At a lovely June outdoor graduation ceremony, Mike was proud. He felt well-established in Fairfield, and enjoyed delivering a lively speech that a friend had sent him. We soon learned that the president of Coca Cola had first delivered that speech. A disaffected individual filmed the graduation ceremony. Mike's speech ended up being broadcast on a popular Boston TV news station in a split screen, with the lines of the original speech scrolling beside Mike's almost verbatim delivery. Mike had provided no attribution, simply unaware of the original source. The media, eager to highlight negative news, can be destructive, and reported a charge of plagiarism. The school board felt the media report damning, injuring the community's image. The charge from some parents was, how could students be held to a higher standard of documenting sources if the superintendent plagiarized? The school board didn't sufficiently value Mike —who'd worked so hard and turned schools around —to defend him. One parent group offered to help Mike, but he felt he could extricate himself alone. With other parents' complaints, no one stepped in to support him, with school board members relying on town voters to remain in their positions. Such conflict over what can be a small issue easily addressed isn't uncommon. A superintendent can be caught in an act some think is okay, others condemn. Fine superintendents are ousted over relatively trivial issues, which may hide other concerns.

Mike had always played to those who wanted to see the schools improve, who were in abundance here. Superintendents can easily be blindsided. Three-hundred-and-sixty-degree awareness is hard, especially when others don't alert one to concerns. A teacher who filmed the graduation, and Mike's speech, precipitated the plagiarism charge by sending the video to the press. The principals identified this teacher; they believed they knew who it was. The school board, unfairly in my view, was more concerned about the poor public view of their town generated by this negative publicity than they were in protecting this good superintendent who had turned schools around, propelling it to tops statewide. Mike provided the explanation for how he'd come across the speech, just receiving it in an email from a friend, but no one wanted to listen. There were other ways of dealing with such a dilemma, but since it's hard to please one hundred percent all the time, this school board chose to not support him. He'd made a difference, building a school system from mediocre to great, hiring new principals, overseeing construction of two new schools, turning teaching and learning around, but all that comes with a cost. And one's supporters step back when they see negatives rolling forward.

Mike was now out, a new superintendent came in and cleaned house. He fired many who I believed brought much of value to the schools: the fine head buildings custodian, who lived in town; a great, energetic new athletics director. The Special Education

Director was ousted, with inevitable complaints in a challenging job. The high school principal who'd shepherded the move out of one shared building into the expansive new building, a lively time, left. The highly capable middle school principal left, wary of the new superintendent. The superintendent following Mike began to build up cases against a couple other principals. After five years of successes, I too was out, due to my close alliance with Mike and his drive. One principal, I eventually too late figured out, was happy to denigrate me to the new superintendent.

Coming from a challenging urban district, this new district leader had sharp political skills, needed for survival, and therefore despite not being an educational leader, lasted long. Mike found a fine position, where he excelled, in his home town of Cambridge. My next new journey was rocky, though I continued to delight in bringing good new ideas and practices to other schools. We'd turned a mediocre school system into high performing. We'd pushed, and it was time to move on. There's satisfaction in that. One doesn't stay long when pushing for change. District leaders who negotiate rough seas well and stay are rare. Factions collide without two-way conversation across gaps. Locating and winning over critics takes time, effort, skill, and it's hard when they hide.

CHAPTER TWENTY

Sussex: More Types of Challenges

I was thrilled to move to my next new job of Assistant Superintendent for Curriculum, Instruction, Assessment and Professional Development in Sussex just outside Boston, a city with more diversity, my five years of work in Fairfield completed.

I continued to oversee teaching and learning areas, and nailed down helpful large grants. In my brief stay, before a budget crisis wreaked havoc, we had important victories. But unfortunately, my zeal to race to the top in academics wasn't met with the same enthusiasm in the schools and community here as it was in Fairfield. And it's easier for the wealthier communities such as Fairfield with more ambitious families to garner town votes for better schools, ever-increasing budgets.

But I did have an early breakthrough victory that was a joy for me, and helpful for children. It was the standards and the test that helped in the crucial area of pinpointing a needed early reading skill, and correcting a gap. We learned from looking at the third grade test that it tested close reading, and students hadn't been well prepared for this. When this skill was explicitly taught, those scores spiked up. Leaving third grade without that key skill would have been malpractice.

First, though, upon my arrival, the superintendent Andrea right away told me she wanted to see written curriculum documents. Andrea said there had been here lots of discussion of teaching and learning, but there were no documents to solidify and communicate expected learning. Nothing was in writing. It turned out I was lucky to have brought the colorful, beautiful written Fairfield's arts program's K – 12 curriculum booklet with bright color print artwork to my interview for this position. It sealed this job for me.

I arrived here in July and before summer ended, with no one in the schools, all dispersed for the summer, I'd sufficiently garnered teacher work to complete both print and online curriculum products. My first year here was full of accomplishments. In my second year it was clear I'd worn out my welcome. The superintendent here didn't have the drive for better learning that Mike had had. And that old thorn of special education students in math continued to burn, my nemesis. But we made a huge simple leap in early reading development. I posted these score jumps charts on my office wall.

Beautiful Art Work is a Hit

I'd worked mainly in just a supportive way with curriculum writing in Fairfield. Our art teachers in particular took this project and ran with it, on their own. In just one year they created a beautifully designed kindergarten through high school curriculum document in which they collected, scanned in and printed with color print magnificent art pieces for each grade that illustrated the art expected for each year's work, exemplars, along with bullet points as grade level guides. The Fairfield district arts chair, Marion, modified a format I'd set out, to make it more visually appealing. When I offered to Marion to take this work of art to the printer for her, for multiple copies, she insisted on taking the material to the printer herself. Marion wanted to have just the right paper weight, binder, and color shades. Our flush funds available for this printing meant what's often a dreary text-heavy document was itself a work of art. While Marion didn't say she wanted to make sure herself that each detail was exactly right—diplomacy always welcome in an often fractious job —I smiled as I knew well that Marion didn't think I'd get it all correct, as artful as they'd planned. She was probably right. Passing around this published document at my Sussex interview screening cinched the deal. One never knows for sure what a district is looking for or wants to avoid, so this was pure luck.

The process for the Fairfield art curriculum product was the ideal. Empowered to create their own artistic document, I'd just run interference for these art teachers as glitches arose. Marion picked up exactly what was needed and moved on it. She initiated the art curriculum writing project at the school year start with an outside arts leader in the area speaking to all art teachers. Under Marion's leadership the teachers ended that school year with their fine, elaborate curriculum document completed and printed, even with a break to hang the end of year art exhibition of best work many schools have, selecting and displaying exemplary student work. On one full-day professional development day during the year, I stopped into the expansive, well-lit new high school building's art room. Every teacher here, kindergarten through high school, was intent on selecting art pieces and words, and scanning artwork, a well-oiled machine. Marion, determined, a fine artist herself, had the respect of her art teachers and the leadership skills to get everyone working together for a visually appealing curriculum document. They didn't need me.

Conversation to Spell Out What's Taught When

Since the superintendent Andrea here in Sussex was more of a "Let's get things done, now," take-charge leader, while Mike had left me alone to note needs and move as I saw fit, we completed almost all curriculum documents my first summer here, though no document reached those art teachers' high bar. I created and posted a reader-friendly new format online and teams began meeting to fill in the areas needed for each subject. I surprised even myself by having departments pretty much complete this full work in two months, working mainly remotely. One department that never completed the work though was the art area. One never knows for sure until too late where talent is, and where it's lacking. This makes school work interesting, to see leadership take hold or bust.

A curriculum document captures in writing what's taught at each grade and in each subject. It collects information and keeps teachers on track. The final product is helpful, and reassuring that there's a guide, but the best part of creating such documents is the conversation teachers and subject leaders have together in open two-way discussion on what should be learned at each grade level. The final written document brings more grade level focus and commonality within grades, and builds learning over the grades, helping to reduce chaotic, overly personalized, teaching. As many succeeded in completing the particular subject and grade levels documents here in Sussex, moving to some consensus, most importantly, educators had open discussion on what's to be taught in their content areas. Always, the state curriculum framework is the good guide for grade level expectations. One subject area head in another district told me he was sorry that their content area didn't yet have a final state-developed curriculum guide, because he wanted to measure his work against that expectation. Not every department leader had that interest, preferring to have just the school expectation, often to their detriment to miss out on high expectations.

The full completion of more substantial written curriculum was completed by the time I left two years later. It had been the high school principal good communicator Ed who early on informed me that written curriculum was a big deal for the superintendent. She wanted to see these documents. I didn't take this helpful alert lightly. However, a tension was that I tended to be more excited than others here about moving along high quality teaching and learning. I'd never find another Mike, championing exemplary learning.

The Test Helps Solve a Key Reading Problem

But the best victory here was early on pinpointing a specific reading skill needed at an early grade level, and correcting this. It was the state test that revealed the reading problem. Upon my arrival here, many district leaders bemoaned a drop in third grade MCAS reading scores. I looked at the scores, and as Andrea was casually watering the plants in her office, I told her that the test scores weren't a big drop from the previous year, but what we had was a four-year downward trend. She set her watering can down. We were on it. At that crucial early grade level, annual declining reading scores was not good.

To her credit, Andrea was a woman of action. Mike hadn't attended my curriculum meetings, trusting me, and allowing me to make some errors, always applauding risk-taking for steaming ahead. We now had many meetings, small and large, with the superintendent attending—to help people pay attention—and including all the third grade teachers from the three elementary schools, no doubt all feeling under the gun. One of our schools' reading specialists, Claire, moved quickly.

Kay speaks with teachers

While I hosted full meetings on reading development in general, our reading specialist Claire read through the test passages and questions. She pinpointed the problem. Claire easily saw that the test was mainly testing for close reading, asking questions on what the reading passage states. But the focus here had been on helping students connect reading to other familiar areas. If a reading was on a child's mother, students were to think about their own mother and compare the reading to one's own experience. This helps provide context to understand passages. With children taught to go outside the reading text and compare with their own experience or to other readings, this is a good way to develop reading ability. But the test tests specifically what's stated. One's own mother was irrelevant. Close reading has always been a main skill tested on the state tests, and we'd missed this here.

Our strong reading specialist Claire went right into every third-grade classroom in her school and taught the children to closely read stated words in text. By reading what text states, we learn new thoughts and information. Test scores spiked that one year from thirty-five percent Proficient to seventy percent Proficient. It wasn't that our students lacked reading ability in general. It was just that one skill they needed. Without that outside test, literacy learning doesn't always develop well. It takes a skilled leader, as Claire was, to note the error, focus on it and bring it alive in classrooms. Claire conferred with the reading teacher in another school, whom she'd mentored, and that school also had a sharp jump in English Language Arts scores. The reading specialist in the third elementary school here found it hard to have teachers allow her into their classes, and that school's scores remained low. That principal there was not happy.

The Math Problem Never Goes Away

But middle school math for special ed students was a Gordian knot never solved, an albatross. There was no simple solution. This was true here in Sussex, and also common statewide. It was a toothache that never went away, a permanent pain.

I initiated lots of professional development on math learning strategies. We purchased some new math books, hired new teachers, and replaced the middle school math department head a couple times (each not happy about this), but we were never able to raise these scores. Now even I—loving the ambitious test for each child—questioned the fairness of when one school has poor scores in one subgroup area, the full district has that cloud of the lower rating casting a shadow on the district as a whole. That cloud followed me.

Meanwhile, the high school here had a superb extracurricular advanced math team, which won math team league competitions around the state annually. Once I walked by the classroom where the math team was working: The dedicated math coach wasn't lecturing and writing out algorithms on the blackboard, explaining. Instead, he was walking around the room looking at students' work, as each student, head down, labored over thinking through and solving a math problem. He'd point out an area to look at. When the school was closed due to a snowstorm the math coach opened school up for the team to practice; they all showed up. At a retirement party for the math coach, graduates lauded him for pushing them. He continued to lead the extracurricular math team even after retiring. A dedicated teacher pushing higher achieving students is special also, seeing reward in student success, and appreciating parent and community recognition, a hard-won prize to ever replace. Pride in the math excellence at the high school compared with the middle school's dilemma didn't go unnoticed.

It wasn't until years later that publishers' math programs at long last flooded the market with books teachers could use that helped teachers align learning with what's tested. As Common Core State Standards swept the nation, now at last educators had the right math materials to better guide the work. For this earlier time, in my quandary of not meeting the mark, I brought in the same math consultant, Grace, who'd helped well in Fairfield, improving even special education middle school math. I had trusted Grace so much in Fairfield that I even let her work on her own with those teachers, and there special ed scores improved. Grace knew the math tests well, and provided new learning strategies, modeled classwork, provided a curriculum format. But here in Sussex none of this made a difference, an ongoing headache. Those scores wouldn't budge and it was a mystery why not, an annoying common dilemma statewide.

A Math Problem Solution

As I cast about wildly to find the key to solve this dilemma, in another attempt to find what might work, I took our Sussex special education and math teachers to visit one of the few schools in the state that didn't have a problem with their middle school special ed math scores. I didn't expect to see a solution. This was just try anything to see if it helps. Here in Weston, we observed a program centered on a supplementary math class, meeting three times a week. The middle school teachers, who knew the students, on their own scheduled selected students for these extra classes, not leaving it to other school schedulers. The math teachers took charge. Selected by whoever needed the most help, all the students in the supplementary classes were special education students, those students formerly dismissed from higher level learning altogether in earlier days.

Here all the math teachers knew their curriculum well because they met regularly on the grades six through twelve math curriculum. These teachers knew that parents were ambitious for learning here, and the teachers too were eager to do well. Parent involvement here was intense. Because these math teachers each cared, I sensed there wasn't always consensus, with somewhat different opinions, but they settled on loose agreement. Those discussions were lively, and key as they worked out a good plan. In the supplementary classes, teachers either forecasted concepts that they knew were coming up in the regular classes, or spent more time on skills to nail down learning, or just provided supplementary big idea concepts for math understanding, such as working on projects with manipulatives. No one dictated to the teachers what to teach in the supplementary classes, and there was no math program book to follow. The supplementary work was teacher-created and teacher led.

In one class we observed, the teacher sat on the floor with students as together they discussed building a tower that involved math concepts. Another classroom we visited focused on a math understanding concept the teacher developed with the students. All these classes were taught only by math teachers, not special education teachers, who are skilled in understanding special ed students but didn't necessarily have the deep math understanding. No special education teacher was in the classroom, probably breaking a state law. The supplementary teacher also was intentionally not the regular course teacher, so that students could learn from a different person. When I asked one teacher how many of these students in his class were special ed students, he had to turn around and look. "All of them," he said. He didn't see them as different, just his students.

These students here whom we visited each had a disability that interferes with learning. Spending more time on learning benefits special education students. But later research informed that additional math has to be learning that aligns with or complements the regular course. The math teachers coordinated well all dimensions of this learning. While they didn't always agree on every specific feature, they shared the same goal of developing math understanding.

One student told us visitors, "This class takes the stress out of math." They saw their teachers cared. In these smaller classes, at one point I observed the teacher crouching down and explaining to a single student, eye to eye, using the six-inch conversation. We were never able to reproduce that model in Sussex, but I was hugely encouraged to see how well such dedicated and skilled teachers made this work.

This wealthy Boston suburb where a supplemental supportive course worked wasn't just riding on their demographics to get their high scores in math that few elsewhere matched. Time, planning and the school systemwide value of focus on learning made math work for all. Their middle school-high school math department chair ensured focus. Dedication and skill were developed in the frequent meetings. Since every math teacher knew the middle school through high school curriculum, the understandings and skills for each year, the learning fit the curriculum. The process that helped was streamlined. Nothing was haphazard.

I thought as I left the school happy, even though I couldn't replicate this, "How nice to see a program created that really works." This was inspiring. It was always a delight to see high scores, and then explore further to see how it was that this happened. Means of empowerment varies. The public state tests simply confirm great learning, and showing advanced work for the most struggling students and how this happens is exciting to see.

"New Kids" in Town

While we never conquered the special education students' math quandary, there were other victories. My other big challenge in Sussex was that I was hearing from all sides about "new kids" in town. It turned out that new low-income housing was burgeoning. Families from racially diverse nearby communities were filling the schools. "New kids" was the code word term for low-income African-American students now entering classrooms. It was said these students behaved differently than long-term town low-income racially different students. I finally located a person who recorded data, and saw in racial group numbers that this increase in population wasn't just myth or rumor or perception—the Black students percentage had increased substantially in just a few years. Since I wasn't in classrooms, I couldn't assess behaviors, but teachers and principals reported that these newer to town students were often more recalcitrant. The charge of difficulty was leveled too at their parents, who boldly advocated for their children. This pervasive term "new kids" implied that these weren't families who'd gone through this school system, to learn the content and behaviors here. I worried about this issue of acceptance of more challenging students. I went into action.

With the refrain that these students were different from the Black students who were born and raised in town, and who went through the elementary schools, where they'd learned (at least in teachers' minds) to be more school-oriented, I sought a way to help. Since I wasn't in the schools much, but located in the central office, plus new to the town myself, I had no idea if this seemingly pervasive belief regarding "new kids" was accurate or myth. I do know it was a dominant belief among Sussex educators, and had been presented this way even to the school board, that Black kids acting up, less cooperative in behavior, and doing more poorly academically weren't "Sussex kids." The concept that we'd seen in Weston of embracing and lifting students not up to par seemed a foreign concept here. I wanted to act on the racial divide issue, to help "new kids" adjust, and help others see the need to better help.

Challenged to better acclimate principals and teachers to a more diverse student population, I went to work, first inviting African-American administrators from other districts to meet with and enlighten administrators. I then located a dynamic African-American principal, Troy, in another district, and brought him to speak with our principals. Our rattled middle school principal Tom—with the dual problems of poor math scores in special ed and more challenging students and parents—told me he was soothed by Troy's statement, "These parents want what we all want, the best education for their kids." Tom hired a Black assistant to just walk the halls all day, to serve as a role model.

Reading Helps Change Minds

I located a common reading that seemed to speak to racial differences, *Why Do All the Colored Kids Sit Together in the Cafeteria?* This book explains affinity groups, to help develop more understanding of and empathy for students of color. In general, students will naturally meet with those more like themselves. I purchased piles of copies of this book and called a meeting in the summer—unpaid—for Troy to discuss this book with teachers. Fifty teachers showed up, representing all our schools, in the middle of summer, with relaxed, tanned faces, in summertime dress, happy and eager to learn. They just wanted to figure out how to best work with their students. This summer reading discussion was a turning point.

When school resumed in the fall, I began to hear from teachers about more of their Black students coming to their classrooms to visit after school, a sign that these classrooms became more welcoming. Complaints about new kids dissipated. Having had a common text reading with discussion, and outside of school, in more relaxed summer, helped open up minds. This intervention of openly discussing how to accept those of racial difference, with administrators and teachers, set a tone that new kids or not, all students merited respect and support. There was no question that more of both was needed. Discussion with a common reading and an outside discussion leader of color helped re-orient thinking and practice.

Forever Budget Crises

With the third grade reading dilemma addressed, full kindergarten through high school curriculum writing moving smoothly, "new kids" issues discussed, desperate and failed attempts to improve math, all in one year, plus my acquiring competitive state grants, now the superintendent casually mentioned in my second year that we were headed to a budget crisis.

I'd been well aware of this quagmire of budget problems that upend schools' smooth operation. As the high-tech economy rose and fell, Fairfield had been dependent on its one small high-tech company that grew and contracted with national technology ups and downs. The drama of failed town votes and painful planning regarding which staff members to "cut"—who to fire —was familiar to me. And I knew well too from Scottsdale the harsh impact of budget constraints. It's the educators in classrooms who keep schools great. Staff cuts are not only painful in losing a person but also hurt everyone's morale. Class sizes soar. But at least in Fairfield, the parent group on steroids had bailed the schools out, every time, always rallying votes to pass a new increased budget. In Sussex, though, that fierce parent support was lacking. Parents here weren't as intensely involved. I rarely saw parents, who were everywhere in Fairfield, turning out at open school board meetings, meeting with us administrators, around every corner, but not in Sussex. A parent push is needed to promote a town vote to override a budget limit. I read the tea leaves.

In forewarning, I'd been told by teachers upon arrival that the Sussex schools had a year earlier lost a community vote to protect some school positions, but the school board then saved these positions with some last-minute town funding. This to me at the time seemed irrelevant to my job here, but now I better understood. I began to attend open community meetings, and meetings with town officials and the town finance officer, to keep an eye on what was going on with the budget. Though these discussions were anxiety-producing to sit through—no one mentioned the quality of learning—I didn't want to again be blindsided by something like the school board vote to eliminate professional development days or fire the business manager that I'd seen in Scottsdale.

So I paid attention, while the superintendent was away, making a four-week tour of China with an education group, when at one evening meeting, the town business manager made the ominous statement I'd heard so often in Fairfield, "The schools have to tighten their belts." Bells went off in my head. I knew what that euphemism meant: teacher cuts, limited resources, a tight next year's budget, low morale, moving backward instead of ahead. Plush funds help. Tight budgets constrain learning.

Here in Sussex a teacher had told me of one book that would work well for third grade students. I thought about its value, and ordered the colorful, child-friendly hardback books. This teacher then later smiled and thanked me. She knew I'd simply ordered them. I trusted her judgement. This type of support, of ordering a helpful text, easy at one time, with funds available, would not continue with a budget crisis.

A district curriculum director's job is invisible especially to those outside schools. In Fairfield, a small, involved town where word flies quickly, I knew parents there saw my work. I'd been invisible to the community in Scottsdale, with one kind principal telling me the administrators were protecting me, keeping me out of sight, so as to shield me from becoming a budget cut target. They liked me in that basement. A school system business manager and watchful superintendent protect funds from getting out of control, not a popular role, but essential. But in these summer meetings with town officials, with the town business administrator wailing about the town's tight budget, I knew my position was vulnerable. When townspeople are voting their own money away in higher property taxes, a relatively highly paid assistant superintendent, even one influencing better learning, is less valued than a kindergarten teacher for one's own child, maintaining small classes. I once again looked around to check out other job openings.

Everyone Understands a Leaky Ceiling

The Sussex superintendent retired the next year. The school board hired as new superintendent the experienced, articulate Wellesley Middle School principal, who'd worked closely with the superintendent there, the right person for the Sussex job of winning a budget vote. A politically savvy guy coming in from an involved-parent community and used to working well with parents, John knew how to win town votes, including mobilizing parents. He quickly posted a clear, simple and visually appealing, reader-friendly PowerPoint on the district web site home page stating exactly what would go next if the new town budget vote for school funds didn't pass. But this was after the devastating blow to the schools of a failed budget vote. Teachers were let go, class size exploded, I left. I wasn't going to sit around to watch a school system self-immolate.

Another school in this same town though, before John arrived, knew exactly how to win a budget vote. I wasn't required to attend town meetings, all focused on votes on budgets, not my favorite issue, but my earlier districts had taught me to pay attention. There was always theater. In my first year's attendance at a Sussex town meeting to vote for the coming year's school budget approval, I saw the importance of dramatizing the need for funds. Sussex's vocational school made a vivid plea to fund repairs to a leaky ceiling. This trade school that was outside the town school system but still a part of the town on its own taught specialized work skills such as cosmetology, carpentry, electrical skills, training for good jobs, a nice support for students to move right into paying jobs. We were competing for the same town funds.

At this school budget community vote, held in the spacious high school auditorium, the energetic vocational school leader stood at the front of the auditorium, commanding attention. He spoke heatedly on the need for ceiling repairs, and pointed upward. We could see the water pouring in. Everyone understood a leaky ceiling.

Rumor later was that the vocational school wasn't going to use their new funds for a leaky ceiling. That leaky ceiling didn't exist.

The vocational school was smart enough to make their desperate plea for funds in an auditorium packed with taxpayers. Also, a surprising number of new people joined this meeting right at the time of this vote. This group came in late in the meeting, and with perfect timing, sat, voted, and walked out. Their increased budget vote passed.

Our own schools presentation, on the other hand, was only a flimsy call to support the public schools, "for the children," with no specifics. I knew we were doomed. Now with the looming budget crisis, I went into action. Practiced now in the job hunt, I snared a new job over the summer, this one in an affluent community. No budget worries, I figured. When I met with the Sussex principals in late August to talk with them about my leaving, one principal commented quietly, with the looming budget vote coming up, not at all accusingly, "So you're the rat leaving the sinking ship?" This was Bill, who'd been on the search committee that had hired me. I responded from the heart, "I feel bad about that." Bill smiled and said kindly, "You have to protect yourself." Surprisingly to me, this empathy was a common sentiment. I met with a teacher whom I asked to take over one of my large grant-funded projects, and she looked at me and said on my departure, "You'll do well there." This was a generous thought when she didn't know if she, as a new teacher would soon lose her own job, since it's always those without tenure, not based on quality of work, who get cut.

The January budget vote, after I'd left, failed by fifty votes. The plan was to have first one vote, then expect a second to win when voters saw the losses coming with the first vote. But now district leaders were told to not even try to have that second vote. It would have been hard to continue to try to help make the schools better when teachers didn't know if they'd have a job. There was a massacre of firings after the first vote failed. I was gone by then.

When I later called the principal Bill—as I was safely now off in my new high demographic district—to congratulate him when the new superintendent rallied community members to pass a new more costly budget, Bill said poignantly, "It's hard to ever recover from having over thirty students in a third grade class." I saw sharply now how, though I could bring in funds for my own projects, a district leader has to attend closely to budget issues to protect the schools from setback with lack of funds. A recent educator salary hike, always proposed by teacher unions, had increased the Sussex budget. And not everyone values district leadership on learning, that invisible but in my view essential puppet master role, one who keeps a sharp eye on academic needs and attempts to salvage a tip in the wrong direction, often successful, always the guardian.

CHAPTER TWENTY-ONE

Paradise: Strong Teachers, Engaged Students

I was thrilled to be next offered the district curriculum director position in a dream spot, Glastonbury, known for its top schools. I'd always seen this small district as a bright, shining school system, a lighthouse, with enlightened leaders and dedicated teachers helping students to be the best of the best. Having seen missteps in other schools and districts, I was delighted to land in a place where I believed things worked smoothly, even elegantly, making wise decisions in civil discourse. With quality of learning a priority here, I was confident I'd be welcomed as head of teaching and learning. It didn't take long for me to discover that under the placid surface things were not always so rosy.

For their part, educators enjoyed their bright, respectful, fun, kids, and school was all about education. Through humor and good will, teachers maintained good rapport and high expectations for students. Classes I visited blew me away. I was impressed and had to smile as clever teachers delicately straightened out off-topic comments. Recalcitrance as a pattern didn't exist.

Soon I discovered other issues. As just one of many projects going awry, the new superintendent who'd hired me, Raleigh, a southern gentleman long experienced in the district leadership role, asked that I take up technology integration as a project, which I was happy to do. I knew that we needed to better harness technology, potentially a huge asset for expediting and expanding learning. Little did I know that the school board had initiated its own technology committee, working on the issue in their own private meetings—a setup for a train wreck. Having different groups separately addressing the same issue shouldn't have been a surprise. I early on saw that if ever there were silos in a school district, this was the model. Everyone here was eager for fine schools, but tripped over each other on the way to bring this about. Meanwhile, teachers excelled, following their own paths to excellence.

As Raleigh wisely wanted me to be out and about, learning new ideas and strategies, a path I was eager to follow, I attended a large statewide school technology conference. Apple's iPad had just come out, and at this conference I saw well-attended presentations on using iPads for schools, and delighted teachers eager to use this new tool. After the conference, I reported at an administrator's meeting on the excitement about this new easy-to-carry manual device. I then learned from Raleigh that the three elementary school principals put together a pilot program based on using iPads and were requesting funds to purchase a set number of these mobile devices. This is what we want to see, principals picking up a good new project and running with it.

Normally I'd have known about the principals' plan earlier, but I hadn't been informed of it, and was just happy they followed up on my tech conference report on iPads to a submit proposal for funding. They had a good plan: Students would select from a range of downloaded books to read on their own, increasing opportunity to develop reading comprehension and fluency. Students could work at their own pace. The teachers had selected specific inexpensive virtual texts for the iPads. The plan was that teachers would take iPads home over the summer to learn on their own how to use them, then introduce these to students in the next year's start. It was a nicely thought-out plan. These principals were an effective team, close and collaborative, meeting together every Friday, though not reaching outside their own schools' common grade level. They were a force that helped their own schools well, but pretty much oblivious to district and other school levels, possibly fearful of constraint if they told others of their initiatives. It turned out that this was a land of silos.

Raleigh asked me to attend a community funding group's meeting that night, at which the iPad proposal would be presented and discussed. One funding committee member at the meeting asked why they were seeking the same number of iPads for each of the three schools, instead of the funds for just one school, illustrative of how others may not understand school issues. The principal Brian responded, "Well, that's ok, as long as it's for *my* school." Everyone laughed. This principal group was a team.

Although I hadn't known the principals were working on this project, I loved the proposal. So we were all astonished when after this committee approved the request, with everyone happy, Ken, the business manager, lashed out at the principals. We later learned that he had been conferring with the school board and served on their technology committee. No one else knew anything about that, nor that the school board committee on technology even existed. The principals were shocked, clueless about why they were being yelled at. They were proud of the plan they'd carefully developed. Fortunately, the outside community funding committee approved the proposal; the iPads got into the hands of students.

This wasn't the only clash, just typical. Initially unaware of these two other groups of the elementary principals and, on their own, the school board too looking at bringing better technology to the district, at Raleigh's request, I formed my own technology committee, which I notified Raleigh of. This must have seemed like spinning plates for Raleigh, a juggling act, but pushing for technology use was in the air at this time, and finding good use made this district very much in line with the times, even ahead of the pack. I chose administrators, teachers, technology assistants, students, parents, and a school board member for my own committee. All five schools were represented. In wide-eyed approval, the district technology director commented on the convening of such a multi-level group, stating "We've never done this before." I realized later that from this larger group, one of the principals, Brian, spun off to help create the iPad proposal, but not informing anyone else, a strange mode in such a small school system, for a small group just going right to the community funding committee for the costs, but not communicating well to others, and bypassing the normal budget development process that's more open. It was a speedy way to get a new project going. I admired the principals' ingenuity and zeal.

At one of the meetings of my own technology committee, I learned about a National History Day class computer project. I asked an eleventh grader, Connor, to report on his experience with a longtime research project in US history courses. His report, which included two research projects he'd completed, one in tenth grade and the other in eleventh grade, gave us all an inside look at what was already being done to integrate technology and learning, most likely unbeknownst to the school board and business manager. The project was excellent.

Student Research Wins the Day

I knew that some schools didn't require all their students to write research papers, often only the "college prep" track, a huge disservice to students, since it's key to preparing students for college and careers. But in this district student research began early.

Starting in fourth grade here, children could choose to do a research project in either science or social studies. They then showcased their projects at a school-day open house, with most using technology for research and presentation. One student's project was on Title IX, the federal regulations for gender equity in school sports. I watched, impressed, as this small child led her audience through a superb PowerPoint presentation on this subject, explaining how Title IX required schools to include females as well as males in sports activities. Her work showed that this accomplished fourth grader had researched the subject well, taken notes, built the PowerPoint by herself, and reported nicely on her findings to parents and other outside guests.

Then, since this district had the middle school and high school in the same building, the history department met for grades six through twelve with the history department chair supervising that full grade span, nicely connecting the two schools, the one link I saw here. So, academically, since the department chair had initiated the National History Day research projects, middle school students also participated every year in this project which Connor now reported on that operated through the national social studies organization. This project was entered in school and regional competitions, requiring students to sharpen both research and technology skills by creating a well-researched report and presenting to varied audiences, evaluated in public by community members and subject experts serving as judges. Such presentations prepare students for real-world work as well as college level research and presentation.

What was different about this research project is that students created a web site to present their information in place of the traditional drudgery of researching on one's own, writing a research paper and submitting that just to one teacher. Students worked in teams to build the web site, not off alone: The learning potential multiplied with tech use and teamwork.

I asked Connor to present at my technology committee meeting. He described two different team projects, one on the Spanish-American War, the other on the theme of innovation, with the national organization setting a theme to study each year. On innovation, Connor's group had decided to research the development of guitars under innovator Les Paul, with teen appeal, a winning project, using primary sources in interviewing guitar players. As Connor easily toggled back and forth between his two websites on the conference room's projection board and talked about his work, I watched, impressed. Every step was exactly right. I marveled too at how all of the literacy Standards were developed in this one project. His work reflected exactly what school should be. This project integrated student engagement, teamwork, Standards-learning, and research. It was like someone had turned on the lights.

The National History Day organization provides students with strict guidelines. The project centers on collaboration. Students work together to build a website using the organization's online template to submit team-approved posts, and then report on their project to a school and community group. As with science fairs—another team-based project common especially in high schools—a committee of teachers and outside judges assesses students' final projects and selects winners, who then move on to regional, state, and national competitions. Seeking public recognition—not simply turning in a rushed research paper—inspires good work. Engagement spikes learning.

Glastonbury's students regularly triumphed at the National History Day national project competitions in Washington, DC. Their work involved the same kind of research activities many schools require, such as citing sources to avoid plagiarism, but with the added more engagement of the team approach to learning, and the opportunity to build a website to post their results. Ted Sizer would have loved this project. It used his preferred method for assessing student performance, one that demonstrates the learning process through a presentation of information, which Sizer called exhibitions of learning.

As the students on Connor's team delved into their topic and conferred with each other, new ideas arose. They determined their focus and sharpened their research, employing Sizer's student-as-worker Principle. Technology allowed for easy revision as students' understanding evolved, or as they located better information, just deleting an earlier post. When the group felt they were too confined by the national organization's provided template, Connor used his programming skills (normally worked on only in another unrelated course) to break through the template walls and expand their website.

As the team worked together to select information and cite appropriate sources, they also enjoyed locating graphics to match content, developing the national literacy Standard of "compare visuals and text." They loved finding the best political cartoon to suit the topic, building their capacity for critical analysis. The thesis statement posted on the website home page is limited to thirty words. Honing this for a concise statement of findings was a learning opportunity in itself. No meandering.

While the students were highly engaged with this project, teachers monitored their work, to ensure focus. Working with these self-motivated students was a delight, with learning coached, not lectured. Teachers provided Boston Public Library membership access to online databases, so students weren't confined to their school library or having to trudge into Boston, or always checking to validate a site. As team members scoured the databases for the best material on their topic and the right graphics, they also selected brief video clips that conveyed relevant information, and figured out how to place them in the best spots on their site, always analyzing. They took care because this would go public.

Our technology committee members too were dazzled as Connor confidently toggled between his two projects. He casually reported that one student on his team had located all the Boston area professors who were experts in the specific historical period they were researching. They emailed all of these professors a question. One wrote back, "Usually I don't respond to outside questions like yours, but since you've asked such a good question, I will," instilling pride in these tenth graders. The team interviewed the professor via Skype. He must have loved sharing what he knew with these eager kids.

In this project, the team members mastered, with self-directed learning, all of the English Common Core Standards of close reading, comprehending informational text, noting central ideas and supporting details in text, conducting research and documenting sources, collaboration on writing. And by studying one area in depth, they learned research skills they could then apply to other studies. The history project demonstrated Sizer's Principle of "Less is more," with more focus on just one topic. The meeting of minds developed in teamwork would serve these students well. Connor's ease with presenting would also take him far. It seemed ironic that students were developing the communication skills and consensus-building lacking at the upper power levels of the school system, where discussion across borders was nil.

This kind of history project is Standards learning at its best. The fact that these teachers hadn't aimed to have students develop all of the national literacy Standards shows how much the Standards are just key basic learning expectations. And online research developed from a need to know serves students well in life.

When the history department head Kevin thanked the school's other subject department heads at a meeting for allowing students to work on this project in their classes, the art department chair, who taught computer graphics, said, "Well, they were doing computer graphics." It's rare for teachers to let students work on another faculty member's project in their own classes. Here collaboration and mutual respect reigned, among teachers.

Judges Aren't Always Right

Outside judges of student projects can vary. Connor's team won at their school, but not at the regional level. Other projects from the school were successful at both the regional and state levels and then went on to the national competition. When their young history teacher respectfully approached Connor's team to ask if they were ready to talk about their loss, they casually said, "Oh, yeah, we overheard our judges saying in advance that they didn't like projects presented with all the bells and whistles, so we knew ours wouldn't win." They were analytical about the judging, and took this rejection in stride. They understood that those particular judges, with their own expectations from an earlier era, would question the more skilled technology use, possibly consider it diverting, as the students delighted in using digital skills to take the product as far as they could, learning as they went. These students had the objectivity and resilience to face rejection needed for the real world. They knew they'd learned a lot and were proud of their work.

Although Connor's team's history project didn't receive the recognition they deserved, his team's science project won at the state level, in a competition held at MIT. The university website immediately posted the titles of all the participating science projects, incomprehensible to a non-science person, along with the names of each student participant, a nice online recognition. MIT also held social events where these budding scientists enjoyed talking about science among peers, in advanced conversation. When I saw Connor in the corridor one day and congratulated him on his win in science, he told me he'd been surprised. I wasn't. The collaborative skills, leadership, and research ability sharpened by the history project carried over to the science project. All I could think of was, watch out for Connor. Connor went on to George Washington University to major in political science, and now works for a Washington, DC digital research company.

Exceptional Teachers Strategize Learning

Glastonbury's teachers also treated lower-performing students with care, respect, and the right amount of pushing, always expecting the best. Their credentials were impressive. One high school math teacher had worked for Microsoft; he told me he chose to take a less lucrative teaching position in order to be able to see more of his family. A middle school science teacher had been a finalist to join the Challenger spaceship team of astronauts. These exceptional educators maintained high expectations of their students and worked with each in a collegial, supportive way, always keeping the bar high.

In another example of collaborative excellence here, one day I was looking at various online MCAS reports. By accident, I located an astonishing graph. The ninth-grade science test scores were off the charts, the biology scores consistently high, and consistently well above the state average. I sent this high-performance data chart to one of the teachers. She passed it on to her colleagues with a self-congratulatory "WE ROCK!" When I asked her how this had happened, I expected the usual response of, "We had good kids that year." But no, Lisa emailed me that the teachers had gotten together and aligned their course with the state biology Standards—a curriculum director's dream. Whatever they wanted to teach that was not in the Standards, they taught after the test. It usually takes moving to the bottom in state tests for many teachers to learn to do this type of careful analysis and planning on the Standards work. These dedicated teachers had simply done it on their own, without prodding. They wanted to show that their students had not only learned, but learned what was expected.

In another small scale victory here, a sixth grade teacher asked me for students' scores from their fifth grade tests, taken at the three elementary schools. The next time I saw Sherry, her face glowed; she stood tall, walked with a bounce. She delightedly told me she'd taken a Saturday to pull her students' scores out of the fifth grade lists, and compared those scores with the scores from her year with those same students. She had worked on the common writing tested, and saw their writing scores had improved immensely, smoothing out the varied writing coming from the elementary schools.

I happened to say to her, "You probably can tell which fifth grade school your students come from." Sherry replied, "I can tell what teacher they had." Varied teaching style is fine. Varied learning holds the risk of cheating some students.

Addressing a Challenge

At the same time, despite superb work accomplished in so many corners of this district, third grade reading scores in one of the three elementary schools had fallen into the category of "Needing Improvement," below "Proficient." Since it was my job to maintain standards, I had to be the one to deliver this bad news to the principal, Brian. As federal law required, he wrote a letter to parents. We hoped not many would notice his note. Parents noticed. The low rating struck fear into their hearts.

Bravely, Brian called an evening meeting to explain the issue to parents. The superintendent and I attended to show support. The school's teachers also showed up; they weren't going to leave their principal out on a limb alone. It was a dicey yet courteous meeting. No one yelled. However, I overheard anxious kindergarten parents sitting behind me express worry about whether their child would be able to learn in this school. They wondered if they should transfer somewhere else. But one parent asked if they could have more meetings like this one. It was refreshing, she said, to be able to talk about schoolwork instead of whether cupcakes should be banished at children's school birthday celebrations, considered by the principals not healthy, but to parents' and student disappointment. Brian would have greatly preferred to have the cupcake discussion.

Meanwhile, I went into action. I visited teachers' classrooms, talked with them, purchased new materials, and provided extra professional development. I invited teachers to the superintendent's office and walked them through the third grade reading test so they could see exactly what skills were tested, an exercise I knew was tedious and painful for them, perhaps trying to avoid this later by improving those scores. As I'd hoped, this unwelcome, annoying meeting got their attention. I didn't tell them what to do to ensure students learned these skills; I intentionally left it up to them, with the hope they'd correct their practices. It worked.

In a stroke of luck, I learned that national literacy expert Irene Fountas was presenting on the topic of helping struggling readers. I asked Brian if his teachers could attend. It was just four weeks before that year's state test, and I was afraid he wouldn't want anyone out of the classroom. Most principals wouldn't have agreed, not valuing as much as I did professional development that can spark new ideas. But Brian said yes.

Fountas's professional development session was pivotal. Teachers heard this national expert's ideas on how to develop reading ability at a time when they felt most pressured and most discouraged. The teachers told me that one of them, who'd that year moved from kindergarten to third grade, a whole new level, spoke individually with Dr. Fountas after the session. Everyone was thrilled that this happened. All were re-energized, armed with new skills, and inspired to push harder, especially with slower students. It was the perfect time to be exposed to new strategies and thinking. The reading scores that year jumped, moving this school back up to a higher level. We all breathed a sigh of relief.

Excellent Remote Math Professional Development is Dismissed

A virtual math professional development grant-funded project too worked. Even in this high-income district, middle school special education students weren't reaching proficiency in math. We needed help. In response to this challenge, I was able to garner a $100,000, two-year state grant to improve math. Top state-based national math consultants would work with our middle school math teachers in remote professional development sessions, along with others statewide, making grueling travel unnecessary.

This small, all-white suburban district appeared all wealthy, and had fairly good test scores, not the conditions needed to win competitive state grants. We weren't the kind of low-income diverse district the state wanted to provide extra funds to, so I arranged to team up with a larger urban district to acquire the grant. I participated in the department of education grant meetings and drove to the in-person sessions held in the other district for the involvement required. But I put the work of coordinating with teachers in the hands of one of the capable eighth grade math teachers. We stayed in close touch.

As I was walking through the corridor one day, this school coordinator ran out of her classroom to rave, "This is how it's going to be!" I had no idea what she was talking about. She raved about how helpful the convenience of remote learning was for her and colleagues. They appreciated the regular communication with math experts experienced in remote work, the excellent new electronic resources perfect for their courses, additional computers, and the fact that special education teachers were learning alongside the regular education teachers. This was also a nice connection of the two very different districts, with me conferring with the other district's grant liaisons, the state people and the math consultants, and special ed and regular education math teachers.

But when I started to report on this complex but smooth-running project at a school board meeting, I saw glazed eyes. It was dead quiet. I felt all the oxygen was sucked out of the room. No one there had children who needed more help with math, so this project was irrelevant to them. Plus, with its silos, the school board possibly harbored other complaints which I had no idea of. I sat down, relieving them of having to hear about assistance for students who weren't their own. Although math scores improved as a result of this professional development, and the middle school was lifted from the lower rating, no one at the top level of leadership cared.

Although such professional development projects such as the valuable math new ideas and resources brought impressive results, and teachers at the high school were a model of collaboration, the adults in power positions were locked in warfare, unwilling to confer across lines. I found myself dodging bullets. It was sad that though classrooms were exciting, communication and collaboration among adults outside of classrooms were so lacking in this otherwise fine school system. Being in the schools and working with the teachers was a haven for me in this otherwise challenging spot of landmines always just a step away.

CHAPTER TWENTY-TWO

Trouble in Paradise

I learned more fully from my experience in Glastonbury that involved parents can be a double-edged sword. Parents can be wonderfully supportive at home, backing up teachers by urging their children to complete homework, get good grades. Parents contribute to school improvement by raising legitimate concerns. When they unite to lobby townspeople on heavily contested issues such as voting for more funding to help schools meet ever-growing needs at the cost of increasing their own property taxes, parent group assistance is crucial.

But parents can also intrude in educational areas where they understandably aren't aware of complexities. It's not uncommon to have a school board member lobby for his son to play more on a basketball or football team; coaches are given instructions. When parents intervene in school issues, stepping over boundaries, it's disconcerting. When parents band together on a controversial issue, it can result in warfare. And when individual parents, coming from their successes in the business world, serve on the powerful school board, and are used to having people move at their command, it can be the biggest disaster ever.

Glastonbury was charming, on the exterior. Just a fifteen-minute drive into downtown Boston, residents either worked from home remotely in tech jobs, owned their own companies, or commuted in to well paid big city jobs. I found many community members and parents well-educated, intelligent, handsome, ambitious, high-powered, supportive of first-rate education, and open to two-way conversation. But others were the worst.

Many parents in high demographic communities volunteer in schools, helpfully taking on the drudgery of photocopying materials for teachers and assisting in classrooms. Often parent groups host celebratory lunches for teachers, providing a welcome break from classroom demands and a chance to visit among themselves while being served and treated like adults. Such relaxed occasions are a way parents show their gratitude for those who teach their children.

In Glastonbury, a local foundation initiated by community members fundraised to help the schools. These were super-nice people with impressive credentials, some with experience and expertise, devoted to helping the schools. The foundation's co-chairs, polite, accomplished professionals, visited an administrators' meeting at the start of the school year and asked us what we wanted. This group had earlier ensured that every classroom had a computer projection system, unique for the era, a nice collaborative effort using a combination of district funds, grants, and the foundation's funding.

However, others were not so helpful. Because some parents and community members were empowered in the work world, they assumed they also knew best about schools. As employers, some were used to ordering others around. But schools are different from the business world. And protected by tenured positions, educators aren't always responsive to others telling them what to do. School is trickier to work with, more layered than the business world, where an end product is clearer.

Teachers often work hard to establish good relationships with their students' parents from the start of the year to avoid unexpected conflict later. But sometimes a glitch in effective two-way communication occurs. When sparks fly, a parent may go directly to the school board or superintendent with a complaint. This is easier than going directly to a teacher with an issue. A parent might demand out of the blue that a teacher be fired for assigning a low grade to his or her child, a situation that happened elsewhere that I got involved with that took some time to negotiate.

Normally, when working to make improvements in a school system, the superintendent leads the way. He or she hires staff, including a person to lead teaching and learning efforts. The superintendent carries responsibility for all aspects of a school district. Directly tied to the superintendent is the person in the school system who is most involved in teaching and learning—in this case, me. The curriculum director does the nitty-gritty work of grants acquisition, keeps a close eye on learning improvement, observes classes to check on practices, creates various teacher groups for needed projects, and provides the school board with updates on progress. In this community here, however, it seemed my position was considered superfluous since many strong-willed parents, often bosses in the workplace, felt they knew best.

A curriculum director's reports to the school board at evening meetings are a tricky enough job in a normal district, since one has to explain the technical aspects of school practice to people who have spent their lives in other professions—as real estate agents, lawyers, technology experts. None of what I did in my new position met with approval from this district's all-powerful school board. The new superintendent who'd brought me in, newly hired himself in July, was fired well before the school year ended.

In theory, a school board, made up of elected representatives of a community, is responsible for overseeing school district policy development. Superintendents know they have to spend a lot of time cultivating good relations with school board members, who often hear complaints from parents or others in the town. The arrangement works well when the board confers with the superintendent on issues raised in this way. Compromises are made, a superintendent may speak with a teacher, call a meeting. Ideally, the board and superintendent meet frequently. A superintendent usually drops everything to hear from a board member. But when a rift arises, the superintendent is always outnumbered. If the dispute is not resolved successfully, the board has the power to fire him or her. There's usually a "payout" deal to soften the blow, which doesn't begin to heal the pain of sudden firing, often for a misstep that sneaks up from behind. A superintendent will go along with a school board's directive, just to keep the job. Sometimes that isn't the deal made.

It can be even harder for the person responsible for curriculum to communicate with a school board, but sometimes both sides tolerate one another. I had a lucky moment in Monson when the superintendent was late to a school board meeting, so members asked me to report on the after-school math tutoring program I had initiated and oversaw. Given time and attention, I was able to explain the project to people who otherwise had no understanding of what I was doing in my job. It happened that the superintendent, when he arrived, nicely backed up the information I'd presented. But this was a unique situation for me that never happened elsewhere. A wise school board, or a representative, meets to confer with a curriculum person off-camera to clarify issues.

Some community leaders inspire civility in a school system, and help non-educators understand issues and situations. Others are unable to. Here in Glastonbury, Raleigh was always civil, articulate, polite, able to converse,. But during my time here, neither tolerance, discussion, nor explanation was valued. The school board, normally supportive on school issues, here was tightly connected with the community, their neighbors, who voted them into office, and it seemed everyone felt they knew better.

With the curriculum person tied to the superintendent, any ill will between school board members and the superintendent spills over to the curriculum director. Then there's little chance of positive communication, let alone survival. This district—despite having so many bright, involved, and seemingly enlightened constituents—was an extreme case of school board-administration dysfunction, not uncommon.

I'd never before heard of a superintendent, especially an experienced, highly competent one, such as Raleigh, in a blow-up over the budget, being yelled at by a school board member. This contentiousness, apparently a common mode in the district, was new to me. The conflict only worsened over the year, with a bloodbath starting in the spring. Meanwhile, despite the chaos at the upper level, superb teachers cared for their students, emanating support and connection. In the end, it was the teachers who moved collaboratively to correct the dysfunction.

An example occurred here of the school board wanting to impose an electronic system on the schools without understanding faculty issues. The school board, claiming to represent parents, wanted the high school to adopt a new electronic reporting system that would allow parents to monitor their children's work, a decision normally made within a school, and after conferring with others. Teachers at the high school told me they'd already been required to learn three new electronic programs within two years. The time wasn't right for another one. Not everyone can easily master four different new electronic applications while overloaded with classroom work.

There wasn't just a communication breakdown in this case. It was the school board's belief that as the ones running the district, they could simply demand adoption of this new tool for parental oversight. When the longtime, personable, and knowledgeable district technology director, a favorite among administrators and teachers, didn't instantly respond to the board's bidding, he was fired. There was no discussion. It was just one of many dramas.

It seemed strange that with this school district just a small town, without the bureaucracy of a big city, there was distance among groups, brick walls isolating groups. Here school board members and parents ran into each other on the street, in the grocery store, and on social occasions, promoting varied views, while teachers and administrators, most of whom did not live in the town, with pricey housing, were absorbed in another world, the bustling world of school. At one evening meeting in the superintendent's office, a community member came and spoke to gain approval to tear down one of the elementary schools to build a mall, for town income. The board agreed to his proposal, bypassing school input.

Informal school board meetings in the superintendent's office were fractious. There was a lot of shouting. When a new member asked a more experienced one what it was like to serve on the school board, she paused, and said, "It's like being in a blender." In addition to tight ties to community members, board members seemed to primarily look out for their own children. Who doesn't want the best for their child? But explaining complicated teaching and learning issues to such an especially entitled group was difficult, if not impossible. No one asked for explanation.

Charming Town, Entitled Parents

In addition to having a fractious school board, the town's involved parents behaved less than ethically. In many districts, community members receive training in how to volunteer in schools, including maintaining respect for privacy since it's important that they not spread around town something they may not understand. Parents are cautioned in volunteer training sessions that it's not their role to judge or to circulate what may be misleading information. But some in this district were happy to report to others whatever they saw. They pervaded the buildings, showing up in main offices and in classrooms, peeking around and spreading rumors. Talk spread through the town like wildfire. I soon got caught in this trap.

One parent volunteer decided I wasn't in my office enough. It then hit me that volunteering in schools was a great way to spy. In my previous jobs in various districts, I hadn't stayed in my office a lot, because I was out visiting schools, sitting in on classes, attending district and state level meetings, essential with the fast-moving state initiatives. And in this position, my boss, Raleigh, wanted me to be out and about, learning what I could about what would benefit the town's teachers and students. But word swept through the town that I wasn't spending sufficient time where they believed I belonged. When Raleigh told me not to leave my office, constraining my work, I knew it wasn't his idea. He was just trying to keep a lid on a frantically boiling pot. This accusation against me I found amusing since many if not most adults here worked remotely—not sitting in a prescribed office anywhere. Sitting in my small office hidden off in the middle school limited my ability to work effectively, though at least I avoided the fireworks going off over in the central office.

A Darkening Budget Forecast

Added to the who's in charge and over-involvement issues was the hot topic of the district budget. Setting school system budgets that all approve can be easy or a challenge. Having a sufficient budget is essential. The school district budget can be a concern to community members, but there's always negotiation with town officials, and usually a proposed budget is accepted by the schools and town officials as a compromise. A town vote is often just pro forma, as details are explained to citizens, and the elected official experts in each area work things out. The school system administration and school board agree on a budget, and the community usually trusts the town officials' approval. Glastonbury, as with many small suburban communities, had no industry helping to pay taxes for school budgets. It was all on the shoulders of property taxpayers. Here residents had had enough of rising taxes. In high demographic districts where parents care deeply about good schools but where many community members struggle with high property taxes this divide can be a dumpster fire waiting to happen.

As an illustration of the tight budget here, because vocal parents made sure each budget vote was passed, making property taxes a stretch, there was a unique arrangement that the middle school principal was also principal of the high school. These two large and very different schools were physically connected, which allowed for cross-school communication, but the principal still had two full-time jobs, constantly moving back and forth between the two parts of one building. It was a setup for failure. The previous superintendent had cut the high school principal position as a cost-savings. Such a dual role is rare.

While I knew this town had always voted for increases in their property taxes to fund education, I hadn't understood well before coming here the stretch it created especially for senior citizens on fixed incomes. Funds for schools made up a high percentage of the town's overall budget, well above ability to pay. I knew my curriculum position was vulnerable, considered expendable, though I had a three-year contract. The district budget was a hot-button issue.

The Hatfields and McCoys

In other towns, school board meetings are not well attended since they can be viewed from home on local cable TV. But in Glastonbury, these meetings provided no-cost theater, with the many strong and differing views. Community members came to watch open combat, and to make their presence known. I made sure not to miss school board meetings, but I attended from the safety of the audience, never choosing to be on stage.

In reaction to ever-rising property taxes, the older, retired, long-time town residents on fixed incomes had formed an official organization called "Enough Is Enough" (EiE), with a dedicated following and a polished website. On the other side were the wonderfully supportive but also uber-aggressive parents who wanted the schools to be the very best for their kids. They had their own organization, called "Save Our Schools" (SOS), and a website. EiE was outnumbered, but managed to strategically gain power. Soon they were able to have all the school board members voted out of office.

When EiE members came to meet with the superintendent and me early in the school year, they went out of their way to be pleasant and diplomatic They were a delight to talk with. Each calmly spoke at length about how much they supported education. One volunteered that she was a former teacher herself. EiE had no agenda for this meeting; they simply wanted to introduce themselves to us. They were nice people. But they were also highly well organized and had a strategic leader. EiE representatives attended every evening school board meeting, sitting up front as a group, making their presence known to the school board and to the public, keen-eyed yet silent. They didn't miss a thing.

SOS was also well-organized and effectively led. These members would scatter themselves around the audience at each school board meeting, listening closely and paying attention to people's reactions. It's normal for a community to have differing viewpoints on taxes and schools. But in this district it was open warfare, and the school board meetings were the battlefield. I was flabbergasted when at one televised public meeting, the chair began the meeting by chastising the EiE members seated right in front of him. The blatant hostility of publicly admonishing people only gave EiE ammunition. They sat quietly and let the chair show his lack of tact and sensitivity.

As in other wealthy communities, all SOS had to do was send out a notice to their parent group to vote in favor of a budget increase. As every budget vote passed, funding for education continually grew, with ever-higher taxes. But now EiE was digging in its heels, determined to stop the momentum. Discussion between the two formal groups was nonexistent. They didn't speak. They fought.

Budget discussions tend to enliven a meeting since developing and gaining approval can be a difficult process. Planning for the coming year begins in January, and after months of work trying to meet schools' needs and also satisfy town officials, the superintendent presents the proposed budget at a school board meeting often held in March. At that time, there may be little discussion, since all that's needed—in normal conditions—is for the agreed-upon budget to pass in an open town citizens' vote at special town meetings. But in Glastonbury, the town open budget approval meeting was like tossing kerosene on a fire. People came prepared, ready to fan the flames. Everyone, it seemed, had a complaint.

After the budget presentations in March, SOS called a meeting with school officials. They were angry that they, as a self-appointed force in the town, hadn't been consulted on the budget. Raleigh invited me to this evening meeting with SOS members in his office. The group's leaders had been characteristically efficient in arranging a time when key participants—outspoken power-players—were available. I admired their logistics in inviting and accommodating the right people for their case. Over a dozen community members, SOS leaders, and parents packed the office that evening. Their behavior was alarming with its vitriol. It began with shouting. One immediately tore into the superintendent, lacerating him for his budget errors. I didn't even understand what the issue was as they pounced on him. Raleigh paused after hearing the attacks and wisely responded, "Well, I should have met with you all before we finalized the budget." I'd never heard of a superintendent having to meet with a community group such as SOS to get their approval, nor to have to take this kind of beating. But here, such groups seemingly had long felt empowered to command attention and influence decisions.

Outside that meeting, things only got worse. One teacher told me that previous school boards had been highly supportive of the schools. Members would warmly hug teachers. One parent, Andy, served on the school board especially well. He'd been head of Mass Insight, a top notch Boston-based education organization, was knowledgeable about schools, and Andy helped the other board members understand why some things would or wouldn't work. He bridged the gaps. Andy had moved to California.

When it seemed things couldn't get worse, at one town meeting, a town official adamantly called for scrutiny of the special education budget. She was right that such programs can be costly to attend well to students with learning disabilities. But Elizabeth, the superb district special education director, had worked long and hard with the previous superintendent to build programs within the schools that averted the high price of sending special education students to expensive programs outside the district. She was saving the district thousands of dollars, and students could stay in the town's schools. Although there was some cost for the local programs, they created huge savings compared with sending students to the costly out-of-district special schools.

But in the war zone of budget discussion, this in-district program was a concept apparently beyond the grasp of hypercritical townspeople focused only on money, and where to cut. From her office, Elizabeth watched the taped, highly charged town meeting demanding examination of the special education budget. She understood that a study of her special education area's budget meant an attack on her well-designed cost-saving programs, and she knew that few would bother to listen to an explanation. Elizabeth had no trouble finding a new position in a nearby quieter town. But many in the district, including school board members, parents, and teachers had greatly appreciated her intelligent, devoted work. Her leaving was a huge loss for the schools.

Elizabeth wasn't the only administrator to leave that year. I'd been hired in August by Raleigh, with his twenty years of experience as superintendent. He was gone in May. He told me that at one meeting with the school board in his office, he'd looked at his hand and it was shaking. He couldn't stop the shaking. His wife ordered him to resign because, she told him, she "wanted to have someone to retire with." Fired on camera at an open school board meeting, with his lawyer present to negotiate lost salary terms, Raleigh came in the next day, packed up his belongings, and was gone. I'd seen dysfunction before. But this took the cake.

After Raleigh was fired, Ken, the business manager, was put in charge as interim superintendent. But when meeting with the high school teachers prior to the new appointment, they asked him if he'd ever been a teacher. He said only that he'd "once thought about being a music teacher." That sealed his fate. Ken didn't last long. A couple of teaching assistants noticed an error in their small paychecks. They went to the head of the district teachers union, who wrote a scathing note to the new school board chair, and Ken was ousted.

With bullets flying that spring, the middle school–high school principal Matt, reacting to the school board making school decisions over his head, not even informing him, also leaped at another job. I was moved out of the middle school to the otherwise empty second-floor of the central office. Working alone in that space allowed me to complete the tedious district grant applications needed to supplement the district budget for the coming year, and to also apply for other jobs, hopefully finding one less dysfunctional. It's hard for teachers to do well in their work with warfare at the higher levels, and administrators leaving in droves. Those working in classrooms worry what new initiatives might be expected of them, how things will change with all new superiors. Morale shifts.

PART FOUR

Re-Envisioning School

CHAPTER TWENTY-THREE

Making A Paradigm Shift Work

The Covid era created a national crisis. The sea change caused by the 2020 pandemic left educators reeling. Going remote was the unthinkable. How could school work without being in school? School changed, dramatically, and not for the better. How to cope was the daily struggle. Educators were advised to do what they could to just try to stay connected with their students remotely. The national statistics on learning loss only reflected what educators knew well: Learning dropped in the absence of school and the classroom. The National Bureau of Statistics reports that one million students left school during the pandemic. Teachers too left.

What's not reflected in national statistics but strikes every teacher's heart is that by students not having been in the tight structure of school day expectations and with classroom required behaviors and protocols, not only is learning level years behind, but errant behavior, from students not having been in classrooms during key formative years, means new techniques to establish the right classroom behaviors for the needed protocols for school to make learning flourish challenge even the most adept teachers. It becomes hard to have the smooth-running school and class behavior of the pre-Covid era. That one or two disrupters in a class who might be mollified earlier now exploded in numbers, to educators' chagrin.

Even in more middle class socio-economic communities, experienced teachers became challenged by erratic behavior by students freed up from the classroom expectations of pre-Covid times. Now it seemed the dam had broken, as recalcitrant behavior multiplied since students had had more freedom when they weren't in school. The absence of social norms for too long at young ages means classes don't run as smoothly anymore. New means for the needed protocols for school to make learning flourish challenged all. "I never wanted to teach my ninth grade students who now behave like and have the learning of seventh-graders," smilingly comments a poised, accomplished high school department head whose classes include AP courses, with even these students set back. She tells me, "I only ever wanted to teach high school, or college." Now longing for the old days means in 2023 longing for the relatively smooth-running 2019, just a few years earlier. Now new ways of working again are required to address the achievement decline coupled with a drop in school norms that hit everywhere.

The dramatic change forced by Covid constitutes a paradigm shift. A new way of thinking and working is needed to address the challenge that remains, even though we're back in school. It's no surprise school doesn't just bounce back to pre-Covid times after being hit by that hurricane force.

My head was cleared during my graduate studies when I read science theorist Thomas Kuhn's landmark book *The Structure of Scientific Revolutions* (1962), describing the process of change in the scientific community caused by a new discovery that transforms scientists' world. Such a discovery, Kuhn reports, is similar to the reaction of early explorers learning the world isn't flat: Disbelief reigns when discoveries introduce something different, then comes adjustment and gradual acceptance. It's Benjamin Franklin out in a lightning storm discovering electricity; Roentgen consistently seeing a strange blue light to discover the x-ray. It's Sizer changing school, a pandemic shutting down school. The change one is forced to make with new conditions doesn't come easily.

Kuhn reports the steps a scientist takes with a discovery that breaks from early beliefs and practices to move to acceptance of the new belief and way of working. Those who can't accept the new belief and practice don't do well, Kuhn reports. The belief that all students can learn led to transformation of schools: With all students expected to learn, this first stirred havoc, then the move to successes. The Covid set-back meant school faced remote, not in-person, for educators and students, and old ways of working, even of just a few years earlier, no longer worked. In post-Covid years, students no longer are up to grade level and in-class behavior. This poses a change to be recognized and addressed.

Covid Era School, and Its Aftermath, Constitute a Paradigm Shift

Kuhn created the term "paradigm shift" to explain the major changes in a field required to take place as a result of a discovery that forces a change in belief and actions that's earth-shaking for scientists. In reading Kuhn, I saw that it connected directly to school work in a time of change. Kuhn's work reads as a treatise on school change, and reflects more recent upending of school as educators struggle with students different from earlier.

Kuhn states a paradigm shift isn't the opposite, just different: "Ducks become rabbits . . . It's as if a professional community has been transported to a different planet." With the change forced by Covid, and with the appeal of Sizer's changes, and expected with accountability, Kuhn points out that "the failure of existing rules is a prelude to new ones." When a crisis occurs, attention must be paid to new ways in which to work. Moving from in-class to cyberspace is no small step.

With the forced paradigm shift in the pandemic school shutdown, school at that time had to change, and quickly. Everyone in the Covid crisis was caught in a surprise that called for a new way to work, and at a moment's notice, not the gradual change over years seen in the long, slow move to acceptance of accountability. With school doors locked during Covid, out of necessity now everyone had to work remotely. Change was forced. For those few who had earlier picked up technology for teaching, and for districts that had built up "one-to-one" computers for each student, and encouraged digital learning, the shift to remote was relatively easy. But most educators were left behind, stymied on how to work in a different way. Yet each picked up new digital skills. Earlier attempts to train teachers on using technology were surpassed by this sudden requirement. It's as if one's house burned down and one had to pivot to seek shelter, immediately. Educators as a group learned new tech skills in days what earlier would have taken years. Google Docs to easily collect and view files became essential. Who had ever heard of Zoom before Covid?

With school lockdown a shock, the paradigm shift from in-class teaching to remote was devastating; Quickly re-thinking work forced a tectonic shift, so it's no wonder that many left teaching and many students dropped out. Kuhn writes that when scientists cannot make a shift in a crisis, many, unable to adapt, "leave the field altogether." Those otherwise little-known in-school tech support experts who helped others make the shift became heroes who unlocked access. Support for a change helps make the shift happen. District leaders, bombarded by often contradictory demands, to open school or remain remote, mostly weathered the storm, but some then left voluntarily, others later forced out. It wasn't a superintendent's fault that the pandemic had created a storm. From reading Kuhn's delineation of how the transformation to a new way of thinking and working occurs when a new discovery is made, forcing a change, at the time of my reading Kuhn's work, I now understood why it was that Sizer's new way of working caused consternation among many, because it was so different. The strictly leveled classes with lecture often the mode had to change. Teaming was different than the earlier isolation. Then next testing all students forced a wider expectation than only just some following Sizer's revolution. I saw from reading Kuhn why educators were distraught when accountability disrupted what had always been believed and worked under those earlier beliefs such as that some can't learn. I saw too in Kuhn's study how the Sizer shift in work and also the accountability expectations were no small changes for educators, but world-shattering, shifting one's world view. Covid era work was uniquely striking because the sharp forced shift of school closure hit quickly and nationally and wasn't a choice. But next educators had to face the results of the effects of remote work on re-entering brick and mortar school. Students returned different.

Kay and Ted Sizer's widow Nancy

However, each new major change, forced or not, as in scientists' world, brings new learning that helps a field move along better. Franklin's discovery of electricity, Newton noting gravity, Edison's telephone. Einstein's theory of relativity with his famous algorithm introduced a new framework for all of physics by proposing new concepts of space and time. Those not making a paradigm shift change are left behind.

Kuhn reports that making the shift affects different people differently and it takes time to adjust. "Adopters" come to new beliefs and practices in different ways, Kuhn notes, citing that initial early believers, whose thinking is close to the new thinking—tech support experts, young tech savvy teachers—open the path for others, then eventually most in the field accept and adapt to the change. It's remarkable how well educators across the country adapted so quickly to teaching without a classroom in which to teach, the rug pulled out from under them. One posts, "It's like spinning plates while on a roller coaster." Others posting to the national education publication *EdWeek* in December, 2020 write these chilling comments to capture the spirit of the time:

Everyone is at the breaking point.

Sad, depressing, weird, house-bound. Strange.

So many losses, but we're surviving.

I can't hear you. You're muted!

No one in my family died.

Hello class, can everyone hear me?

So many losses, but we're surviving.

Grace and patience while we pivot.

We must do better next time.

The superintendent cried during our interview.

First year teacher: crying and trying.

I have no motivation for anything.

Hardest year of teaching so far.

I'm sure I have no idea.

One exhausting Zoom meeting after another.

Unpredictable, violated, angry, dismal, shocking, progress.

Unimaginable blessings among completely unexpected challenges.

We're doing the best we can.

8:58 wakeup. 9:00 meeting. Made it.

My students need more of me.

Challenging, resilience, experimentation, learning, grace, community.

The Process in Moving to Change

The discoverer who initially introduces the reason for a change, Kuhn reports, is often someone outside the field or new to the field and therefore more open to new ways of thinking. University professor Ted Sizer wasn't a public school classroom teacher, only an observer, but steeped in education research and practice, who bravely chose to take on the job of making a change for schools. It was state governors and US Congress that urged accountability, stemming from the civil rights movement and Japan's meteoric economic rise, with an overview perspective, for a goal of school improvement and equity. Early leaders in using technology for education were valued helpers in assisting the shift to remote learning, but had seen earlier the advantages of technology, and then jumped in to assist others not so tech-oriented. The need to change wasn't questioned with the global pandemic with forced isolation. People suddenly dying was evidence enough to require isolation.

In the accountability shift, I saw over time that many if not most Massachusetts educators later came into public education with a belief now learned in their university training that more students could learn. And eventually this concept of helping all was most often the guiding belief of the school system new teachers moved to. Since many new teachers had taken that test as students themselves, taking the time away from classes for state testing became more accepted in schools as just part of the way school worked. More today use the test results to inform their teaching. Post-Covid, test scores are needed to check on learning loss, and, ideally, improve. It's understandable that testing, especially as Standards and the test increase in demands, are less than well-accepted after school closure. But keeping the bar high helps as a guide.

Covid's Break with School

'It's hard to imagine a greater change imposed than the pandemic force. With school shutdown, one's own classroom, desk, paper, books, class materials such as a whiteboard and computer projection system, and seeing colleagues in person, often helpful, all were gone. And not only did the workplace disappear physically, but the threat of contracting Covid permeated what had been the place for school. Many, understandably, feared going back into that familiar building. As administrators struggled with how to have school without a school, some accommodated teachers who were reluctant to return to the building, with a practice of a teaching aide in the classroom and the teacher remote. Still, that distance was less than ideal.

Making matters worse, early on in the pandemic, frightening national news stories appeared on deaths for educators not as careful with the needed distancing, to compound the anxiety of sudden remote work. Three elementary teachers in Florida worked together to try to figure out how they'd teach. All three caught Covid, one died. An experienced teacher went in to school to monitor students taking the SAT test, for which teachers are paid a small stipend. He caught Covid and died. A student in the room at the time said there was one student there who kept coughing. But it's no wonder that parents, with their children now stuck at home, often having to pick up the struggle to keep their children connected via a computer, pleaded for schools to open, while teacher unions argued to keep teachers remote and safe. But out of this crisis, new ideas and ways of working emerged.

The Hybrid Compromise Just Doesn't Work

Attempts to "fix" things don't always work. A new way to teach contrived as a compromise to address the competing cries for in-school and the need to social distance bombed. As administrators struggled to meet the parent demand for students to be in school and with teachers eager to return to classrooms but reluctant to risk their health, a poor hoped-for solution widely implemented was the hybrid mode. This draconian approach aimed to minimize the number of students in classrooms to allow for some distancing, but only taxed educators and students more. Teaching with half in-school and half remote at the same time didn't serve anyone well.

In summer, 2020, a strong teacher in my online course tells me, distraught, that she's been assigned students in her classroom for the fall, but half of her students are scheduled to be in another part of the building, online, rotating daily. Even this fine, optimistic, inventive teacher was stunned, found it hard to think how this bizarre contrivance could work. Soon hybrid was the trend nationally, believed by those not teachers to be a good middle ground. But this ineffective mode of using the contortion of two different teaching modes—in-person and remote—at the same time only put new stress on educators. Students wondered why come in to school when one could watch remotely.

With hybrid intending to ensure that students remote and in class would get the same learning, it was decided these two modes should happen at the same time, with this administrative decision illustrating the management-teacher divide views. An excellent special education teacher in a high demographic district of privileged families tells me "Hybrid is so awful I can't even talk about it." Others call hybrid the worst of both worlds, constraining what the classroom could do while also not serving well those remote. That educators complied showed cooperation but also frustration that anything would work.

To multiply concerns, the same teacher disconcerted to receive the hybrid assignment is then excited because she's asked to pick up an in-person summer school course, because the assigned teacher had contracted Covid. I worried for her. Just hearing these stories was distressing, as it wasn't only about school deteriorating but also about life and death. One teacher in my online course completes a four-week course in one week, to my amazement. She'd had to complete reading the full required text and post in response to many different discussion questions. She tells me they're asked to go into school, and her partner is an essential worker. She tells me she doesn't know what the coming weeks will bring.

A Silver Lining

Yet in a time when good problem-solving was most needed, at least one school system did find a better solution than hybrid. A district in New York state devised an online unit template for teachers to complete that had won state approval to count student completion as school day class work, to satisfy the state requirement for the required number of school days. This meant only at-home online work on alternate days, with students working on their own, replacing the simultaneous hybrid. Teachers sat together at the year's start in a computer lab to try to figure out how to fill in this complex online unit, and helped one another complete the templates with their course material. Such outside-the-box thinking worked. "I did love that I only ever had eight students in class," reports a fine veteran fifth grade teacher here. But she adds that Covid teaching "was like every teacher was a new teacher," overwhelmed in a new world.

Surprisingly, a pre-school teacher in a high low-income district tells me it was her best year ever. In a helpful state decision, pre-school children were the first allowed back into the building, and the only ones there, a quiet environment, with lots of space for an age group that direly needed socialization and age-appropriate learning. Other teachers of young children in upper grades were deeply frustrated using remote, with just trying to gain children's attention, to have them sit properly and for a time.

Success in a Dark Era

But this period also forced dramatic positive change for all. Not only did widespread new technology means for learning soar during this

Making A Paradigm Shift Work

era, but also creativity and innovation broke through. And instantly reaching out to others, seeking or sharing new ways to work, proliferated. Learning for educators surged as they struggled to stay afloat, and found new ways to work and engage students. With school turned upside down, re-thinking teaching exploded. An elementary art teacher tells me her third graders gave her helpful tech tips. But a teacher teaching summer school in which students make up course work that they'd failed, teaching remotely, found it frustrating when parents would pull a student off to do errands during the online summer school time. She called home frequently and soon this irritant stopped. Reaching students and parents by any means necessary taxed educators, and they would often find a way. "Work-arounds" became a new schools term.

In addition to the gigantic leap to new use of technology, and creativity in how to break through the brick wall, or work in cyberspace, to try to connect with one's students, was also the desperate need to connect with anyone who could help with tech skills. Now veteran teachers teamed up with skilled young new tech-savvy teachers who had grown up with technology, "technology natives," reversing the tradition of veterans mentoring new teachers in how to adapt to school. Younger teachers weren't new to remote work, and thrived on it, and were happy to help, life savers for others. They now became the experts others looked to. Pre-Covid, colleagues buddied up often out of physical proximity. With everyone remote, now the accident of proximity wasn't relevant: It was who knew what, and whom one could connect with to help, that brought new ties. Collaboration across schools, grade levels, and subject areas now blossomed, more intensely, efficiently and effectively, self-started, because so many needed help. It was all about connecting, remotely.

With such collaborative help, openness to new online tools and strategies exploded, quickly. Who had heard of Edmodo, Prezi, Canvas, Flipgrid before? As skills and ease with digital work grew, some teachers learned how to remotely have students work in small groups and monitor each group's work, simple in the classroom, not as easy remotely. Now educators were immediately thrust into the tech world that many in business had been operating in for years, to help boost learning through new interactive tools, better suited to the world their students thrived in.

Successes Through the Covid Nightmare

The miracle is, we came through this, though like battered soldiers. The pandemic constituted a paradigm shift in which people learned and moved on with important new ways of working. We can't go back.

Now that teachers have new tech skills and know they can easily reach out remotely to any other person who might help, not blocked by physical location or years of experience, we must continue with these new abilities forged from the fire of Covid. All teachers became more inventive during remote work, to attempt to connect however possible, striving to connect with students, less reluctant to contact parents for help, failing but continuing to try.

These three new ways of working of tech skills development, urgent calling on others for help and freely sharing information, and increased creativity must be retained so we can move in a different way post-Covid. Teachers broke through common traditions and familiar practices and colleagues to now attempt to maintain school as well as possible, tenuous as it was. We must retain these newer ways of working, not simply move back to old school ways now considered "normal," which didn't work all that well anyway.

We must continue to move ahead, in part because learning levels during the remote period dropped so far so fast, and student in-school appropriate behavior was shredded during shut-down. If educators can continue to build on their tech skills for coming years, innovate, and continue to seek aid from whoever whenever, not stay in one's comfort zone or retreat back to one's old way of thinking and working, there's the potential to be able to provide the greater support so needed today and in the future. Teacher teams sharing the same students for more ownership; ensuring that advisory groups are the teachers' actual students they teach, as we had in that long ago Sizer era; advisory groups are the teachers' actual students they teach; the problem-solving in school day meeting time together is on the team's own students' needs; and reaching out, by any means necessary, to the team's own students and homes in the event of behavior issues or absenteeism, can help immensely with including all students.

If schools can move ahead to better use of time and collaborative teaming, embrace Standards learning, and continue with innovation and constantly share best practices, using technology to expedite and maximize learning, we can move closer to the promise of no child left behind.

Hope High School

Appendix

Ted Sizer's Coalition of Essential Schools Ten Common Principles
Common Core/Massachusetts English Standards

COALITION OF ESSENTIAL SCHOOLS TEN COMMON PRINCIPLES

1. The school should focus on helping adolescents learn to use their minds well.

2. The school's goals shall be simple: that each student master a limited number of essential skills and areas of knowledge. "Less is more" should dominate.

3. The school's goals should apply to all students.

4. Teaching and learning should be personalized to the maximum feasible extent; no teacher should have direct responsibility for more than eighty students ... decisions about the use of students' and teachers' time and the choice of teaching materials must be unreservedly placed in the hands of the principal and staff.

5. The governing practical metaphor of the school should be student-as-worker.

6. The diploma shall be awarded upon a successful demonstration of mastery—an "Exhibition" that may be jointly administered by the faculty and higher authorities. As the diploma is awarded when earned.

7. The tone of the school should explicitly and self-consciously stress values of unanxious expectation of trust and of decency, parents are essential collaborators.

8. Principal and teachers perceive themselves as generalists first, specialists second.

9. Ultimate administrative and budget targets should include substantial time for collective planning by teachers, competitive salaries for staff and an ultimate per-pupil cost, not [to] exceed those at traditional schools by more than ten percent.

10. Adopted in 1997: Democracy and equity: The school should demonstrate non-discriminatory and inclusive policies, practices, and pedagogies. It should model democratic practices that involve all who are directly affected by the school. The school should honor diversity and build on the strength of its communities, deliberately and explicitly challenging all forms of inequity.

Common Core State Standards

COLLEGE AND CAREER READINESS ANCHOR STANDARDS FOR READING
Key Ideas and Details

1. Read closely to determine what a text states explicitly and to make logical inferences from it; cite specific textual evidence when writing or speaking to support conclusions drawn from a text.

2. Determine central ideas or themes of a text and analyze their development; summarize the key supporting details and ideas.

3. Analyze how and why individuals, events, and ideas develop and interact over the course of a text.

Craft and Structure

4. Interpret words and phrases as they are used in a text, including determining technical, connotative, and figurative meanings, and analyze how specific word choices shape meaning or tone.

5. Analyze the structure of texts, including how specific sentences, paragraphs, and larger portions of a text relate to each other and the whole.

6. Assess how point of view or purpose shapes the content and style of a text.

Integration of Knowledge and Ideas

7. Integrate and evaluate content presented in diverse media and formats, including visually and quantitatively, as well as in words.

8. Delineate and evaluate the argument and specific claims in a text, including the validity of the reasoning as well as the relevance and sufficiency of the evidence.

9. Analyze how two or more texts address similar themes or topics in order to build knowledge or to compare the approaches the authors take.

Range of Reading and Level of Text Complexity

10. Independently and proficiently read and comprehend complex literary and informational texts.

COLLEGE AND CAREER READINESS ANCHOR STANDARDS FOR WRITING

Text Types and Purposes

1. Write arguments to support claims in an analysis of substantive topics or texts, using valid reasoning and relevant and sufficient evidence.

2. Write informative/explanatory texts to examine and convey complex ideas and information clearly and accurately through the effective selection, organization, and analysis of content.

3. Write narratives to develop experiences or events using effective literary techniques, well-chosen details, and well-structured sequences.

Production and Distribution of Writing

4. Produce clear and coherent writing in which the development, organization, and style are appropriate to task, purpose, and audience.

5. Develop and strengthen writing as needed by planning, revising, editing, rewriting, or trying a new approach.

6. Use technology to produce and publish writing and to interact and collaborate with others.

Research to Build and Present Knowledge

7. Conduct short as well as more sustained research projects based on focused questions, demonstrating understanding of the subject under investigation.

8. When conducting research, gather relevant information from multiple print and digital sources, assess the credibility and accuracy of each source, and integrate the information while avoiding plagiarism.

9. Draw evidence from literary or informational text for analysis, interpretation, reflection, and research.

Range of Writing

10. Write routinely over extended time frames (time for research, reflection, and revision) and shorter time frames (a single sitting or a day or two) for a range of tasks, purposes, and audiences.

Source: **Massachusetts Curriculum Framework for English Language Arts and Literacy**

Acknowledgements

Thanks to my husband Peter for allowing me to write instead of accompanying him on walks, and over the years out of the blue suddenly demanding of him a synonym or a word that describes something or someone. He never asked why, only always tried to help. Always pleading for short sentences.

Brown University non-fiction writing professor Catherine believed in this book from the first and kept believing in it when I began to falter. She read the first terrible manuscript and kept reading drafts, never critical, always encouraging. This constant delicate support of a great coach made this book happen.

Ted Sizer's assistant the highly competent Kathy, at the calm center of the hurricane Ted created to make school better for all, kept me in that lively past of turmoil and energy as together we laughed about those good old days over many many lunches together, keeping that energy and spark of that tempestuous period alive for me and this book.

Mike Ananis, best superintendent ever, gave me the support to do my best as we changed a school system from mediocre to great, to be able to write about this success story from our brief time together.

Thanks to Vicky and Dave, among my many readers, who read through an earlier draft and told me they thought the manuscript made sense.

Thanks to my brother Phil who caught word errors I never thought I had, and gave sage advice.

I thank all the great teachers I admire and that I've had the joy of working with who pioneered and sustained great teaching. You helped me stay sane. You know who you are, the lonely hard-working saints who thanklessly give of themselves to help kids grow, and inspire others.

Thanks to John, who made team teaching so much fun.

Thanks to our son Peter, who never questioned this six years of effort.

www.ingramcontent.com/pod-product-compliance
Lightning Source LLC
LaVergne TN
LVHW021951060526
838201LV00049B/1666